To Sara Bubba Bateman
with my compliments
A.J.J.M.

Growing Up in New Orleans

Alvin G. Gottschall

VANTAGE PRESS
New York

Published by Vantage Press, Inc.
516 West 34th Street, New York, New York 10001

Manufactured in the United States of America
ISBN: 0-533-12095-0

Library of Congress Catalog Card No.: 96-90548

0 9 8 7 6 5 4 3 2 1

To my sweet and lovely daughter,
Anne Hilton Gottschall Purvis

Contents

Preface

Several years ago my daughter made the remark that I hadn't told her much about my early life. I thought I had, but she insisted that wasn't the case. So, I tried to accommodate her request by writing her some letters. They began by my describing things that I recalled almost from the time I was born. The more I wrote, the more I remembered many other things, people, events, etc. One-page letters ultimately became much longer.

Toward the end of my writing about life in college, I started thinking that this material might make a good book someday. I really wanted to sign off upon completion of the letters about college, but my daughter encouraged me to continue, so I wrote another hundred pages about my naval career in World War II.

In order to increase the readership universe, I did some research and included as an addendum the lists of graduating classes of most of the high schools in and around New Orleans where I had friends during the period roughly from the mid-thirties to the mid-forties. This information is reasonably accurate and should stimulate interest.

Perhaps the title of this book is somewhat misleading since I added the letters describing my naval experience. This led to suggestions that I use titles like *Growing Up from New Orleans* or *Growing Up in New Orleans and Elsewhere*. Nevertheless, I was compelled to retain the title as shown and trust that most readers would approve.

Not all of what I have written is without some margin of error, but it is the best of what I could recall about real people and real situations in my early years.

Acknowledgments

To Elsie Brupbacker Martinez, who planted the seed that someday I might attempt to complement her work on New Orleans life in *Uptown / Downtown*.

To Lucy Goodson, whose invaluable assistance with a word processor made my effort much easier.

To my son, John Austin Gottschall, who advised me to take all the risks involved and "go for it."

And, of course, to my daughter, Anne, whose inspiration gave me the incentive to write these letters in the first place.

Growing Up in New Orleans

Part I

The Very Early Years

December 31, 1993

Dear Anne,

    This could be the beginning of a long, continuing epistle, but you have an excellent idea, and since I have revealed little about my early life, it might be worthwhile. At least you have given me something to write about.

    Before I start, Mother and I want you and John to know how much we appreciate the VCR. I finally got it installed and working. Still wading through the myriad of instructions.

    Well, Annie, I was born on September 20, 1922, at Hotel Dieu Hospital in New Orleans, Louisiana. Mother and Dad were renting a small cottage on Eagle Street. They had been married since October 12, 1921. Dad was a reporter for the New Orleans *Times-Picayune.* I believe he met Mother when she was a secretary there. Dad had saved some money and a year later bought the house at 1716 Pine Street for $8,500 cash. You always had a good memory of your early days and, I guess, so have I. Aunt Jane came along in 1924. My earliest recollection of anything was pushing my sister on a backyard swing when I was four and she was two. There were lots of children in the neighborhood. My best friend at the time was Ray Courter who lived across the street. He was a year older (like five). He could cross the street, but I wasn't allowed so he would often tease me about being afraid to come over to his house. I started kindergarten at Lusher School just two and a half blocks away. I remember three classmates in kindergarten—one was Leonard King (who eventually married a girl who lived in Mother's neighborhood in Laurel, Mississippi), another was Betty Grant and another was Parker Schneidau, who was the bad boy of the class and always got into trouble. In later years, he turned out to be quite different. His older brother, Gayle, and I became close friends when we worked for Gulf Oil. Well, this is enough for now. I will try to limit these letters to one page. There will be many more to come.

    Our best to all the boys in your family and have lots of good fortune in the year ahead.

Love you much,
Dad

January 10, 1994

Dear Anne,

Continuing on with my "biography." I have vague memories of the time I was in first grade at Lusher School. The grade was divided into two semesters—1A and 1B. I do remember my 1A teacher, Ms. Dixon, who was very good and very patient, but my 1B teacher, Ms. Lee, was tough. She scared us into studying hard under the threat of being kept after school. It's funny, but I don't remember any of my classmates in first grade. I can remember walking the short distance to and from school with friends, but can't recall their names.

My neighborhood friends were Ray Courter, the "big guy" across the street and Thayer Fichman who lived in the next block, and then Clifford Roberts who lived around the corner in one of those shotgun duplex houses. Cliff had several brothers and sisters. They were very poor. I'll never know how they all lived in that half of a shotgun. I can remember Cliff inviting me into their kitchen and sipping coffee for a drink. They didn't have enough money to buy milk. That coffee was nasty tasting stuff! Anyway—I should mention this now—Cliff's older brother, Nash, went on to LSU (Louisiana State University), became a meteorologist in the Navy in World War II and afterward started the first TV weather program on WDSU-TV. He held this position for many years, became a famous weather consultant and retired a wealthy man. Never knew what happened to Clifford, because they moved away from the neighborhood.

This takes me to the summer of 1929. My father had progressed at the New Orleans *Times-Picayune* to become an advertizing manager for the newspaper. I remember Dad coming home one day in the summer and announcing that we were going to move to Shreveport, Louisiana. "Where's that place? . . . What for?" Well, he received an unsolicited offer from the Louisiana Oil Refining Company of Shreveport to be their advertising manager. This was a growing integrated oil company in that area. He must have thought this was his big break and the higher income appealing, so we moved to Shreveport in August of 1929—a memorable year. More later.

Love you much,
Dad

January 18, 1994

Dear Anne,

Many thanks for your nice letter and pictures of the new bathrooms. Mother and I may take a short vacation to Orlando in February.

In moving to Shreveport in 1929, Dad decided to rent our house on Pine Street. We then rented a very nice house in Shreveport at the corner of Cresswell and Robinson Streets. This was a smart move on his part. I remember at that time there was a big valley of pine woods behind us. I began to notice the sounds of robins, mockingbirds and crows. Never forgot those sounds. My best friends were Baby and Jerry Mize next door as well as Jimmy and Caroline Haywood two doors away. Across the street were "big teenagers" who had bought a Model T Ford and raced it up and down the street at sixty mph. For Christmas I got my first two wheel (sidewalk) bike. The Mize home had no basement, just a dirt crawlspace underneath with plenty of headroom for us. We used to build castles and forts, etc. there. I broke up some of Dad's Caruso records to make one of our forts and got punished for it.

We were only two blocks from the Cresswell Grammar School. It was across the street from a beautiful park where we used to go down to a lake and catch tadpoles (which later turned into frogs). At the other end of the park was Byrd High where Jerry Mize later starred in football and was an outstanding running back at LSU. We bought our first car—a 1929 Dodge—and took trips to Hot Springs, Arkansas, and East Texas where the roads were still dirt and/or gravel. We went fishing on Cross and Caddo Lakes where Dad's company had producing oil wells. Downtown Shreveport was a memorable place—had a new, white, six-story courthouse surrounded in the square by shops, the local hotel, and a movie theater. The first movies I ever saw were with Harold Lloyd or the Marx Brothers. Also remember a movie that showed a body floating in the water. Ugh! The first songs I remember were in Shreveport—one called "In a Little Spanish Town," also "Ramona" and "In Old Monterey." The big shock of the year was the stock market crash in the fall of 1929 and the beginning of the Great Depression. Dad lost his job in the spring of 1930. After school was out we traveled to Dallas and Houston, Texas to look for another job. At least we had a car—Dad was able to store our furniture somewhere. We stayed overnight in places called tourist homes or boarding houses for three dollars per night. I can remember the tremendous meals at those boarding houses. We finally went on to live in Houston, Texas.

More later.

Love you much,
Dad

January 26, 1994

Dear Anne,

After school was out in 1930, we left Shreveport and took a long journey into the state of Texas. Drove through Dallas, Austin and San Antonio to Houston where Dad finally got another job with the Houston *Post* (or *Press*) in the advertising department. We rented a house on Park Street near Welch Avenue and two blocks from the Woodrow Wilson School where I started third grade. I was in "heaven" because it turned out that my next door neighbor was Billy Langston—same age, same grade—and we became inseparable. We did everything together. We would hike or ride our bikes to Buffalo Bayou near River Oaks and run up and down the trails that bordered this stream. We built forts in both backyards with cut up stalks of bamboo that grew abundantly. We had lead soldiers, cars and trucks running all over the place. I remember my big Christmas present was a complete tool chest and I put it to good use.

Several blocks away was a large shopping center. Dad and I would walk over there every Sunday to get the paper. This edition was most important because the comic strips were in color—and the best one was Buck Rogers and his girlfriend, Wilma. This was the 1930s version of *Star Trek* and Buck Rogers was my big hero. Occasionally my father and I would go to a "railroad car" restaurant in the shopping area and have waffles with Log Cabin maple syrup. Once Billy Langston invited us up to his grandfather's place in Lovelady, Texas—had a great time. We also took trips down to Galveston on the Gulf Coast and played in the surf. I think I almost got black from the sun and have had an olive complexion ever since.

Across the street was a large two-story home occupied by a family that kept pretty much to themselves. Even their children was unfriendly. One morning I was awakened by fire engine sirens. The house across the street was engulfed in flames. After the fire was put out the firemen learned that it was started in an upstairs back bedroom where these people had operated a liquor still and made moonshine whiskey. For a week after the fire the whole neighborhood smelled like alcohol. We never saw the family again.

By the summer of 1931, my father decided it was time to move back to New Orleans. More later.

Love you,
Dad

February 7, 1994

Dear Anne,

In the summer of 1931, we moved back to New Orleans. These were difficult depression times. Dad had to look for another job. We couldn't move back to Pine Street yet because the lease to Dr. Browne didn't expire for another year, so we stored our furniture and moved into a furnished shotgun-type house at the corner of Maple and Short streets. We were there only three months. The only significant thing I can remember was that it was across the street from the New Orleans Mounted Police headquarters, where they kept their horses. Also diagonally across the street was a grocery store run by an Italian family named Castrogiovanni. Dad got a job with General Outdoor Advertising Co. (billboards) and we found a house to rent in Metairie on Bonnabel Avenue. This was "out in the country." We were in the second to last house on one side of the street. Beyond this and across the street was a wooded swamp. This old house had a cistern, a large circular wood structure that caught water from rainfall. Used it for washing clothes but we had city water also. Next door was a French family whose grandfather cultivated a vegetable garden and lived by himself in a shack in the rear. They called him "Grandpere."

Because the nearest public school was miles away, Jane and I attended a Catholic school three blocks away on Bonnabel. The teachers were nuns. This was fourth grade for me. Our teacher was very strict, but good. I also had to learn a lot of things from the Catholic catechism, including several prayers. Do you know that I still pray every night and recite these prayers I memorized from fourth grade in 1931! Several good friends were Dick Blanchard, on the next street back of us; Ashley Schexnailder, who lived next to the school; another boy who lived in a big house across Metairie Road—but can't remember his name—and also the grandson of Mr. Bonnabel who lived in a large house. Then there were two beautiful looking blonde sisters who attended school and lived in a nice place—surrounded by a fence—on the way to my house. I was too shy to get acquainted, but used to daydream about protecting them from the forces of evil.

I often went across the street into the swamp to catch crayfish. Once I stepped on a huge water moccasin. Scared the hell out of me! Never liked snakes after that.

In the summer of 1932, the Gottschall family was emancipated and moved back to 1716 Pine Street.

More later.

Love you much,
Dad

February 27, 1994

Dear Anne,

Mother and I had a marvelous time in Orlando, Florida. The best exhibit was Epcot Center. It made you feel good about your country. Sea World was also outstanding. Disney's Magic Kingdom is about the same as Disneyland in California. When the boys are seven or eight, you and Charles should visit.

To get on with my life's history, we moved back to 1716 Pine Street, New Orleans, Louisiana, in the summer of 1932. The 1932–35 period was a time when I greatly expanded my network of friends as well as my confidence and self-esteem. It took in fifth, sixth, and seventh grades at Lusher School. I distinctly remember the principal, a Ms. Serjax, a very capable old battle-ax. Then for reading (and homeroom) it was Ms. Hereford; for geography Ms. Hay; for arithmetic, a Ms. McCabe; English was Ms. Gravely; history was Ms. Lawes; for writing and music, it was Ms. Valles and for woodworking or manual training, Mr. DeFraites (the girls took sewing and cooking) and for gym it was Ms. Bergeron. How about that for memory?

Students from fifth grade up moved from room to room. Before classes, every morning we all gathered in the center hall of the school for a prayer, the Pledge of Allegiance to USA, and sang about six songs. I'll never forget an Italian song, the tune of which I can still whistle. Once every month we would also go to the hall to hear the then famous Walter Damrosch and his symphony on the radio. In his children's program he described in detail the different instruments and what the music was all about. He would always begin by saying, "Good morning, my dear children," in his unusual accent. While we had a cafeteria, Mother fixed our lunch to take to school. We did get milk at school, mostly chocolate. There was also a place near school where you could get poorboy sandwiches and all kinds of candy. We had a mid-morning recess (fifteen minutes) and an hour for lunch. School was out at 3:00 P.M.

I remember playing marbles in the schoolyard under a huge oak tree, which is still there and you can see it from Pine Street. Playing marbles introduced you to the fierce world of competition among boys. You played for keeps, i.e., if you knocked another guy's marble out of a ring, it was yours. There were lots of fights.

There was no eighth grade. You went on to four years of high school that wasn't co-ed. Well enough for now.

Love you much,
Dad

March 6, 1994

Dear Anne,

We sent you and Charles a box of oranges from sunny Florida. Hope they arrive in good condition.

Moving back to Pine Street was something we all looked forward to. Dr. Browne, to whom we rented our house for three years, liked the neighborhood so much that he bought a house almost across the street from us. As I have said previously, the 1932–1935 period, during which I attended fifth, sixth and seventh grades, was a wonderful experience as far as I was concerned. While the whole country was in the depths of an economic depression, it didn't impact too much on children. We didn't have a lot in the way of material things, but we had a ball—at least I did. Before writing this letter, I made a list of all the things I still remember during this time that I want to relate to you—and it came to nearly fifty—so bear with me.

I looked forward to seeing my "old" friend, Ray Courter, again, who used to tease me a lot. We were several years older then and became the best of friends. He had an older brother, Buddy, and a sister named Sweetie. They were Catholic and attended Mater Dolorosa parochial school, but that made no difference. Then there were Thayer and David Fichman, sons of Rabbi Fichman, also older, but I learned lots from them. Most of the other kids were much older, like three or four years, namely Andrew "Poulka" Wolert, Bob Cosgrove (next door), and Billy Coats, Charlotte's big brother. Next door on the "lake side" of us were the Englands—Frances and Mary (high school), Norton and Harry (in college). Directly across the street was Captain Low and his family. All his children were college age or better. I became a very close friend of his grandson, Jack Sequin, about whom I will tell you later. Oh, I forgot about Ruthie Low (age unknown), who was retarded and at the time the ugliest person I ever saw, but harmless. In the big house on the corner across the street was another sea captain, Captain Breen, and all his children were over twenty-one. On the other corner were Harold and Katherine Cornay (college age). At the other corner on our side was the scoutmaster of Troop 22 at Lusher School, but can't remember his name. All others in the block had no children. All of the above were neighborhood acquaintances in the early thirties—others moved in later.

I got a nickname early in life. It was "Gootch" because they couldn't pronounce, much less spell, Gottschall. It stuck with me up through high school, college and even the Navy.

More later.

Love you,
Dad

March 15, 1994

Dear Anne,

I'll never forget the good old summertime. What a glorious period. No school for over three months! Sure it was hot, very hot and nobody had air conditioning—always in the nineties (degrees Fahrenheit) and over 90 percent humidity. We wore almost nothing—just shorts—and went barefoot. If we got too uncomfortable, we just sat still in the shade or found somebody's porch that had a ceiling fan. We didn't think much about how our fathers had to dress up for work in suits and ties and may have had to pound the pavement downtown.

When it was too hot to exercise, we played all kinds of card games like battle, hearts, Bouray, also checkers, and when we got a little older, it was poker, blackjack, seven and a half, Canasta, chess and Monopoly.

We would read lots of books too. Wish I could remember them. I do recall reading *The Adventures of Tom Swift,* a series of maybe sixteen books, also *The Rover Boys,* and for serious reading, Mother and Dad bought *The Books of Knowledge,* which was an outstanding twenty-volume pictorial encyclopedia for children eight to twelve years old. I was also fascinated with *Popular Mechanics* magazine—worthwhile for kids who liked creative ideas on new machinery.

When the evenings weren't too hot, we played outside games like Hunt the Hay and Kick the Can (Kick the Stick when the neighbors complained of the noise). The whole block was "in bounds." On Sundays, we'd listen to the popular radio shows like *Jack Benny, Fred Allen, Fibber McGee and Molly, The Hit Parade,* and *Mystery Theater.* Even liked to listen to classical music, but must admit it put me to sleep on the living room sofa.

We used to play hockey in the street on roller skates and took up the length of the block for a rink. We carved out hockey sticks from royal palm tree branches. The puck was a square piece of wood. Didn't worry about cars because only one would come by every fifteen minutes, and the neighbors all parked in their driveways. Nobody parked on the street! We had some fast and fierce games. I still have a scar above my eye from a hockey stick blow.

When we got tired of all of this, we made skatemobiles. We'd break up the skates and nail them to two-by-four pieces of wood and race them all over the place. And when we got completely bored we would sit on the curb and try to identify the cars coming up the street. Every Friday night was the time to go the neighborhood theaters (the Poplar or the Mecca) and see cowboy movies starring Tom Mix or Hoot Gibson. In addition to the feature was a Disney cartoon and a scary serial short featuring the Wolf Man. All for about twenty-five cents.

More later.

Love you much,
Dad

March 24, 1994

Dear Anne,

More on summertime events as a grade schooler. Several times a week, we would get up at 6:00 A.M. and walk or ride bikes to the swimming pool in Audubon Park. We got there early to avoid the crowds and the heat. After putting on our suits we had to dash through a tunnel of ice cold showers before we reached the pool. We fooled around playing all kinds of games until midmorning. Afterwards, we'd go over to the bend in the Mississippi River in front of the park where there was a huge sandbar and have mud fights.

In the evenings sometimes we would take long walks—about two miles—to the Cloverland Dairy on Carrollton Avenue and get huge double-dip ice cream cones for a dime.

Although I hate to admit it, we had switch fights when we were bored with everything else. We made the switches from long young shoots from lugustrium trees. I can remember Jack Sequin and I deciding one day that we had been tortured enough by Thayer Fichman. We knew Thayer often took naps on his upstairs sleeping porch. So we got some good switches and sneaked into his house, sneaked by the cook in the kitchen and found him snoring away and buck naked. We really laid into him with our switches and ran away as fast as we could. He followed us out of his house before he realized he didn't have clothes and gave up the chase. We got mad at each other often, but made up quickly.

Then, we had rubber gun wars. The guns were pieces of wood shaped like pistols or rifles. The bullets were elastic rings of rubber cut from old auto tire inner tubes. They were stretched from the end of the barrel back to a clothespin nailed to the handle, or stretched back to notches on the barrel under a piece of cord. When you opened the clothespin or pulled the cord, the rubber would fly and hit anything fifteen yards away. I can remember being initiated into Ray and Buddy Courter's Rubber Gun Club. They put me in the back of their garage and a half a dozen kids let me have it with their rubber guns. They could really sting. We would build forts (mine was in a tree house in our backyard) and have rubber gun wars with other groups of kids.

More later.

Love you,
Dad

March 28, 1994

Dear Anne,

A couple more summertime memories. Thayer Fichman (about two years older) was always setting a bad example for the neighborhood kids. We had a vine that covered our backyard fence and grew unusually large leaves with prickly stickers all over them. We called them "washrags." Anyway, one day in late August when the vine dried, Thayer broke off a bunch of six-inch sticks from the vine and induced us to light up and smoke them. Boy, did we get sick! Also got punished.

You may recall that there was a large cemetery in the block behind our house on Lowerline Street. Most of it was used by colored people (that's what they were called then). Occasionally, those of some means would have large funerals. They would parade slowly from a nearby church to the cemetery, complete with hearse, several limousines, followed by maybe twenty-five cars and perhaps a hundred people on foot shuffling slowly in rhythm. Everyone was dressed up in their Sunday best and their shoes sparkled. The procession would include a twenty-piece band playing the saddest music. Whenever we heard the noise, we would run over to the cemetery, slip through holes in the whitewashed fence and creep up to the grave area. Colored people seemed to take funerals very hard, especially the bereaved family and countless relatives. We also heard that there were professional wailers added to make matters more dramatic. They would cry, shriek, swoon and sob loudly and a few would try to throw themselves into the open grave. As we witnessed everything, the black crowd paid absolutely no attention to us. Sometimes there were singers with the band. We actually saw Louis Armstrong singing at one funeral. After the burial ceremony was over, some attendants had to carry away the wailing, struggling family members back to the limos. Then the tempo of the music changed and everyone marched away down the street at a brisk rhythmic clip with the band playing "I'll Be Glad When You're Dead, You Rascal, You." I think later they all went someplace and got drunk. Most of the bereaved families were not rich, but we were told that many colored folks would save a little money all of their lives just to be able to afford a first-class funeral.

Love you,
Dad

April 10, 1994

Dear Anne,

I should tell you that even though the thirties were depression years, the Gottschall family managed to take vacations. Dad moved from General Outdoor Advertising to the advertising department of WSMB, a thriving radio station affiliated with NBC. He was successful enough to take two-week paid vacations all at one time so the family could go on extended trips somewhere (in our 1929 Dodge). I can't remember all the places, but we did go to the Florida Gulf Coast around Fort Walton, Destin and Panama City. Also trips to the mountain area near Ashville, North Carolina, and trips to Tennessee and Virginia where his mother's relatives were located. Besides getting tired of visiting relatives, we always had to stop at every historical marker on the highway to read what was inscribed, which I found boring at the time. I enjoyed reading the series of shaving cream signs that attracted your attention. The best one being:

> Each Time
> The Stork
> Brings a Boy
> Our Whole Factory
> Jumps with Joy
> Burma Shave

The most exciting trip was going to the Texas Centennial in Dallas in the summer of 1936. I believe it was similar to a World's Fair in those days. We still have a nice enlarged photo of the whole family walking down one of the concourses—and there I am, about thirteen years old, in knickers.

Mother, Jane and I made several trips to Harrisburg, Pennsylvania to visit Grandmother Gottschall and Aunt Glenn, an old maid who cared for her. They lived in a nice house on North Second Street, a block north of the Harrisburg Military Academy where Dad attended school from kindergarten all the way up to the second year of college! The first trip was when I was eight. I can remember making friends with two boys my age in the neighborhood—one was Joe Joe Dahl. Made another trip there when I was twelve and became very close to Henry and George Tillson who lived on Front Street overlooking the beautiful Susquehanna River. I can remember playing ping pong daily with both Tillsons and winning most of the time. Also visited Uncle Amos Gottschall, a psychiatrist, who was the head doctor at the Pennsylvania State Mental Hospital at Embreeville, Pennsylvania. He lived in a huge house on the grounds. All the help, like the maids, the cook, the gardeners, etc., were patients. They were harmless (said Uncle Amos) but sometimes weird and downright scary. A couple of times Amos broke the rules and took me and several of the inmates (patients) to Philadelphia in his big touring car to see a major league baseball game. Uncle Amos said it was "good therapy."

Have to go.

Love,
Dad

April 18, 1994

Dear Anne,

When we moved to 1716 Pine Street in 1923, there was a young mulberry tree in the backyard. Every spring it was covered with light-colored mulberries that were edible, but the silkworms always got most of them. It grew to a great height over the years and became the foundation of lots of activity. Dad installed a long, heavy four-by-four between the mulberry and a camphor tree nearby, and then put up some swings, a trapeze, a set of rings and a nice climbing rope. They were used constantly by all the kids in the neighborhood. The mulberry tree itself was my favorite. I used to climb up in it as high as I could. Later we built a solid deck within its three trunks about fifteen feet high with a trapdoor in the middle. This was my treehouse, my domain. With the trapdoor shut, the only way to get up was to use the climbing rope. If you could get up by rope, you could be a member of my tree club. The treehouse was also used as a fort, particularly in rubber gun wars. It wasn't too long before the tree grew to a tremendous height—higher than any of the live oaks around there. I established a second perch way up near the top of the tree just big enough to squeeze in two of us. From this vantage point you could see the Tulane football stadium on Willow Street—also the Hibernia and American Bank Buildings, the two tallest New Orleans skyscrapers downtown. Later, when I organized track and field meets in the backyard, we suspended a rope from one of the mulberry tree's highest branches and created a new field event that we called the rope vault. We built a pit in the corner of the yard for high jumps, broad jumps and rope vaults. In the rope vault you would take the rope back as far as possible and run toward the pit, flinging yourself up in the air and over the bar into the pit. We would rope vault higher than sixteen feet, which was higher than the world's record for the pole fault, at that time. Unfortunately, the day before I was to go to Camp Salmen, a boy's camp near Slidell or Covington, Louisiana, I came down head first from rope vaulting and broke my arm. A terrible disappointment because I never got to go to camp.

I can remember taking one of Jane's friends, Betty Morphy, up to my mulberry tree perch one night and kissing her. She made us climb down in a hurry. The tree continued to grow to even greater heights. Other activities in high school and college separated me from my tree.

When I returned from service in the Navy, I found that Dad had the tree cut down because it was too large for the backyard. It was a sad day.

Take care.

Love you much,
Dad

14

April 25, 1994

Dear Anne,

Within a year after returning to Pine Street in New Orleans, my best friend, Ray Courter, moved to Atlanta. The Courter family was charismatic and very active socially, so it was a real disappointment to learn they were going to leave us. I met Ray only once, years later. The Courters had a very handsome dalmatian named Zep. We also had a sort of hunting dog that we called Spot. When Spot was a puppy, he used to jump all over Zep, but the senior dog always ignored that frivolous little half-breed. However, Spot grew up to become the intelligent, well-respected pet of the neighborhood. He had a bad habit, though, of chasing Dad's car or me on my bicycle. On the day of my high school graduation, I raced on my bike to the florist to get a corsage and didn't pay attention to Spot who got a late start in chasing me. I returned home by a different route, got dressed, went to the exercises, etc. The next day nobody could locate Spot. Finally, after looking everywhere, I retraced my trip to the florist and found Spot dead in the middle of the street. He had been hit by a car. We buried him in our backyard.

My main activity between ages ten and thirteen centered around Lusher School. When I returned there to the fifth grade, I had to reacquaint myself with everyone and, in the process, got into two fights. One with Richard Andry who was a grade ahead of me. I think it had something to do with playing marbles. Anyway, he beat the heck out of me. Later, we became good friends. The other memorable fight was with Raymond Ball, and to my knowledge, it all started because our peers wanted to see us fight. I can remember throwing Ray down and sitting on him, but when I popped him good in the mouth, he really got mad, rolled me over and pinned me down, hitting me with everything before our audience stopped us.

We had a snowball man, Charlie Palmissano, who came around daily in the summer in his 1930 Austin that he converted into a truck. Charlie scraped the ice by hand and had perhaps twenty different flavors. My favorites were spearmint and chocolate. Snowballs were so refreshing on a hot day. The cost was about five cents apiece. One day Sen. Huey Long's son, Palmer, came by in his Model A Ford. (He was only fourteen versus our age of around twelve.) His father somehow got him a license to drive. Palmer was a very obnoxious kid. Anyway, Palmer pulled up behind Charlie's truck while we were giving him our orders. He pushed us aside and demanded that Charlie make as many snowballs as a dollar would cover. So we had to wait forever for Charlie to serve the great Palmer Long. Palmer then dumped all of those juicy snowballs (but one) into the street and drove away howling. The things you can remember!

Love you,
Dad

May 2, 1994

Dear Anne,

To continue with my early life during fifth through seventh grades, I began to broaden my friendship with a number of people. However, I must tell you of an unusual experience. I think it occurred in fifth grade. A new boy came to our class. He moved to town from Texarkana, Arkansas. Name was Coulter Prescott. The family bought a bungalow on Lowerline Street, just a half block from Lusher School. We became good friends in no time and did lots of things together in the second half of the school year. For some reason, his family decided to spend the whole summer back in Texarkana. I was very sorry to see him leave, because there were things we had planned to do during summer vacation. Anyway, when school started again in the fall, Coulter didn't show up. I checked with other friends, with teachers, etc., but no one knew anything. I checked his house and it was still closed, but it looked as though the furniture was there. A few days later my home room teacher called me aside and revealed that shortly before the Prescotts were to return to New Orleans, they went fishing and there was an accident. Mrs. Prescott and Coulter had drowned and Mr. Prescott could only save himself. What a tragedy! I just couldn't believe Coulter wasn't alive. Many years later, I worked for Gulf Oil. It turned out that Mr. Prescott was also with the company and eventually became the Southern Division General Manager (maybe a vice president). Before leaving Gulf, Prescott had give me a couple of special assignments and seemed pleased with my results. During my eight years with Gulf I had never discussed my relationship with his son. Upon leaving, I felt compelled to tell him of my friendship with Coulter when we were in the fifth grade. Perhaps I shouldn't have, because tears came to his eyes.

I made friends with guys who lived all over the Carrollton area. A few lived over on Audubon Boulevard between Willow Street and Claiborne Avenue. This was a pretty well-to-do area (and still is). Played lots of sand lot (tackle) football in the side yard of Billy and Roy Hodges. Others were Raymond and Ronnie Ball who lived on Audubon Street behind the Hodges' house. Also there were Charles Hanson, Sammy Eaton, Larry Merrigan, Wilmer Thomas and a Verlander kid. Others in my class who lived on Audubon Boulevard were Irwin Isaacs, Staigg Ray and Dale Stancliff. They weren't the athletic types but I had lots of fun with them, either trading postage stamps or playing games in Irwin's huge attic. He had an elaborate electric train system, pool table, ping pong table, etc. He lived in a beautiful pink stucco house next to the Bestoff mansion (K&B Drugs).

Have to go.

Love you,
Dad

16

May 8, 1994

Dear Anne,

More memories of friends in grade school. I became good friends with Charles Schwartz, who lived on Broadway behind Billy Coat's home on Pine. Charlie Schwartz came in and out of my life on several occasions and for different reasons, which I will describe later. He and I attended grammar school (Lusher), high school (Fortier), and college (Tulane) at the same time. Some people will want to understand why I had several friends who happened to be Jewish. At that age there was no strong discrimination. Also my parents were very broad-minded and certainly influenced my thinking. I suppose my Jewish friends may have thought I was of the same faith, because when Gottschall is pronounced fast, it sounds like Godchaux. We didn't associate with black kids, not because we had any animosity toward them, but because they just weren't around. Due to the social code in the South, they were simply excluded from our lives, had different schools, churches, public transportation, restaurants, neighborhoods, etc. Remember the lyrics in South Pacific—"You've got to be taught . . ." Anyway, getting back to Charlie, he was the only child of parents who came from Romania. We were walking home from school one day and I told him we had a few chickens in our backyard and they were laying eggs. He had to see this so I took him into one of our whitewashed chicken coops, raised a hen off her nest and there was an egg. This thrilled Charlie so much that he had to sit there staring at it. Charles and I were good friends with another classmate, Irwin Isaacs, who lived over on Audubon Boulevard. His family owned Marx Isaacs department store downtown. The three of us did lots of things together in the sixth grade. They insisted that I join their cub scout troop that met in their synagogue facilities at the corner of Calhoun and St. Charles Avenue. I was the only Christian in the bunch, but what really interested me were the football games we played in Audubon Park. I was a pretty good runner (and dodger) but I learned that Jack Gordon, another member of the troop, was a little better than I. We respected each other's ability. Charles also got me briefly into a dance club where kids my age were taught all the steps. While I didn't mind learning to dance, I was less interested because the girls weren't too attractive—except Jean Hirsch. Anyway, I dropped out because there were other things to do and people to be with.

Love you much,
Dad

17

Dear Anne,

During the 1930s, we had a wide assortment of children that lived in our immediate neighborhood. I recall the big boys as David Fichman, Andrew Wolert, Bob Cosgrove, Billy Coats, Buddy Courter, Jack Robinson, Oscar Schneidau, Dave Melville, Jimmy Dwyer and Joe Joe Dale. A few more that lived nearby but hung around were Pat Murphy, Ed Leverich and Graham (?). The big girls were Sweetie Courter, Valerie Sequin (visiting at the Low's house), Frances England, Cecile and Katherine Stuart and Wandahope Bailey. The little guys were Sonny and Tommy Bailey, Ed Talbot, Donald Reinackle, Guy Mioton, Bill Milkeild, S. J. Weiss, J. C. Randall, Harold Melville, and the very little Jackie Weinmann and Seymour Weiss. A few others hung around like Billy Arbogast, Allen Favrot, Bobby Zetzmann and Ralph Chevis. The little girls were my sister Jane, Charlotte Coats, Betty White, Babette Fichman and Ruby Wolert. Then there were those roughly in my age bracket like Ray Courter, Thayer Fichman, Jack Sequin (visiting the Lows' house), Bob Dunwody, Charlie Schwartz, John Miazza and Roy White. These folks will not be of interest to anyone except those mentioned or their descendants, but I thought it appropriate to reveal.

Beginning in about the seventh grade, I became an avid stamp collector. This was another way of broadening my array of friends. I traded stamps with a number of people, including Noalie Cire, an "older lady" in her twenties who lived two doors down from us. Noalie's claim to fame was getting $500 from the Coca-Cola Co. for submitting the slogan in a contest that said, "The pause that refreshes." Some award for some slogan! She introduced me to the Crescent City Stamp Club that met occasionally downtown in the Roosevelt Hotel. I'll never forget winning the door prize at one of those meetings. It was an unused block of fifty-cent Graf Zeppelins. Probably the most valuable in my collection—even today. It is slightly marred by a brown smudge that came from my eating a Hershey Bar. I traded stamps with people like Ed Wynne, Charlie Steidtmann, Ivan Mattes, Jordan Brown, David Kleck, Irwin Isaacs, Delbert French and many others. My Aunt Glenn in Harrisburg, Pennsylvania, had a friend who owned the Moorhead Knitting Mills. They received correspondence from all over Central and South America. One of their secretaries would send me a pile of stamped envelopes every so often. Then I really hit the jackpot! Bob Cosgrove's father (next door) had a collection, but Bob had no interest whatsoever. So one Christmas day, Mr. Cosgrove came over and gave me his entire collection. This greatly increased the volume and value of my collection. I still hold on to it, though I gave up collecting long ago. Everything is in an old Dobbs hat box that I haven't touched for many years.

Have to go.

Love,
Dad

May 23, 1994

Dear Anne,

      What I am about to relate may seem childish, even corny, but the subject was something that occupied our time and our thoughts when I was growing up. The Gulf South in general and New Orleans in particular, had an abundance of bugs, insects and little animals due to the prevailing warm temperature and humid climate. As a consequence, youngsters came in contact at one time or another with many kinds of creatures. In the wetland areas of the city we found tadpoles that eventually turned into frogs. There were several varieties of frogs, from little green ones to the large brown ones. We would catch (never kill) them and put into shoeboxes punctured with holes. Of course, there were all kinds of snakes, from small green ones to the large black garter snake that was scary at first, but not harmful. We'd try to kill any of them before they could slither away. The one dangerous snake was the poisonous water moccasin—we stayed clear of them. We had crawdads (a kind of crayfish) that built mud mounds in the drainage ditches. And then there were all kinds of turtles, both those that lived on water and those on land. This reminds me about the folks who made either Colgate or Pepsodent toothpaste. They offered live miniature green turtles that you could obtain after sending in a certain number of coupons that came with the purchase of the toothpaste. Along with the turtles (which were no bigger than the palm of a five year old) came some turtle food and instructions on how to care for them. They always died eventually. We had heard that these turtles came from a swamp in Louisiana, but never could verify. Then there were the lizards that climbed vines or porch screens and changed color depending on what they were clinging to. They were only four to six inches long and we had fun trying to catch them by their tails. There was another reptile that was the size of a lizard that had shiny black skin with an orange streak down his back. We called them scorpions, but that was a misnomer.

      At certain times of the year we had lots of lightning bugs (fireflies) that came out at night and lit up the air. We'd knock them down with our hands, but their glow left shortly afterward. Also in the evenings we heard the crickets and locusts in concert. Locusts were fun to catch, but you couldn't locate them unless it was daytime and they were almost dead. We also had quite a few bats that would fly around very fast on summer nights. I never saw one up close, dead or alive. We had some mice, but not too many as I recall. An occasional rat would come out of the sewers and run along the top of your backyard fence—always at night. We heard that the rats came from the foreign registered ships that came into New Orleans to unload on the river. The rats would escape to the docks on the ship-handling lines. The constant pests in New Orleans were the roaches—all kinds, all sizes, fast and slow-moving—and you would try to step on them every time you saw one. We never got rid of roaches. Just had to get along with them. They were the year-round insect. Of course we had ants, all kinds: black, brown or red. Never leave any food around inside or out of the house—they'd find it. Also had carpenter ants that chewed on wood anywhere. Also termites, either in the flying or wood-eating stage. They were devastating to wood that touched the ground, and in some cases would build mud tunnels over brick or concrete to get to the wood. Homes in New Orleans were always being repaired for termite damage.

Of course we had millions of mosquitos most of the year and often gnats to go with them. Both were so bothersome whenever you sat outside. We were somewhat thankful for the mosquito hawks (dragonflies), which feasted on mosquitos. The hawks were fun to catch and hold in your fingers. They would try to bite, but your skin was too tough for them. Like most everywhere else, we had flies that were bothersome, especially when you were concentrating on something. Some flies could really bite. Then we had those big bull flies that would somehow get into your house and then knock themselves against your window or screen trying to escape until they were exhausted or you executed them. I forgot to mention that sometimes when a mosquito lit on your arm and you tightened your muscle, the thing couldn't pull his sticker out. Then you killed him with your hand and found your blood and dead mosquito all over your arm. We'd do this sometimes whenever we were completely bored.

Then there were worms—brown, gray or red, fast or slow-moving—which were always found in the ground under a piece of embedded wood or slate. They would also come up out of the ground or a crack in the pavement after a hard rain—made good fishing bait. We also had tree worms, like the silk worms in mulberry trees. Along with the ground worms, you would find cute little gray doodlebugs. These harmless creatures were fun to have crawl across your hands. There were also some white-ringed worms found under objects on the ground but I never learned what they were or why they existed. We had "thousand leggers" too, which were no fun except to stomp on them, if you were quick enough.

Then there were caterpillars—the black or brown hairy ones and the ominous-looking green ones that smelled when you squashed them. There were all kinds of beetles: stink beetles, bright orange or black beetles, a few Japanese beetles, and also June bugs, which I thought were flying beetles.

And . . . we had bees, hornets, wasps and yellow jackets. I'm sure every kid has been stung at least once. You just stayed clear of them but sometimes you couldn't avoid getting stung, if you walked around barefoot in the grass or sat on clover.

We had gorgeous butterflies in all sizes and colors, and there was always a huge array of yellow ones that migrated from Canada to Mexico every year. Also had swarms of grasshoppers, both brown and green.

There were all kinds of spiders: black, brown, yellow, and gray. Just leave something alone for a few months and a spider would spin his web from it. Once in a while we would see a poisonous black widow.

Only once did I see a huge praying mantis—out in Metairie. What an odd looking creature! Every so often we would uncover snails in damp places and watch them slowly move along. Never harmed them. Well, enough of this subject.

Love you,
Dad

May 27, 1994

Dear Anne,

    I had another hobby—building model airplanes—but it was brief. I spent several weeks putting together a PBY—a large amphibious airplane. About the time I finished the fuselage, which was made up of hundreds of pieces of balsa wood, mother called me to lunch for the third time. I jumped up from the card table, laid the model on my chair and raced to lunch. Afterwards, I dashed back to my project, only to sit down on my model, crushing it completely. I gave up building model aircraft.

    Sister Jane had been taking piano lessons from a very talented lady who was graduated from the University of Michigan School of Music. Name was Sarah Nadler. She was very much in demand. One day she stayed for dinner and the during the evening she mentioned that she would teach the two of us for the price of one. I was stuck despite my strong objections. I became a prime example of the kid who was forced to take piano lessons, while my friends would stand outside and tease me about it. I had these lessons for about a year and learned very quickly—hated to read the music and memorized everything. I can remember playing at a recital in the Hodges home on Audubon Boulevard. I was the only boy in the class! Some of the others were a Bernstein girl, sister Jane, Gloria Thomas, Ann Legendre, Ann Springer and Evelyn Hodges. We had a beautiful baby grand piano that took up much of our living room. I could still play some of the pieces ten years later. Dad sold the piano to Elaine Schneider's family.

    Sometime between ages eight and thirteen, I inherited a magazine route from Bill Barnes. I delivered the *Saturday Evening Post, Ladies Home Journal, Colliers* and *Liberty* magazines. Had about fifty customers all together. I would pick the magazines up weekly from a sales rep's car and deliver on my bicycle. My territory stretched from Fontainbleau Boulevard to St. Charles Avenue and from Lowerline to State Street. Years later I got acquainted in college with the children of some of my customers. Two were girls whom I flirted with, but they didn't mind—in fact, looked forward to my coming to the front door. The hardest part of the job was collecting the money. I also took over a *Times-Picayune* newspaper route for three months one summer. Had to get up at 3:00 A.M., ride the bike over to where they dumped the bundles, folded them up so you could throw, if necessary. My route was a six square block area. I'll never forget delivering a paper (at say 4:00 A.M.) to a big house with a porch full of rocking chairs. The family had a retarded son much older than I. Once, when I put their paper on the porch, he wheeled around in one of the rocking chairs and screamed, scaring the hell out of me. I quit delivering newspapers.

    Take care.

Love you,
Dad

May 31, 1994

Dear Anne,

By now you might guess that my favorite sport was football. One of my disappointments in life was not being big or heavy enough to play varsity ball in college or even in high school. What really griped me was many of my friends that I played sandlot ball with as a youngster somehow grew bigger and went on to play varsity ball in school. The earliest football I can remember was in the Hodges side yard on Audubon Boulevard. This was a rough-shod tackle game with not much protection in uniforms. Later we graduated to larger fields of play on portions of the Tulane campus near Willow Street. There was also the prep field where the Tulane University squad sometimes scrimmaged. Anyway, the procedure was to dash over there every Saturday morning in the fall and winter months. We'd choose up sides of anywhere from eight to thirteen each and played hard tackle ball. Some of the kids were the Ball brothers, Raymond and Ronnie, Oscar McMillan, Elmo Fischer, Donald and Marion Wellford, Paul Tessier, Billy McCord, Charles Hanson, Sammie Eaton, and one of the D'Antoni boys who always had the complete uniform. I just had a helmet, shoulder pads and Keds. Paul Tessier became a terrific player in high school, and had a neat stutter step. Elmo Fischer made the best flying tackles (now outlawed). We played in all kinds of weather and came home completely exhausted—and often injured. My forté was running with the ball—I was a "scat back." One day a big, strange kid arrived to play. I took the kickoff and weaved and dodged around everyone but this guy. I took the chance of running into him at full speed since I was so close to the goal line. He knocked me unconscious. When I woke up I learned he was Doc Blanchard, who went on to West Point after playing at St. Stanislaus in Bay St. Louis, Mississippi. He made All-American at the U.S. Military Academy and played in that famous backfield of Davis, Blanchard, Anderson, McWilliams and Tucker. Carl Anderson was at Fortier High just one year and transferred to Rugby Academy before going to GMA and the Point.

We also played a lot of touch football on the field in back of Fortier High or in the street on Pine. I remember playing touch ball during the lunch hour or gym hour at Fortier with Ray Ball, Ed Vales and Dave Dixon. We used either a regular football or a tennis ball. Touch ball was right down my alley because I was so light and skinny. I could bob and weave all over the place before being touched. When we played in the neighborhood on Pine Street, Roy White was a good player. In fact, he later made the varsity team at Newman High. John Miazza was also a good, intelligent player. We also had Bob Dunwody and Jack Sequin and even let the little guys like Sonny Bailey and Bobby Zetzmann play with us.

Oh, I forgot to mention that I also played a little football (as well as baseball) in the (then) open field between the Tulane Sugar Bowl Stadium (now gone) and Claiborne Avenue. My memory of who the regulars were is fuzzy, but I do remember kids like Jack Dane, Tom Lennox, a kid whose last name was Constantine, and a great little runner that I'm almost sure was Johnny Martinez, whom I got to know so well at Tulane and thereafter. I've mentioned before that I joined a cub scout troop that met at Sinai Synagogue (on Calhoun and St. Charles), mainly because they played a little football in the front of Audubon Park. I was the only Gentile in the group, but that didn't bother me. One kid I respected in playing football over there was Jack Gordon, who was killed in World War II.

Must stop.

Love you much,
Dad

P.S. Forgot to mention in a previous letter that I'm guilty of a little bit of graffiti. I scratched my initials on the sidewalk at the uptown/river corner of Pine and Hickory Streets. It's still there.

June 8, 1994

Dear Anne,

During my grade school and high school years one of my closest friends was Jack Sequin. His mother was the daughter of Captain and Mrs. Low, who lived directly across the street from us. The Sequins (a Swiss name) moved down from Garden City, New York, when I was about twelve. While Mr. Sequin was looking for work, they stayed at the Low's house. Later, he started a business in Dallas, Texas, but for some reason Jack and his older sister, Valerie, spent every summer, Christmas holidays and other long weekends at their grandmother's house. Every time Jack came to town we did all kinds of things together. He had a wonderful personality and a great attitude on life. I can remember going swimming or hiking or going to the movies or on long bike rides, etc., with Jack. He blended in perfectly with all the neighborhood kids. Once we set up a communication line between his upstairs bedroom and the clubhouse in my backyard and sent messages to each other by Morse code, until the neighbors and our parents made us take it down. When we didn't have anything else to do we'd play tunes on our okarinas (like "Christopher Columbus"). As we got older, Charlotte Coats (in the next block) had a crush on him and began to "muscle in" on the time we spent together. This attention was aided by the fact that Billy Coats began courting Jack's sister. Eventually, Bill and Valerie got married. Anyway, I didn't blame Charlotte and wasn't really jealous. It was just that whenever I had planned to do something with Jack and the other guys, she would invite him to her house or to go somewhere with her family—even had him spend time up the river at the Coats' plantation at Somerset.

Jack and I corresponded all during high school and college. On one occasion in our college days he came down to New Orleans during spring break with his friend Bill. I was always bragging about the good-looking girls I knew in New Orleans. So he asked if I would fix them up with blind dates. This put me in somewhat of an embarrassing position. I didn't go steady with anyone—was nice to all girls, though I did have favorites. So I asked my three best girlfriends at the time, if they wouldn't mind triple dating—and they all accepted. The girls were Betty Waggaman, Lana Hummel and Harriet Blish—all gorgeous. We went to the very popular (and expensive) Blue Room at the Roosevelt Hotel for dinner and dancing. The orchestra was Xavier Cugat. Had a marvelous time. Had difficulty in deciding on my date. Believe it was Betty. Later, I went into the Navy and Jack enlisted in the Air Force. We corresponded often between my ship somewhere in the Pacific and his B-24 base in England. One of my letters was returned to me un-opened with a note stamped on the envelope that the recipient was missing in action. Jack's B-24 never came back from a bombing mission over Germany.

Must go.

Love you much,
Dad

Dear Anne,

In fifth and sixth grades the girls in the class may have had a crush on some boy, but the fellas paid no attention to them. However, in seventh grade, things changed a bit. To get the boys interested, some of the girls initiated parties. I was torn between my friends who were invited and those who were not. The first girl I paid attention to was Betty Beard. She was not only the best looking but had matured sooner than the others. She did a good job of flirting with the boys she liked. She displayed a figure before the other girls did. I can remember the boys talking about how she shaved the hair under her arms. Anyway, Betty, with help from her family, hosted a truck ride on Mardi Gras day which followed the Rex Parade. It was a huge success, and everyone wore some kind of costume, but I can't remember how we were dressed. I would ride my bike by her house on Jeannette Street just to see if I could get a glimpse of her, but didn't dare to stop. Was too shy and scared. Once when I saw her in the front yard, she asked if I would come inside. This really frightened me and I made excuses that I had to go somewhere else. Her number one boyfriend was Bill Ellis, but she also liked Howard Campbell. Anyway, there were several more parties in the last half of seventh grade (before we went to separate public high schools). I remember parties given by Clara Julia Saunders and by Mary Jim Goodwin, who both lived on Audubon Boulevard. Also a big party given by Bill Ellis and attended by Betty Beard, Clara Julia Saunders, Mary Jim Goodwin, Elise Pixburg and Audrey Reinhardt. The boys were Bill Ellis, Bill Eason, Howard Campbell, Kennon McWilliams, Ed Sanford and me. I remember walking over to the party with Kennon McWilliams. Kennon, as I recall, was sweet on Elise Pixburg. The party was interrupted by Palmer Long and his "gang," who weren't invited so they came by making a lot of cat calls and noise. Bill Eason was a tough kid who could handle most anyone in a fight. He dashed out the front door to catch one of the gang and fell down on his face, knocking his teeth up into his gums. This put somewhat of a damper on the party. Betty Beard was her usual enticing self and had all the boys eyeing her. After starting high school I left the social scene for several years. Once in a while I'd see Betty walking home from McMain Girls High. I was still so shy that I always avoided facing her. The older she got the more attractive she became. I think she started dating boys at Tulane University when she was a sophomore in high school. I never saw Betty again, but used to hear some of the older boys in college rave about how gorgeous Betty was.

Must stop.

Love you much,
Dad

June 24, 1994

Dear Anne,

     I'm going to try to remember some highlights of my association with close friends in the neighborhood during the latter part of grammar school and high school. (I believe you met Bob Dunwody on one occasion when he lived in the Minneapolis area—out near Eden Prairie.) Bob was very much an individual. His father died when he was about ten. He was the only child of Mary Dunwody who was quite active her entire life, and to some extent dominated Bob's life, which caused him to be rather delicate when he was growing up. Bob was very intelligent. His mother bought the Weinmann house in the 1600 block of Pine. We had a lot of good times together—his basement was full of things to do. He had a regulation pool table and we would play for hours. He also had a lot of chemistry equipment and experimented in all kinds of things. I can remember our painting strips of paper with a potassium permanganate solution. After it dried, we'd take it over to the nearest streetcar track and lay it all over the rails. When the car wheels rolled over it, it popped like a firecracker. You could also make noise, if you hit the paper with a hammer, but you had to be careful. Bob's front porch was the place where many of the kids gathered to play Monopoly. The game would go on all day and into the wee hours of the night in the summertime. Mrs. D. volunteered to chauffeur us to high school and even Tulane. We sort of had a car pool, that generated a lot of interesting conversation on the way. Passengers were usually Bob, Roy White, John Miazza, Charles Schwartz and myself. The Dunwodys were originally from Atlanta, Georgia. I think Mr. D. owned or operated a naval store's plant on Broad Street before he died. The family was known to have a fair amount of Coca-Cola stock—a very wise investment that helped Mrs. D. and Bob for many years. She was a staunch member of the Little Theater group that performed in the French Quarter and was responsible for my family attending many of the plays. Among Mrs. D.'s many friends was a sociable bachelor, A. Watson Chapman, who was chief chemist at the Celotex plant across the river. I enjoyed many conversations with him. Bob and I crossed paths later in life when we lived in Cleveland, St. Louis, and Minneapolis. He was based in West Chester, Pennsylvania and lived near my Uncle Amos. We visited Bob a couple of times when I was on Naval Reserve training duty. He also contacted Jane from time to time depending on where she was located. Last time I saw Bob was at our fiftieth reunion at Tulane. Well, that's enough about Bob.

Love you,
Dad

July 2, 1994

Dear Anne,

Then I had a crazy kind of friend, in S. J. Weiss, who lived in the big house across the street on the corner—the former Breen house. S.J. was a year or two younger than I. He was the son of Jack Weiss, who managed the ladies clothing department at Godchaux's store downtown. Mr. Weiss moved to Pine Street after his wife died in an automobile accident. He came with his two sons, S.J. and Seymour, as well as his wife's parents, who looked after the two grandsons. Jack Weiss always drove a Packard or a Chrysler convertible and wore very stylish clothes including a tam on his bald head. S.J., Jack Sequin and I palled around for a while. S.J.'s uncle was Seymour Weiss who managed (and later owned) the Roosevelt Hotel, the most prestigious in those days. Uncle Seymour had political connections with the great Huey Long, etc. He lived on the top floor of the hotel in a very elaborate suite with his wife Faye. The Roosevelt was famous for its Blue Room nightclub that was on the circuit for many famous bands and entertainers. Anyway, on several occasions, S.J. would have Jack and I downtown for lunch in Aunt Faye's suite on the top floor of the Roosevelt—very impressive for a thirteen year old. S.J., himself, was a character. Very comical at times—a born actor—he would show us how he could bring tears to his eyes singing "Red Sails in the Sunset." He could also belch loudly anytime he felt like it or when anyone asked him. We played lots of games on their huge front porch in the summer months—all kinds of card games from poker to blackjack to seven and a half, to hearts or canasta and bet with chips. We had chips all over the place. Also played lots of chess. S.J. had a terrible temper at times. Once he had something upset him and went to the side door of his basement and found it locked. So he screamed for someone to open it. When nobody responded he began to kick at the door. He kicked for maybe thirty minutes before the maid finally let him in. S.J.'s brother was a little tot and in constant care of a black nanny (Annie), a very fine and patient woman in a spotless white uniform. As S.J. got older, he became very despondent. There had been problems which we didn't understand at the time. The situation got so bad that S.J. locked himself in a bathroom and turned on the gas heater. Not long afterwards his grandmother came out of the house screaming for help. John Miazza and I dashed in and broke the door down. S.J. survived but may have had some brain damage. Later the family moved away and S.J. disappeared from my life, although I heard he joined the Marine Corps and served his country well at Guadalcanal.

Have to go.

Love you much,
Dad

July 8, 1994

Dear Anne,

Another friend was Roy White, who lived next door to us. The Whites moved in around the mid-thirties. He was my age but a year ahead of me in school. Roy's father was a dentist and the Gottschalls used him for years for all our dental work. Roy attended Newman school and graduated with honors. He went on to Tulane Medical School and had a residency at the Mayo Clinic where he met his wife. Roy's sister, Betty, was even younger than Jane, but I will always remember her playing hopscotch or jacks with the "little girls." Roy was a lovable guy full of laughs and jokes, and used a number of expressions like "Judas Priest," "Job Jammit" and "Son of a Bull Finch," etc., as a substitute for cursing. He was rather heavy and played on the line in football at Newman High. Roy liked to come home and tell stories at length about whatever happened at school that day, what certain students thought about other students, or what silly things his professors did. He wasn't necessarily bragging—just made it enjoyable to listen to. He was the same way relating stories about his football team or his fraternity brothers or medical school classmates—or teachers, like Dr. Hathaway at Tulane crawling on top of his desk to demonstrate how some insect or animal behaved. Roy was an agile athlete despite his size. He had a ping-pong table in a special room in his basement. We played for hours at a time. He held the paddle like a tennis racquet and would slam the ball all over the place while I nearly always returned it with my fountain pen grip on the paddle. Roy would work himself into a frenzy playing this game. I'm sure he would lose five to eight pounds in a match. He would finish literally dripping wet, while I was so skinny I didn't have any fat to lose. I have always enjoyed table tennis, but will never forget the days when I could beat Roy most of the time. Roy would rarely quit—he would keep on insisting that we play again and again. Unfortunately, Roy died at an early age when he operated a medical clinic out in Arizona. I will never forget Roy's hearty laugh or his jovial attitude. Roy was a serious student. He was also an ardent church attender, although the rest of his family never went to church. He would walk to the Carrollton Avenue Presbyterian Church every Sunday without fail to hear Reverend Fortna deliver his sermon. I admired him for this.

Must stop.

Love you,
Dad

July 21, 1994

Dear Anne,

Still another close neighborhood friend was John Miazza, who moved in the mid-thirties to the next block across the street from the Bailey house. John was a year older and a year ahead of me in school. He was very smart, an excellent chess player, and at the same time quite athletic. John was very reserved, didn't say much, but was a good companion never the less. He had a very fair complexion and consequently looked pale most of the time. John tried to interest me in attending his church PF (Pilgrim Fellowship) classes on Sunday evenings, which was like a social hour for teenagers. The Christian Church was small and located on the river side of St. Charles Avenue near Henry Clay (or Webster Street). Some nice people attended this church—like the Saunders family (Clara Julia and Cappie), the Jennings family (Jim and Ed), the Fraser family (Carol Jean) and others that I can't remember. John was influential in my joining SAE (Sigma Alpha Epsilon), the social fraternity at Tulane, but that story will come later. John also asked me to be best man in his wedding. His mother was a house mother for SAE for a while. She was quite active in a number of social things and was friendly with the Davies family (Harry and Sandy) and the Ryniker family (Sam). I was well acquainted with the children. John had a somewhat sad early life. His younger sister died a tragic death and Mr. and Mrs. Miazza were divorced before Mrs. M. moved to Pine Street. Mrs. M. was very devoted to John, like Mrs. Dunwody was to Bob. Forgot to mention that John and I invested, fifty-fifty, in a new Lightning Class sloop, several years after we came back from the service.

I developed two other short-term friends in the seventh grade. Both moved to New Orleans from the St. Louis, Missouri area. One was Frank Kiddoo, who was an out-going individual with an unusual Midwestern twang. He lived over on Versailles Boulevard. His father was the manager of all Woolworth stores in the New Orleans area. Our relationship started with stamp trading. Frank was the object of jokes from my classmates but never let this get under his skin. However, upon entering Fortier High, he became sort of obnoxious toward everyone and I couldn't understand it at the time. Anyway our friendship faded about the time they moved back to St. Louis but I always remembered his better days. Years later, when we lived in St. Louis, I located him through Ed Young, one of my salesmen, whose father was also with the Woolworth Company. Poor Frank had gone to pot for all of his ability. He ended up being a used-car salesman on Kings Highway.

The other friend was Emerson Burnett, who also came from St. Louis. Again, the contact was initiated through stamp collecting. He lived in Leonard King's parents' apartments at Pine and Plum Streets. He was a real nice guy. We happened to build model sailboats together in manual training class. We would work in pairs gouging out the hulls from blocks of mahogany. Worked at both ends with sharp chisels. I missed once and gouged my chisel up Emerson's hand and arm. I never saw so much blood—I even got woozy and almost passed out. To this day I can't stand the sight of blood, or even watching someone who's been cut. I don't even look at inoculations on TV. This was the main reason why I didn't go to medical school when I had the chance. Emerson stayed in New Orleans during first year of high school and then moved back to Kirkwood (St. Louis), Missouri. A few years later Cal Hadden, Carky Guillot, Jack Sequin and I made a three-week trip up north and passed through St. Louis. I looked up Emerson and we had a great time one night at a spot called the Wigwam in Webster Groves. The place was a structure in the shape of a tee-pee that had a bar, dance floor and a nickelodeon for music. The kids all drank beer and jitterbugged, Missouri style. One of the steps was for the girl to swing around from side to side 180 degrees while her partner did his thing—real neat to watch. I loved to dance but for some reason never caught on to jitterbugging. Incidently, that night spot in Webster Groves was still there when we moved to St. Louis years later, but it had been abandoned and was about to fall down.

  That's all for now.

Love you much,
Dad

July 25, 1994

Dear Anne,

At some point in time after moving back to Pine Street our family started attending the Carrollton Avenue Presbyterian Church. The minister, a Reverend Fortna, had a warm, sincere relationship with the entire congregation and was an outstanding speaker. He also happened to be from York, Pennsylvania, near Dad's roots. Jane and I attended Sunday school fairly regularly. There were a lot of fine, substantial people who were members of this little church. Wish I could remember some of the names. I do remember a Mr. Wishart, a crusty old Scotsman, who was probably an elder or trustee who would walk around the Sunday school area like a sergeant-at-arms. The church choir consisted of just four people—two men, a baritone and a tenor, and two women, contralto and soprano. They were very talented. Some of the boys in Sunday school, as I recall, were Jimmy Alexander, David Crais, Don Balovich, Merlin Markel, David Dixon, Lee McCrocklin, Hunter Early, Bradford O'Leary, George Riviere and Frank Norman. Only girls I can remember were Lucinda Hill, the Ivey sisters, and Clare Shannon. For a while we had a great Sunday school teacher, Dr. Hardy Bethea, who had recently finished Tulane Medical School. I'll never forget his sister—she was the only real natural platinum blonde I ever knew. She was beautiful, but much older than I. Once I took a friend of Jane's on a church picnic. She was "Punky" Smith. Had a good time except for a guy by the name of Carroll Johnson who tried to muscle in on the date. Later, in college, I switched my allegiance to the St. Charles Avenue Presbyterian Church. Some of the girls at this church influenced my decision.

I hate to go back to football, but forgot to mention playing ball and doing many other things with the Frantz family who lived in the 1800 block of Broadway. There were Roy and Phares Frantz, and their cousins, Ludy and Billy Frantz—all about my age. Besides football, I enjoyed going over to their house to work their jigsaw puzzles and play cards and other games in their basement. Roy had a girlfriend in Betty Prestiss that I thought was kind of cute. Her family had emigrated from Brazil. Ludy Frantz was a comedian—kept us laughing all the time. While it may not be of interest to you, I feel I should document something somewhere before I lose it. My association with Lusher School and the Carrollton area must have a special place in my memory book. Not long ago I sat down and tried to list all of the kids I had ever known, or was aware of, in the mid-thirties and came up the attached. Think I put down just about everyone in my class. However, I should emphasize that the names in the class groups other than my class might not be in the right place.

Must go.

Love you much,
Dad

R. M. Lusher Elementary School

AGG's Class—1935–39

Edward Fischer
Helen Levy
Raymond Ball
June Beyer
Leon Klinger
Roy Keeney
Audrey Reinhardt
Alvin Gottschall
Kennon McWilliams
Charles Blanchard
Frank Kiddoo
Bill Eason
Mary Lou Marks
Richard Halpern

Saul Feldman
Delbert French
Howard Campbell
Staigg Ray
Coulter Prescott
Charles Schwartz
Epifanio Tusa
Mary Jim Goodwin
Elise Pixburg
Charles Hanson
Emerson Burnett
Edward Sanford
Betty Beard

Gwendolyn Phillips
Tericina Cotourié
Irwin Isaacs
Bradford O'Leary
Mary Allen Monroe
Edwin Taylor
Rosemary Reimuth
Clara Julia Saunders
Conley Von Salzen
Sam Eaton
Bill Ellis
Darrell Griffin
Roland Cockreham

One-half to One Year ahead of AGG's Class

Leonard King
Rich Andry
Betty Grant
Barb McMillan
Rich Queyrouze
Joe Dale
David Monroe
Roy Frantz
Bobby Reinhardt
André Horcasitas

N.C. Cromwell
Betty Beyer
Harold Marx
Elsa Hoehn
Ivan Mattes
Marvin Joseph
Clay Spencer
Dale Stancliff
Harold Levy
Donald Biewer

Rich Cromwell
Ronnie Ball
Harold Athey
Palmer Long
Nellie Ivey
Paul Tessier
Elise Cambon
Donald Levy
Bill Sanford

Two to Four Years Ahead of AGG's Class

Steve Guice
Walter Sessums
Louise Nelson
Betty Sandoz
Bob Cosgrove
Andrew Wolert
Katherine Stewart
John Culbertson
Lloyd Fremaux
Robert Leake
Marshall Ordemann
Cecile Stewart

Walter Grant
David Melville
Charles Nelson
Jane Sandoz
David Fichman
Oscar Schneidau
Wandahope Bailey
Arnold Levy
Jimmy Dwyer
Nester Beyer
Catherine Cornay

Adley Gladden
Pat Murphy
Mary Leake
Billy Coats
Thayer Fichman
Edward Leverich
Edward Merrigan
James Reid
George Leake
Bill Melkild
Harold Cornay

One-half to One and a Half Years behind AGG's Class

Jack Kleppinger
S.J. Weiss
Hubert Clotworthy
Rufus Harris, Jr.
Charles Steidtmann
Ludy Frantz
Noel Genevay
Susie Merrigan
Ricker Schmitt
Nate Halpern
Bill McCord
Billy Zetzmann
Betty Prestiss
Catherine Balmer
Mildred Avegno

Billy Hodges
Robson Dunwody
Aubry Moore
Bob Melkild
Phares Frantz
Harold Melville
Donald Wellford
John Jané
Allen Favrot
Charles Robinson
Leo Lob
Al Bodney
Emile McMillan
Carole Jean Fraser

Cappie Saunders
James Wynne
Margie Rotharmel
Fred Anepohl
Ralph Chevis
Billy Frantz
Charles Farrell
Tom Favrot
Billy Coleman
Jack Queyrouze
Mary Allen Jackson
Parker Schneidau
Joseph Fontana

Jane's Class Two Years behind AGG

Jack Dabdoub
Jordan Brown
Alan Oden
Edward Talbot
Lela Bridger
Roy Hodges
Charles Eshleman
Mary Lou Bonnecauze
Bill Barnes
Amalie Clark
Dan LeGardeur
Punky Smith
Sidney Pugh

Carroll Johnson
Shirley Tessier
Elmo Fischer
May Bridger
Jane Gottschall
Betty Morphy
Fred Guice
Albert Ledner
Patty Phillips
Joy Barrett
Mary Palmasano
Gladys Ivey
Sue Stater

Dorothy Planchard
Jack Rich
Alan Robinson
Allen Shelley
Richard Piske
Louis Burkes
Jack Petagna
Bill Arbogast
Curtis Amuedo
Charles Kahn
Margie Keeney
Larry Merrigan
Evelyn Hodges

One-half to Two Years behind Jane's Class

Billy Balmer
Marion Sandoz
Billy Pugh
Gloria Thomas
Jackie Weinmann
Denise Sessums
Tom Bailey
Guy Mioton
Ruby Wolert

Bill Van Horn
Kenny Robinson
Charlotte Coats
J.C. Randall
Georgia Fischer
Betty White
Sunny Bailey
John Ellis
Anthony Ingargiola

Nollie Felts
Bobby Zetzmann
Tom Hodges
Catherine Clark
Gordon Heffron
Dick Rotharmel
Bill Renaudin
Babette Fichman
Bob Bermudez

Teachers

1A—Dixon
1B—Lee

Fifth, Sixth, Seventh Grades

Reading—Hereford

English—Gravely

Manual Training—Defraites
Sub—O'Toole

Geography—Hay

History—Lawes

Fourth Grade—Vogel

Arithmetic—McCabe
Music &
Penmanship—Valles
Recreation—Bergeron

Principals

Ms. Serjax

Ms. Hildebrand

Part II

The High School Years

July 28, 1994

Dear Anne,

Entering high school was a big thing in my early life. I was such a little guy and so young that I stood in awe of everything that embraced high school. Because New Orleans was predominantly Catholic, it's my understanding that the public school system at that time patterned parochial education, in that there were only seven grades of grammar school and from there the boys and girls went to different high schools. I began at the tender age of thirteen. Being separated from the opposite sex caused me to leave the social scene that had some beginnings in seventh grade. I concentrated on keeping up with my studies and participating in all kinds of sports after school. I attended Alcée Fortier High, one of two public high schools in the city. It was the most recent, having been completed in 1931. It was a huge four-story structure on Freret Street at Nashville Avenue and took up two whole blocks. I'm guessing it was almost a mile from my house on Pine Street. I know that Mrs. Dunwody chauffeured us there in the mornings and we walked the "long way" home in the afternoons. Sometimes I walked both ways, and later rode my bike both ways. Fortier High was governed by a stern principal, John R. Conniff, who insisted on some kind of punishment for any infraction of his many rules. However, this was probably the only way to maintain discipline in a school with 2,500 or more boys, all kinds and shapes, with varying degrees of intelligence and morality. You reported to a home room for about fifteen minutes in the morning before moving to various other classrooms for both required and elective subjects. Mr. Conniff would come in on the public address system from his office—first with a morning greeting, then with significant news and then finally announcing those students who had misbehaved in some way, as well as the punishment he would inflict, usually so many days after school in study hall, Rooms 301 or 302. Some guys would get "continuous service" in study hall until Conniff thought they had learned their lesson. The most fortunate thing about Fortier High was that it had outstanding teachers in almost any subject. Reason for this was because the country was in the depths of a severe economic depression and teaching was the only way these competent people could get jobs. With such a large enrollment, Fortier excelled in athletics and had some of the best sports teams in the state. We always had pretty good teams in football, baseball and even basketball. Had outstanding teams in swimming, track and field, and tennis.

The only social event I went to in my freshman year was a fraternity rush party. Somehow, somebody nominated me to be considered for membership in Phi Lambda Epsilon (PLE). I vaguely remember going to this party over on Fern or Burdette Street, just off of St. Charles Avenue, hosted by some older guys, twins by the name of Schroeder or Schaeffer. I remember very few of the other fellows except for Nester Beyer, June's older brother. There were some girls, the cutest one being Tiny Umbach. She was the main attraction, especially when she danced. I'll never forget the piece they played over and over on the record player, Bing Crosby singing "Small Fry." Anyway, this activity was too adult for me. I got cold feet and turned down the invitation to join PLE. However, I was asked again, when I was a Junior and accepted, but this is another story.

Have to stop.

Love you much,
Dad

Dear Anne,

I had a number of very competent and talented teachers at Fortier High. First, there was the stern taskmaster, a Mr. Blanchard, who taught us Latin. This was a difficult language to learn, much less use, but the advantage in taking Latin was that many English and other language words are derivatives of Latin words. Often, if you came upon a rarely used word that you didn't understand, a good knowledge of Latin could give you a hint of its meaning. Another excellent teacher was a Mr. Martin for general science or chemistry. He was outstanding. He would also give an occasional lecture on why alcohol was a menace to good health and to society in general. Another capable science teacher was Karlem (Ducky) Riess, but I didn't have him. Got to known him better when he was elevated to a professorship at Tulane University. Then there was Ms. Cecelia Grim, who made algebra easy. I was very interested in geometry (plain and solid) and trigonometry, because anything graphic or with pictures was easy for me to understand, but I can't remember the teacher's name—a very tough-talking woman. Ms. Marchal was an excellent French teacher. She not only made you learn the language, she insisted on your pronouncing the words correctly. Mrs. Reed was my civics teacher. She knew her subject cold and made you understand the organization and mechanics of government, the Constitution, the Bill of Rights, etc., and yet she admitted to being a very devout Communist—and dared the school board to suspend her (they didn't). I was crazy about one of my English teachers, a Ms. Williams. She was a bug on making us turn in themes, essays, term papers, etc. She really cut me down to size once when I borrowed a couple of sentences from *Time* magazine in writing a paper on Ignace Paderewski, the Polish pianist/statesman. Mr. Joe Abraham was good in communications. He would record and play back our voices to show how good or lousy we were and to reflect our accents and how so many of us mispronounced words. Messrs. Bierhorst and Tortomasi taught mechanical drawing. They certainly taught this lefthander to forget script and begin printing everything. Elmer Flanders was a sharp civics and economics teacher. Our football coach, Jack Pizzano, held gym classes in his spare time. They usually consisted of nearly one hour of calisthenics. He believed everyone was out of shape except his varsity players. Larry Lashley (football), Dutch Luchsinger (track) and Harry Gamble (swimming) were outstanding coaches, but kind of dull for health and hygiene classes. Then there was a Mr. Leonard Dennena, head of the school music department and band instructor. He became so competent in his field that LSU hired him to be the director of their university band. Other teachers in my memory, but can't match them with subjects were Alma Bittenbring, Joe Carson, Joe Kluchin, Ms. Towles, Mr. Tonglet, Harold Heidingsfelder, Charles MacMurdo, Steve Ozenovich, Mr. Romeo, Mr. Wellinghoff, Ethyl Pinsky and J. Skelly Wright (who later became a federal judge).

I have saved my most impressive teacher for last—Wilma Lilburn, a wonderful person who taught public speaking, debating and dramatics. She really taught me how to get over stage fright. When she accomplished this, she influenced me to go out for the debating team in my senior year and forget about the track team. That took some doing, since these two activities came up in the spring of the year and there was just no time for both. After much practice and effort I became the "fifth wheel" on the Fortier debating team. The first string members were John Roberts and Charles Schwartz (my old grammar school/neighborhood friend). These two guys were super. Years later John became a national executive with either the Rotary or the Kiwanis Club. Charles became a successful lawyer and federal judge. Second string were Dan Verges and Jim Garrison. Dan went into chemical engineering, but never stopped talking, and Jim, of course, was in local politics, district attorney for the city of New Orleans, and had a crazy idea about how John F. Kennedy was assassinated. Remember the movie? Then there was AGG—number five on the team. We won most of our debates, but suffered a devastating loss to a Catholic girls high school team. The school was over on Canal Street near Carrollton Avenue and maybe Warren Easton High. Can't remember the name, but years later I took a train from New Orleans to Laurel, Mississippi, and a lady came up to me to say she was on the team that beat us and remembered my face.

Anyway, getting back to Ms. Lilburn, she was also the director of all the school plays. Very talented woman. She was also a silent recruiter for Phi Lambda Epsilon, the high school fraternity I mentioned in a previous letter. She used her knowledge of students to recruit and her influence to persuade this group to invite me to join again when I was a junior. She was, in fact, responsible for PLE having a great number of first-class guys, most of the key people on the athletic teams, student government, etc.

I should add a couple more things about Ms. Lilburn. She always said that to get over stage fright, you should walk slowly over to the podium or center of the stage, take a slow deep breath and while looking over everyone from left to right, develop the feeling that you were the expert on your subject and you were going to enlighten those stupid fools in the audience. Then begin speaking slowly and distinctly. She also taught us what to do with our hands if there was no podium. Just make fists and bring them up to your waist. It feels awkward at first, but it makes you look confident and relaxed to the audience.

Have to stop. Take care.

Love you much,
Dad

August 13, 1994

Dear Anne,

The first two years of high school seemed difficult for me academically. I passed all the subjects, but my grades weren't so hot. I joined and became active in the Stamp Club. In the spring of my sophomore year I went out for the track team, because I thought I was a pretty fast runner. The 100-yard dash was the only race I was any good at—and only once did the coach clock me at ten seconds flat. I also entered broad jump and high jump competition. I made five feet, eleven inches, only once with the scissors-type leap. I broad jumped between twenty-one and twenty-three feet. I was still a frail kid. The preparation for track was very arduous and time-consuming. We spent late January, February and part of March doing calisthenics and stretching our muscles, followed by running laps (which always got to me and discouraged my distance running). We trained every day after school over at the old Tulane Football Field and Stadium (in back of the Naval ROTC Building). The dressing area was in the dank, dark quarters underneath the stadium. It was deplorable—the toilets wouldn't work and the showers had only cold water and the whole area had the stench of BO. Some of the big guys, juniors or seniors, were Joe Anderson, high jumper, who did a roll-over leap perpendicular to the bar, also Bob Segura and Charlie Vosburgh, quarter milers, and Red Dameron, a fine discus thrower. Wish I could remember some of the others. I trained with a classmate by the name of Clyde. His older brother was on the team. Anyway, I stuck it out, but wasn't good enough to participate in any of the events with other schools. Competition was fierce to make any sports team in a high school with 2,500 boys. I didn't have any better luck as a junior, but thought I had a chance in my senior year, except Ms. Lilburn convinced me that I would benefit more by being on the debating team, so I dropped track. I was crazy about track and field events and followed the meets in the newspapers. Was always interested in Glenn Cunningham's performances in the mile run. Kept in touch with all the world records, and had a strong interest in the NCAA meets, the AAU meets and the Olympic Games, especially the 1936 games held in Germany. I kept track of people like Jesse Owens in the dashes and the broadship, "Slats" Hardin in the hurdles, big Joe Torrance (from LSU) in the shotput and Cornelius Warmerdam in the pole vault.

I tried playing tennis briefly. My only exposure was when my father gave my sister Jane and me a racquet for Christmas—just one racquet for both of us. I can remember Rufus Harris Jr. (who lived down the street) and the son of the dean of Tulane Law School (and later president) asking me to play with his father and another Tulane professor. Well, as I recall, Rufus wasn't so hot and I was terrible. Thereafter, sister Jane started to play tennis more than I did, so I gave it up. In those days, tennis took some money and we didn't have much. Besides, I had many other things to do. Golf was another sport I thought about, but back in the thirties you had to be wealthy to play golf.

During the lunch hour at Fortier High, it took about fifteen minutes to eat something in the cafeteria. The balance of the time was used to play touch football on the athletic field behind school with guys like David Dixon, Eddie Vales, Earl Ittmann, Edwin Stockmeyer, Charles Hanson, Raymond Ball and others.

I will never forget seeing a kid during the lunch hour who always sat by himself behind the athletic dressing facility slowly eating a huge pumpernickel sandwich. He was a weight lifter and wore very thick glasses. He wouldn't talk to anyone but you could always find him there eating that sandwich he brought from home. Can't remember his name. Why do things like this stick in your mind?

Fortier High had outstanding sports teams. While I was there we used to beat everybody in football except perhaps Jesuit High. It's strange, but I still remember the Jesuit fight song, because it had a terrific melody. I can still hum or whistle the tune. Can't remember anything about Fortier's song. Most of the games were played at night at the old Loyola Stadium on Freret Street or out at Gormley Field in City Park. A few of the football players I remember were Jeff Oser, George McCaskey, Fred Wendt, the Richardson brothers, Eddie Fischer (my classmate at Lusher), Benny Lampo, Bernie Lipkis, David Bernstein, Stan Asbury, Louis McFaul, Tom Lennox, the Eason brothers, Emmanuel Defraites, Charles Modenbach, Bill McGinnis, Rudy Bittman and Larry Zibilich.

The baseball teams were fair except for one year when some of the Fortier boys played on an American Legion team that went to the National Finals and when Howard Pollet was one of the pitchers and a couple of the other guys, I think, were Charley Christina and Joe LaCroutes.

Our basketball team had guys like Kennon McWilliams and Gabe Villarubbia.

The swimming team had Bobby Wiegand, who claimed he swam across the Mississippi River once from his home at Nine Mile Point.

The tennis team had some great players like Roy and Earl Bartlett, Billy McGehee and Tommy Stokes.

I think it was my junior year when Fortier sponsored a carnival/fair. There were all kinds of the type games you see at state fairs. I was employed as a barker to get students, parents, and the general public to come spend a little change to throw baseballs at targets. Had the best time shouting my head off.

Adjacent to the Fortier athletic field was Allen School, which housed elementary classes as well as a girls' commercial high school (on the top floor). This was about as close as Fortier boys could get to females with the exception of Richmond's Pharmacy on Freret Street where clusters of girls from Allen hung out after school. It had the usual soda fountain and white ceramic tile floor with a few wire-back chairs and tables. I would slip in and out once in a while to buy something—never stuck around. It was obvious the girls were there to meet the boys (and vice versa), drink sodas or Cokes and smoke cigarettes. The place always had a pallor of smoke halfway to the ceiling. I never gave smoking a thought until I was in the Navy. Never gave the girls much thought either, because I wanted to hurry home to participate in some sports with my friends. That drugstore seemed like a den of iniquity anyway—most of the Fortier boys there were the ones that were in trouble with "Warden" Conniff, our principal.

Love you much,
Dad

August 20, 1994

Dear Anne,

Sometime during my junior year at Fortier High, I was asked to join Phi Lambda Epsilon fraternity. I considered myself fortunate to be invited again since I had declined an invitation as a freshman. Anyway, with the help of Ms. Lilburn (considered the chapter Mother), I agreed to pledge. In those days pledges went through some degree of hazing but I took it in stride. PLE had their meetings on Sunday afternoons in a conference room of the then Roosevelt Hotel. I think it was obtained at a reasonable price because someone in the chapter was close to the hotel management. We had many of the top students as members. It's been so long ago but those I can remember are Edward Merrigan, A. J. Nugon, George McCaskey, Tom Lennox, Louis McFaul, Fred Wendt, Stanley Asbury, Curtis and John Fitzgerald, Milton Singleton, Bob Courtin, John Roberts, H. B. Bradford, Hunter and Forres Collins, Jim Garrison, Allan Robinson, Nester Beyer, and a good many others—probably thirty total in any given year. McCaskey and Wendt were each president of the student body. We had several parties during the year I was active. I think one of them was out at Louie Prima's Penthouse next to the old yacht pen near West End Park and the New Basin Canal. PLE held a big formal dance, but I was a little shy of the girls, so I went stag. Had a good time though. The girls I met seemed to like me, which encouraged my interest immensely from then on forward. I really couldn't be too active in PLE because (1) I was only made a full member in my senior year, (2) I had to excel academically, for reasons I will explain later, and (3) I had a strong interest in the debating team as well as the track team. I also had a social interest in visiting Peggie Baker's house on Saturday nights, which I also must explain later. Two things stick in my memory with PLE. One was the informal initiation when all the pledges were taken to a trucking company warehouse somewhere downtown. We were blindfolded and stripped of our clothing and forced to lay down on our backs on an "altar" which was next to a very hot fire. We were then told to brace ourselves so we could be branded with PLE on our chests. At first the brand seemed like it was going to be scalding hot, but when the thing touched you, it turned out to be very cold dry ice. They made us go through some other shinanegans, but I have forgotten. Several days later, we had our formal initiation downtown at the Roosevelt Hotel. This was a very impressive and serious ceremony. They would take us one at a time from an outer hall into the "inner sanctum." Jim Garrison and I were the last to be brought into the initiation room, and for some reason Jim thought the whole idea was hilarious and started to giggle. It was contagious so I started to snicker as well. All of a sudden the president of the chapter came out in his majestic robe and declared that because we laughed at such a serious affair, we wouldn't be initiated and were subject to expulsion from the fraternity. This development sobered us up real fast, and somehow, later we were forgiven and initiated anyway. Afterwards, when we were pinned and declared full members of PLE, everybody got a kick out of scaring us to death. That night we had a banquet and "Mother" Lilburn was invited and congratulated all the new members.

PLE engaged in a few sports contests with some of the other high school frats, but I'm vague about details. Anyway, Phi Lambda Epsilon was a very nice affiliation and we did maintain a fraternal bond with each other. It certainly helped me to develop a social awareness.

    Must go.

Love you much,
Dad

September 1, 1994

Dear Anne,

While attending Fortier High I developed close friendships with several other classmates. One was with Edwin Stockmeyer, which probably began with trading postage stamps. We got to know each other well throughout high school, college, and for a number of years after our service in the Navy. Edwin was sort of an odd-looking fellow, acted silly at times, but had a very good mind and a sharp sense of humor. He didn't appear athletic, but actively participated in most sports. We would often leave school together and stop by his house on State Street just off Freret. His mother was always there to give us a drink or something to eat. Edwin had an older brother, Carl, who had graduated from Fortier before we entered. Don't know why I should remember this, but once, when we were passing through Carl's bedroom, I saw a big picture of Betty Beard on his desk. You may recall our relationship as classmates back in grammar school. When Edwin and I entered Tulane he was rushed to Beta Theta Pi because his brother was a member. I came close to joining Beta also, because of Edwin and because Roy White, my next door neighbor, was also a member—and he and Carl were good friends. Edwin and I remained close throughout our college years. He introduced me to a number of girls that I eventually dated: Nancy Nunez, Mary Ellen Simon and Virginia Brodie. Edwin was crazy about boats, so he became a frequent companion when I sailed my cat boat out from the Southern Yacht Club. He bugged me for a long time about selling him this boat, so when I bought a Lightning Class sloop, I sold him the cat boat for $550 (Dad had purchased it ten years before for $100 and gave it to me). Edwin was an excellent card player. Sometime after we all married, we helped to organize a poker club, which included Jack Dane, Oscar McMillan, Phil Duvic, Bobby Newlin, Randy Richmond and several others that I can't remember. Edwin and I were in Acheans together. His brother Carl was captain of the balls for quite a few years. I also played a lot of badminton with Edwin and Carl at the New Orleans Athletic Club. Unfortunately, not long after Mother and I moved away from New Orleans (with Pittsburgh Plate Glass), Edwin died of complications. I could never remember Edwin ever being sick.

Another close friend was Jim Garrison, who was a high school fraternity brother, and on the school debating team with me and one of the guys who attended the parties given by Peggie and Wilma Baker (see future letter). Jim was a tall, silent type except when he spoke publicly. He was a real sharp individual who could express himself eloquently, had a dry sense of humor and a keen political awareness and, at times, was a practical joker. Jim moved to New Orleans with his mother and sister from Evansville, Indiana—apparently she divorced their father. Jim's mother was a huge woman with a boisterous, hard-nosed attitude. She happened to be a self-employed oil and gas lease lawyer and did very well financially. At first they lived uptown off State Street somewhere, then moved to the French Quarter and lived on Madison Street, which is only one block long. In fact, they had an apartment next to the one leased by Tennessee Williams, the playwright. Jim's sister developed mental problems and was eventually committed to the hospital next to Audubon Park. Anyway, after Fortier High, Jim and his mother moved to Oklahoma. Several years later they returned to New Orleans, where Jim finished law school at Tulane. Jim and I didn't cross paths again until I worked in Southern Mississippi for Gulf Oil and learned that his mother had moved to Laurel, Mississippi (where there was a big oil strike) and shortly thereafter married Lyon Gardiner, a man of considerable means. All of this occurred before I had met Mother. I would see Jim in Laurel from time to time when he came home from law school or visited from New Orleans. His mother was instrumental in inviting me to several parties in Laurel, one of which was at the Chisholm home where the guests were entertained by her cook's daughter, Leontyne Price. Mrs. Chisholm later sponsored Leontyne's education at Juilliard. Anyway, Jim and I would have long conversations about what we wanted to do in life. I will always remember him saying, "Don't laugh, but I am going into politics and my goal is to be a United States senator." Well, he didn't go quite that far, but he did become the New Orleans district attorney and later a judge. And, of course, there was this JFK thing. I'll tell you about one of his practical jokes. Once, while he was the district attorney for New Orleans, Mother and I were awakened one night about 2:30 A.M. by a policeman at our door. He had a summons for me to go down to the station at Jackson Avenue and Magazine Street, because "I failed to show up in court to explain a number of parking violations." I couldn't imagine how I could be accused of this, because I had received no tickets. Anyway, after I had gotten dressed and gone down to the station and was trying to understand what they had me there for, the desk sergeant finally told me they had made a mistake and released me. The next day Jim called to ask how I enjoyed the experience and broke up laughing about it. As I recall Jim enjoyed shutting down all the honky-tonks on Bourbon Street periodically, although he was probably their most frequent patron.

Another good friend was Michel Fortier whom I first met while working out with the Fortier track team. He and I were close as juniors in high school and often studied together. Although he transferred and completed high school at Newman, we both started at Tulane in mechanical engineering and both joined Delta Tau Delta. However, after our freshman year, his family moved to St. Louis and he elected to finish school at Purdue. Never saw him again.

I was also friendly with Victor Kirschman, whose family owned a department store downtown on Canal Street. He lived close to Fortier on Nashville Avenue. Our mutual interest was in trading stamps.

Still another good friend in high school was Houston Chapman Reynolds (Chappie), but this will take a separate letter, so until later . . .

Think of you always.

Love you much,
Dad

September 6, 1994

Dear Anne,

      To continue telling you about my friendship with Chappie Reynolds, we became acquainted by having the same teachers in English and literature. Chap was a terrific writer and got excellent grades for his essays, themes, etc. I respected him for this and competed with him to see if I could do better and as a result, I improved my ability in written assignments. Since he lived on the way home on Freret Street, we would occasionally leave school together. His father was a professor at the LSU Medical School downtown. His mother died when he was young so his father remarried and Chap had two half-sisters, Charlotte and Gail. As we got to know each other better, we would ride our bikes all over town on the weekends. Once he tried to get me to take our bikes all around Lake Pontchartrain but I can't remember why I didn't go along. Anyway, he went on his own, taking two days and staying overnight in Mandeville. His family attended the St. Charles Avenue Presbyterian Church. One day he asked if I would join him for a visit to the home of Peggie and Wilma May Baker who lived on State Street on the river side of St. Charles Avenue. He had become acquainted with them through church. The Bakers lived in a large comfortable house between Dr. Bethea's and the Lanes' homes. Their father was a doctor at Touro. Anyway, the next Saturday night, we went over there together. It seems that the Bakers had a kind of open house every Saturday evening for friends of their daughters and this was a nice way for the girls to socialize and not get into any trouble. It was also nice for their guests. Although I didn't realize it, these occasions started my social life and renewed my relationship with girls. Peggie and Wilma would have essentially the same group over to their parties. I assumed this was because we were accepted by the girls and their parents. Besides Chap and me there were Jim Garrison, Felecian (Gus) Perrin, Warren Malhiot, Pat Gore, Albert Alba and several others. Besides the Baker sisters, the other girls, as I recall were Jim's sister, Jane, Elise Talmadge, Elizabeth Klipstein, and Polly Lane. After a while the other girls came very infrequently, if at all. All the boys got the impression that the Baker girls wanted us to themselves, but that was OK with us—we always had a good time. We would arrive about 8:00 P.M., sit around their two large living rooms or on a huge screened-in porch and talk about anything and everything. Then we played all kinds of games. We'd listen to the radio and tried to identify the music as well as the bands that were playing. Occasionally we danced. Sometimes we would walk over to the Prytania Theatre, if there was a good movie. The hit of the evening was at 11:00 P.M. when we moved to the kitchen and raided the refrigerator. This was OK with Mrs. Baker because she knew what was coming and kept the pantry and refrigerator full of drinks and stuff to make sandwiches. She and Dr. Baker were discreet enough to retire upstairs, except when she had to come down and insist that we leave by midnight. At first Chap and I would go to the Baker home on our bikes. Later, when I learned to drive, I picked up Chap and went over in our new 1939 Dodge, at least when Dad let me have it. Otherwise, I took the Broadway bus and the St. Charles Avenue streetcar, because I didn't want to wrinkle my trousers or get overheated or have anyone think I was a kid who still had to use his bike. After the parties, Chap and I would walk over to the streetcar stop and shoot the bull for what seemed like forever until the next car arrived. Most of my

Saturday nights were occupied in this way during my senior year in high school and for some of my freshman year at Tulane. Wilma Baker was a year younger than I and Peggie two years younger. They both attended Louise McGehee's School (for girls) and, consequently, I was invited to some of the school's functions. Peggie was the same age as my sister Jane and for a while they went to Wright High School (for girls). The Bakers opened up a whole new world to AGG. This activity was one reason why I wasn't as active socially with my high school fraternity. The Baker girls were lots of fun to be with. There was never anything real serious between them and any of the boys, except that eventually Wilma married Warren Malhiot.

I forgot to mention that the Bakers had an adopted son, Dick, who was years older than all of us. He was never at the house for their parties. Must have been cutting up somewhere. He immediately joined the service when we got into World War II, and was lost in combat.

Well, this all started by my friendship with Chappie Reynolds, so I guess I can thank him for the entrée. He went on to Southwestern Louisiana Institute at Lafayette, Louisiana for pre-law, joined the service, married a Hawaiian girl when he was stationed on the islands, came back and finished law school at Tulane, and eventually moved to the Los Angeles area. I met him again only once after the war when he was in a campus dorm for married students. I had another unusual experience with Chap in the summer following graduation from Fortier high but this will be related in another letter.

Take care.

Love you,
Dad

Dear Anne,

After my sophomore year at Fortier, Dad called me aside to have a serious talk. He explained that he didn't think he would have enough money to send me to a good college and the only way to accomplish this was to somehow secure a scholarship. The one thing I could control was to buckle down and make every effort to obtain good grades during my last two years of high school. I was never an excellent student, but I understood what he meant and so I set some goals to try to gain the highest grades possible in every subject. Dad also knew of my limitations and consequently he didn't push me. Besides the money situation he wanted to see me in a college with the highest academic standards, and being from the Northeast, he was well aware of the good schools in that part of the country. So in spite of all the other activities and interests at the time, I did my best and it turned out that I was graduated seventh in a class of over three hundred boys, with a numerical grade average of ninety-plus, as I recall.

In January of my senior year, Dad learned from an ivy league alumni club downtown that Harvard University had a national merit scholarship program in which full scholarships (tuition, board, books, etc.) were awarded every year to two students in every state of the country who attained the highest grades in a competitive entrance exam. I completed the necessary applications to take the exam. It was held around March 15 at the Isadore Newman School. There were about thirty students present from all over the state to take a series of tests that lasted all day. Well, I was so fortunate and so lucky. Most of the tests were on subjects that I was currently taking or had just completed. Anyway, I thought I did reasonably well, but I was in awe of the competition. Several weeks later we received a letter from Harvard indicating that I was one of the two students receiving the highest grades on the exam. I couldn't believe it, and of course the rest of the family was overwhelmed. In any event I learned later that this wasn't the only hurdle. A couple of weeks before graduation, I was in somebody's class at Fortier and a messenger came to take me to the principal's office. Had no idea what was going to happen. I distinctly remember wearing an old purple sports shirt, open collar, some thread-bare corduroy trousers and beat-up shoes. Mr. Conniff, the principal, introduced me to a well-dressed distinguished gentleman who had come down from Harvard to interview me. This took place in Conniff's private office for about an hour and a half. I didn't realize it, but this was the oral portion of the Harvard scholarship entrance requirement. I think I handled all of the questions fairly well and felt that I impressed the interviewer favorably. The only thing that bothered me was that I wasn't at all dressed for the occasion. Well, I graduated with honors, etc. and began to make plans for the summer, which I'll describe in my next letter. Just before leaving for the long trip, Dad received another letter from Harvard asking that he send a $500 bond to cover the possibility of my damaging any furniture in the dormitory that I would be assigned to. He sent it promptly and got a receipt. Also from the time of the interview we started to get a steady stream of literature from Harvard; school history, school maps, description of all the facilities and the courses that were available, etc. This continued throughout the summer and Dad would forward to me while I was away.

I have to tell you quite honestly that while I was elated at having apparently won a

Harvard scholarship, I had mixed emotions about going. How was a very young-looking, skinny immature kid of sixteen going to make out at the great Harvard University? Way up in Cambridge (Boston), Massachusetts, of all places? Many of my friends were going to enter Tulane, and some to LSU, but no one was going as far away or to a place like Harvard. I was a dedicated football fan and crazy about the Tulane football team. I kept up with all the players and attended every home game without fail for years. When I returned from my long summer trip (in 1939), I was invited to a number of Tulane fraternity rush parties. I accepted, but explained that it was certain that I would be going away to school. That didn't seem to make any difference—they wanted me to come anyway. I attended parties by Beta Theta Pi, Phi Kappa Sigma, Delta Tau Delta, Phi Delta Theta and Sigma Alpha Epsilon.

About the first of September we received another letter from Harvard with some sad news. While I had earned a scholarship, they regretted to inform me that 1939 was a tough year for the university as well as their scholarship program, necessitating a reduction in available funds and, therefore, they could only afford to give one scholarship in Louisiana, and it was awarded to the other student with highest grades on the entrance exam—a boy from Monroe, Louisiana. Well, needless to say, my father was crushed. I didn't take it too hard. I was more embarrassed after all the talking I did about going east to school. As I look back on the experience, I had reached a fork in the road of my life and I went one way instead of the other. I often wondered what I would have done or where I would be today had I gone to Harvard. I wanted to keep their last letter, but Dad was so mad he tore it up and threw it away. At least we got our $500 back from good old Harvard.

Dad somehow accumulated enough money to cover first year's expenses at Tulane and I went to a school that was personally my first choice, just a few blocks away from home.

Must go.

Love you lots,
Dad

September 17, 1994

Dear Anne,

By the summer of 1939 I had finished high school, an honor student with an opportunity to go to college. Plans were made to take a lengthy trip to two different parts of the country—Kentucky and Pennsylvania/New York. The first portion was conceived by my good friend Chappie Reynolds. His grandfather, a retired dentist, had a farm at Kevil (near Paducah), Kentucky and asked Chap to come up there to help work the farm for the summer. Chap in turn asked me to accompany him. This sounded great, but it was the way he wanted to get there that was risky. Chap always wanted a motorcycle and so in his senior year of high school he bought a 1933 Indian for around fifty dollars. It was an old beat-up machine that took lots of work and money to fix. Anyway, it was Chap's idea that we go up to the farm on this thing and have our belongings shipped separately. Well, my parents were against it because of the danger—two people riding over 600 miles on this old bike—Chap driving it and AGG on the back hanging on for dear life. My mother was still saying no when we left.

It took all of a day to go from New Orleans to Jackson, Mississippi. We first went west to LaPlace, Louisiana and headed north on old U.S. Highway 51. Halfway up to where Lake Maurepas meets Lake Ponchartrain, a very swampy, isolated area, we had a revolting development. The cycle drive chain broke. Where were we going to get this fixed? We were so lucky. We hitchhiked back to civilization and the first service station we saw had a mechanic with a spare cycle chain. By midafternoon we continued up 51 to Jackson, arriving at sundown. This bike could only go about forty-five to fifty mph at top speed. We stayed in some motel for three dollars apiece. We didn't get under way until midmorning the next day. Now, while these old cycles had mufflers of a sort, they still made lots of noise. Well, wouldn't you know, halfway to Memphis, the muffler on this contraption fell off and we couldn't put it back on and couldn't carry it, so we threw it in the ditch and kept going. There were a couple of problems though—it made one hell of a noise, especially in passing through those quiet little towns when we had to slow down and then accelerate again. Everybody jumped up to stare at us. The other problem was that the exhaust line was so hot it burned the inside of my pants leg, so I had to hold my leg out much of the time. Forgot to mention that the steel frame I sat on wasn't cushioned well and there were times when I thought I broke my tailbone. Well, we arrived in Memphis, Tennessee that night, but we sure woke up that town with our noise. We were stopped by the local police and had to promise to get a new muffler, but we didn't. Memphis had a law against hornblowing so you can imagine how a muffler-less cycle sounded. Stayed at another motel for five dollars. It had one single bed so we flipped a coin to see who would sleep on the floor. I lost.

The third day we finally got to Kevil, Kentucky, which is about seven miles west of Paducah near the point where the Ohio River enters the Mississippi. Dr. Brittain had a 200-acre farm on a gravel road about a mile east of town. It was really a delightful place—a large two-story frame house with plenty of space, a huge yard, and a magnificent oak tree in the backyard where Dr. Brittain had planted a dental chair. Occasionally someone would beg him to pull a tooth even though he had retired from practice. There was a nice-sized barn, a couple of cows, a dozen pigs, some chickens, a nice pond with some perch in it, a huge vegetable garden—maybe almost an acre—growing corn, tomatoes, potatoes, peas, beans, carrots, radishes, turnips, watermelons, cantaloupes, peppers, onions, snapbeans and strawberries (when in season). It also had an apple orchard, a peach orchard and plum and cherry trees. Then, I'd say a good 150 acres of feed corn, soybeans and tobacco. The farm was actually managed by a black man who had served in the army in World War I. Chap and I were his helpers. We did a variety of things. We were the gardeners for the yard, weeded the whole vegetable garden daily, pulled potatoes out of the ground, picked suckers off the tomato plants, fed the pigs, collected eggs from the chicken coop and did all kinds of odd repair jobs. Didn't fool with milking the cows—they were too temperamental. Besides, I didn't care for it.

For pleasure, Chap and I pitched horseshoes every day, took trips around the country on that stupid motorcycle, helped Mrs. Brittain clean house, shot .22 rifles at squirrels that tried to get into the barn, listened to the radio every night or read some books and magazines. Once Chap and I went to town (Kevil), which was only two blocks long on one side of the street (but had seven churches). The occasion was to hear a traveling evangelist who had set up a huge tent and gave sermons every night for about a week. The place was packed every night—must have had several hundred folding chairs under the tent. This denomination didn't believe in music, so there were no musical instruments and no singing. Chap and I attended one night out of boredom and found the only two empty seats in the first row. Midway through the sermon (you can imagine how the minister preached), we got tickled and started to laugh. The preacher stopped and ordered us from the area. We ran up the center aisle and out the tent laughing louder than ever.

As the summer wore on Chap and I found more and more things to argue about and we ended up fighting each other several times. In time we would make up. Once we had a big argument up in a tree and Chap pushed me hard enough to make me fall to the ground. On the way down a broken bough caught my arm and put a deep gash in it. I still have the scar. Another time he wanted to hike to Paducah to "cut up." I went halfway and then changed my mind. I walked back to the farm, but he went on and came back at the end of the day, but I didn't believe what he bragged about. Once his aunt and husband came to visit for several days from Detroit. He worked for Ford Motor in production.

I'll never forget the wonderful meals that Mrs. Brittain cooked every day. Huge breakfasts with eggs, bacon, sausage, pancakes, waffles, etc., and lots of milk. The really big meal was in the middle of the day that consisted of three or more meats, six or seven vegetables, plus salad and homemade ice cream. The one dish I learned to like was fresh, tender snapbeans topped with chopped raw onion. Still love it. The evening meals (supper) were the leftovers from noon "dinner."

Chap and I got tired of fooling around with that motorcycle. A farmer about ten miles away answered Chap's advertisement for sale in the county newspaper. We took it to him one morning and had to go over a lot of rough dirt roads. It was after a hard rain and all the ruts in the roads and the ditches were filled with water. Chap was driving (he would never let me drive) and I hung on the rear as usual. Well, on one stretch of road, we got into a deep rut and couldn't leave it. The rut led to the ditch and we hit something hard. I flipped in the air over Chap and landed on my back in the water. Chap flipped, too, but held onto the handlebars. I had the wind knocked out of me. It was miraculous that I wasn't hurt—not a scratch. If there hadn't been any water in that ditch, I might not have been around to tell about it. Chap had cuts on his hands, face, and body, but he was OK. Some farmers saw us from a field nearby—came over and helped us pull the machine out of the ditch. Chap finally sold that thing for $100 and two hogs, which the buyer brought over to the Brittain farm. Later we learned that the hogs were diseased and it decimated Dr. Brittain's herd of pigs.

Well, time came for me to leave the farm for another part of my summer vacation. My Aunt Glenn, Dad's sister, who lived in Harrisburg, Pennsylvania, invited me to come up there and join her for a trip to the New York World's Fair which was held at Flushing, New York, on Long Island. This was my graduation present. Didn't think this letter would take so long—I'll have to finish in next one.

Love you much,
Dad

September 23, 1994

Dear Anne,

Continuing with my summer vacation in 1939, I departed from the Brittain farm and left Paducah, Kentucky, on a Greyhound bus. I went through Indiana, Ohio, and Pennsylvania. Had a good seat, first row window, right behind the driver, and got a nice view of the countryside. I stayed in Harrisburg with Aunt Glenn for about two weeks, during which time I renewed acquaintances with George and Henry Tillson. Played Ping-Pong in their game room almost every day. Harrisburg is an attractive town located on the Susquehanna River. The Tillman boys and I would hike up river to the first mountain range, Peters Mountain, and climb it. We also tried to cross the river several times without success. The riverbed was unusually wide, but got very shallow in dry weather. George Tillson was already going to Dartmouth and was very enthusiastic about its campus and facilities. Later in my life I would confirm that it is an outstanding school. During this visit with Aunt Glenn, I finally learned the truth from her about Grandfather Gottschall. I was given to understand he had died years ago. But he was still living—he and grandmother were divorced around 1914. He left her comfortable and bought another house on the other side of town. He eventually married his housekeeper and left her everything in his will. At this point I guess I should elaborate about the Gottschall side of the family, who came to Pennsylvania from Bavaria, Germany, as far back as 1740. My grandfather (your great-grand), Amos Haverstick Gottschall, was a combination lay minister, explorer, naturalist, author and manufacturer of medicines and perfumes. He made a number of journeys out to all parts of the Midwest and West, lived with several Indian tribes, collected artifacts and wrote books about his exploits—about seven books altogether. He came back to Tennessee, married Mary Barker (whose father founded Milligan College at Johnson City, Tennessee) and returned with his bride to Pennsylvania. He settled down and proceeded to manufacture a line of drugs, medicines, ointments, salves and perfumes in Harrisburg. They had five children: Glenn, who remained a spinster, took care of Grandmother until she died and was secretary to the minister of the Harrisburg First Presbyterian Church; Harlan, who was a talented artist but contracted tuberculosis and died very young in Arizona after Grandfather sent him there for health reasons; Paul, who worked for Grandfather and took over the business; Amos, who became a psychiatrist and spent most of his career as the head of the Pennsylvania State Mental Hospital at Embreeville/Coatsville, Pennsylvania; and finally Alvin, the youngest, who attended the Harrisburg Military Academy (two blocks from home) from kindergarten all the way up through the second year of junior college, became a coal broker, a reporter for the *Philadelphia Inquirer,* joined the Marine Corps in World War I, spent most of the time in Santo Domingo, was separated in New Orleans, Louisiana, decided to stay there, met and married my mother and was advertising manager for the New Orleans *Times-Picayune* until we moved to Shreveport, Louisiana. I should add that, coincidentally, Mother's family was originally from Bethlehem, Pennsylvania, and migrated to New Orleans sometime in the middle of the last century.

Getting back to Grandfather Gottschall, when Aunt Glenn revealed that he was still living, I told her I wanted to visit him. She was incensed with this idea and threatened not to take me to the New York World's Fair if I tried. I secretly decided to try anyway but when I got halfway there, my better judgement prevailed and I didn't go through with it. Never saw my grandfather who died toward the end of World War II in his eighties.

Well, let's get back to my trip to the World's Fair. Aunt Glenn and I went with a friend of hers who had a car, as I recall. The fair was quite a sight in those days. Lots of foreign countries were represented, wonderful exhibits, and a terrific midway for the young people. I remember attending the feature entertainment performance of the fair, a musical production called the Aquacades with Billy Rose's orchestra playing behind a huge swimming pool decorated with colored fountains and featuring Eleanor Holm, a U.S. Olympic swimmer, doing her thing in the water with a lot of other good-looking girls. They also had the comedy team of Abbott and Costello who went through their skit of "Who's on First" in baseball. Also remember Abbott asking Costello if he wanted his palm read. When Costello agreed, Abbott painted his hand with a big brush dripping with red paint.

Anyway, we returned to Harrisburg. Before leaving for home, Aunt Glenn took me to Gettysburg to see the battlefields. While it was interesting and scenic, what I really enjoyed was the nickelodeon in the lounge of the inn where we were staying. Some college kids were playing the records, and dancing to Glenn Miller's "Tuxedo Junction," which they played over and over again. They were really neat to watch and I'll always remember that piece.

After the trip, it was back to New Orleans on the Southerner. Seemed like it took forever to get home—made too many stops.

Must go.

Love you, love you,
Dad

Part III

The College Years

October 3, 1994

Dear Anne,

After the Harvard setback, Dad enrolled me in Tulane University and suggested that it would be wise to take an engineering course. I hadn't given much thought to any particular career. At this stage of my life anything was fine. If he felt becoming a professional engineer was worthwhile, I would give it a try. So I elected to take mechanical engineering, not that I was so mechanically minded, but I did set a goal to at least try to understand what was being taught—good grades were not important and probably difficult to achieve.

However, my college experience began with an abundance of social life, which never really made good sense. Prior to any academic activity the big "in" thing to do was to join a fraternity. I continued to accept invitations to frat parties as mentioned in a previous letter. Selection of a fraternity wasn't easy because I liked a lot of guys in all of them. However, my decision was dictated by several influences and circumstances. I was actively sought after by Phi Kappa Sigma; then the Stockmeyer brothers and Roy White wanted me to go Beta Theta Pi; John Miazza wanted me to join Sigma Alpha Epsilon; and some other friends wanted me to pledge Phi Delta Theta. Almost at the last minute Delta Tau Delta gave me a strong rush because George Mayoral, a Delt alum who worked at WSMB with Dad, asked him to persuade me. George gave Dad a big pitch about the Delts emphasizing scholarship, but that was a lot of bull. Still, this went over big with my father, and he was going to pay the bills. Another influence came from A. Lane Plauché, another Delt. He was a significant member of the Tulane Naval ROTC Unit and with the war clouds coming up over the horizon, I was very excited about serving in the Navy. I was still the young underweight kid and felt I could never pass the physical, but Lane pulled some strings with the personnel in the unit and I was accepted.

Anyway, during rush week, I was at many parties. Toward the end of the week, I was at a big party at the Beta house. After a while, Jim Reid, the Rush Captain, pulled me out to a quiet spot on their porch and gave me an effective pitch on joining Beta Theta Pi. Just when I thought he was going to pop the question to pledge (and I think I was going to accept) a delegation from Phi Kappa Sigma swarmed up on the porch and told Reid that I was supposed to be at a Phi Kap party and they were there to take me away. They had an argument about it, and finally asked me what I wanted to do. For some reason I said maybe I should go to the Phi Kap party. However, I told Jim Reid that I would like to continue our conversation later. That evening I had to attend an important Delta Tau Delta function on the roof of the Jung Hotel. This was a huge affair: cocktails, dinner, music, tables packed with people all over the ballroom floor as well as the mezzanine area above. Very impressive. Must have had all the alumni they could find. After lots of food, drinks, songs and speeches, the Delts began to make announcements of those rushees who pledged. Whenever this happened, it was followed by lots of cheering, noise, toasts, etc. Then I was cornered by the Rush Committee and asked to join. I said I would let them know the next day because I had made some commitments that I promised not to break with Beta, Phi Kap and Phi Delta Theta. I especially wanted to see Beta again. Well, all the other frats except Beta asked me to pledge also. I went to my last party with Beta and they didn't bother to discuss pledging, and, to make matters worse, Jim Reid, the Stockmeyers and Roy White weren't around. So after considering all the pros and cons, I pledged Delta Tau Delta—I think mainly to please Dad. I must say there were a lot of fine people in DTD and a number of good friends of mine pledged also. I didn't want to dwell on frats this much, but there are reasons which I will explain later. One of the observations I made about fraternities (at that time anyway) was that there was usually a real spark plug, a dedicated leader in the group who held the chapter together and seemed to be the one most responsible for its overall success. And it wasn't necessarily the president of the chapter. With Delta Tau Delta, it was Stanley Ray, a fantastic salesman, a real mover who continued to attend Tulane for about seven years and had organized several businesses on the side while in school. With Phi Kappa Sigma, it was Karlem "Ducky" Riess who taught science at Fortier, then Newman and finally at Tulane. He did everything to influence me to join Phi Kap. With Beta, it was Jimmy Reid, a terrific guy with lots of charisma. Although I wasn't rushed, the Pi Kappa Alphas had Herb Kaiser and Kappa Sigmas had Jim Oviatt.

I wasn't quite ready for this fraternity social life. You have to appreciate that I really didn't date in high school. My limited relationship with girls had been the Saturday night parties at the Baker home. But I started the dating game with DTD. My first date to a frat party was with Margaret Ann "Sugar" Williams, an out-of-town girl from College Station, Texas (her father taught at Texas A&M). From then on I went wild for the rest of my college days, at the expense of the academics and trying to learn something in mechanical engineering, a very tough curriculum, at least for me. Adding to this were the courses at the Naval ROTC Unit.

As pledges we had to eat lunch at the Delt house nearly every day. I can remember having to say things like "please pass the good Delt peanut butter" or you wouldn't get any. There were many fine boys in DTD starting with Stanley Ray, the Torre twins, Mottram and Douglas, who were really sharp, Hanlin Becker, Phil Jahncke, Barney Phelps, Lane Plauché, George Schneider, Walter Verlander and A. J. Nugon. Others that impressed me were Connie Meyer who was on the Tulane boxing team; Henry Mentz with his humor and quips like, "Well, now I ask you, how about that?"; and Charlie Emling who could really gyrate his rear end when he danced. The pledge class had some great guys too like Michael Fortier, Steed McGee, N. C. and Richard Cromwell, Richard Andry and Kenneth Kahao. Delta Tau Delta had a relatively large number of members and a good reputation on the campus at the time, but for some reason it wasn't a very homogeneous organization. The members usually split off into smaller groups of three or four who were much closer as fraternity brothers. There were parties at the house after every football game. I think I brought Peggie Baker to a couple of these functions, but most of the time I went stag. Later in the school year I particularly remember participating in a skit with the Delts on Campus Night at Dixon Hall, where we made fun of Huey Long and closed with everyone singing "Every Man a King," one of the themes held by this crafty but famous Louisiana politician. Think we won first prize for our performance.

I was really trying to reduce the length of this letter, but can't, so let me get this off my chest. In the midst of all the social activity, I worked my tail off in engineering school. However, I managed to fail one subject in my freshman year—mechanical drawing—in a peculiar fashion. This course consisted of a one-hour-per-week lecture period and two four-hour-per-week lab periods where we had to draw a dozen or more intricate plates of machinery. I made excellent marks on all of the plates, but I flunked the lecture portion taught by Mr. Steffin. He gave only one quiz during the semester, which I failed miserably, because I just didn't study for it and wasn't too interested. The final exam counted for half of the total lecture grade. I passed the exam but not enough to raise the total grade to passing and, consequently, failed both the lecture and lab portions of the course. To make a long story short, I took mechanical drawing again in summer school and had to draw those plates all over again. This time I passed with an A in both lecture and lab.

Failing this course was partially the reason why I wasn't initiated as a member of DTD at the end of my freshman year. I say partially because that was the excuse the Delts gave me, but I later learned on reliable authority that three other pledges and I were blackballed by one redneck out-of-town member who didn't like the way we conducted ourselves. I was stunned. I had never failed to be accepted by anybody or anything before. I was told that I could remain a pledge and try to become eligible in my sophomore year, but I resigned. I think this development caused the ultimate downfall of DTD on the campus and to my knowledge the chapter never fully regained the stature it once held. I had some consolation from a number of Delt members who went out of their way to apologize for what happened. Stanley Ray, who was "the great white father" of DTD, was incensed. He was absent from the chapter meeting when this decision was made and told me several times it never would have happened had he been there. For the balance of my college career Delts would continue to come up to me and apologize for what happened. Naturally, this was a blow to my ego, but I handled it. The experience taught me early on how to manage disappointment. You can't be bitter, angry or attempt to secure revenge. All this does is make you feel worse. Hate usually consumes the hater. There were other influences at the time that mitigated my disappointment. With World War II coming on there was an esprit de corps in the Naval ROTC that replaced the togetherness found in fraternity life. There was also a camaraderie among the students in my engineering class that made up for it. My two closest friends in DTD departed from the scene. Michael Fortier moved to St. Louis and continued college at Purdue and Steed McGee quit the chapter for other reasons. At any rate, life had to go on. The following year, the Phi Kappa Sigmas and the Sigma Alpha Epsilons wanted me to pledge into their chapters. This was somewhat unprecedented. Well, I finally decided to pledge SAE and went on to contribute making this chapter the best on the campus in the ensuing years, but this is another story to relate.

Have to stop.

Love you so much,
Dad

October 7, 1994

Dear Anne,

As the first year at Tulane came to a close, I signed up for training duty that summer with the Naval ROTC group. This was a marvelous experience, because it involved all sorts of training for about a month aboard the USS *Wyoming,* an active battleship, and also meant spending time aboard still active (but old) four-stacker-type destroyers. The freshman class spent most of the cruise aboard the *Wyoming.* Some of the upper classmen were kept on the tin cans. As I recall we left New Orleans on the *Wyoming* and steamed down to Dry Tortugas, the last bit of land at the end of the Florida Keys. There we visited Fort Jefferson, which looked like it was sitting all by itself in the ocean. We then steamed up to Charleston, South Carolina, where we stayed a couple of days and picked up the naval unit group from Georgia Tech. We proceeded on up the Atlantic Coast to New York City. On the way at sea I can remember the captain announcing over the PA system that the Germans had broken through the Maginot Line and the French were in full retreat. Very ominous news! Spent several days in New York and picked up naval unit contingents from Yale, Harvard, Minnesota and Northwestern. Remember going to the Commodore Hotel, Grand Central Station, Central Park, the Empire State Building and eating at Jack Dempsey's Restaurant with David Kleck and Bill Lutes. Still have a photo of the three of us there. We went on north to Portland, Maine, where we had a very enjoyable shore leave. We were invited to a dinner dance given by some beautiful local girls at the Portland Country Club. Next, we moved down the coast to Annapolis, Maryland, where we were given liberty and toured the campus of the U.S. Naval Academy. All of the grounds and buildings were so immaculate and impressive. The mess quarters where we had lunch with the midshipmen was huge—could seat over a thousand.

Before returning to the ship, some of us used the academy's bowling alley in the basement of Bancroft Hall. Then we steamed out of Chesapeake Bay for extensive drills and gunnery exercises. After several days of this, we pulled back into the Bay and docked at the Norfolk (Virginia) Naval Base. After touring all the facilities here, we departed for Charleston, South Carolina.

Throughout this cruise, we participated in various cleaning details, i.e., chipping paint/swabbing the wooden deck area, etc. Also stood all kinds of watches and got involved in navigation and communication exercises. We slept in hammocks on the first deck below the main deck port side aft. Occasionally, we would sleep on the main deck. The group from Minnesota slept on the starboard side aft. I made friends with several of the Minnesota guys. The only one I can remember was a Richard Carlson. Years later when we lived in Minneapolis, I met several people who took the same cruise. We stood many watches while under way. The best spot was to be a lookout on the bridge. Had some great times aboard the old *Wyoming.* Good food at every meal and good movies every night (if you weren't on watch). I remember their having some kind of amateur hour and our Sam Ryniker won a prize for being a very good whistler. Also had song fests singing "Bell Bottom Trousers, Coats of Navy Blue" and the usual " Sweet Violets" verses. Another memorable feature on the *Wyoming* was the ship's band. Every day, it seems, they would play each school's fight song. Heard them so often, I can still hum the ones from Minnesota, Northwestern and Georgia Tech. The band even had a "fight song" for the *Wyoming;* I can still whistle that one, too.

At Charleston we were transferred to one of the four-stacker tin cans that operated with us—the USS *Broome.* We then went non-stop all the way back to New Orleans. This segment of the cruise was really rough. It was the first, and only time in my naval career that I ever got seasick. Anyway, it was still a great experience. Upon returning to New Orleans, I was met at the dock by Mother, Dad, and Jane and—a surprise—my old neighborhood chum, Ray Courter, who was passing through town from Notre Dame to return to his home in Atlanta. Such was the summer of 1940. (The actual logs of our reporting aboard and detachment from the USS *Broome* are attached to this letter.)

I was also fortunate to be included in two other naval training sessions. In the summer of 1941, I spent three weeks at the Pensacola Naval Air Station. We were passengers in every type of naval training aircraft available. Did acrobatics in those Yellow Peril biplanes, which got me woozy. Also, the dive-bombing exercises in those SNJs were scary, especially when you pulled out; you thought you left your stomach somewhere. And when you landed on water in those PBY flying boats, you would think they slammed down on a sheet of steel. Anyway, it was fun. The purpose of this training was to persuade us to leave school and join the Naval Air Corps (which happened to several of us). Also, in the summer of 1942, we spent three weeks at the Naval Air Station, Corpus Christi, Texas. Had lots of classwork and drills, but little flying. We were given the last weekend off in Corpus. I remember about seven of us secured a room at the Driscoll Hotel downtown facing the marina. My good buddies were trying to teach me how to drink. They said I should start easy with a little gin in a glass of Seven-Up. Trouble was they put a jigger of Seven-Up in a glassful of (cheap) gin and I got drunk as a skunk. We all had a good time on the long train trip back to New Orleans. The reason for shore-based training in '41 and '42 was that the Navy didn't have any ships to spare and, besides, it was dangerous to venture out into the Gulf with those German subs snooping around.

Later in the summer of '42, Lana Hummel's father got jobs for John Martinez, Jim Jennings and me at George Sharp, Naval Architects, downtown in the Hibernia Bank Building. Made enough money to pay for most of my senior year at Tulane. Also worked a short while for James M. Todd, Consulting Engineer.

Being part of the Naval Unit solidified my strong interest in naval service—one in which I was so very proud to have played a part in World War II. We had some outstanding officers assigned as instructors to the unit—more about them later—and some very talented and knowledgeable chiefs: Farrell, Webb, Woods and Bernhardt. They were great people.

Must go.

Thinking of you always,
Dad

UNITED STATES SHIP   BROOME (DD210)   Sunday, _____ (40)

ZONE DESCRIPTION __Plus 5.__   **REMARKS**

0 — 4

Steaming on course 235°T and pgc, 231°psc, at standard speed 8 knots, in company with N.R.O.T.C. Practice Squadron, enroute Charleston, S.C., in column distance 500 yards. Order of ships - USS WYOMING (BUPA), BROOME, LEARY, BLAKELEY, and BIDDLE. Boilers #3 and #4 in use. 0332 Changed course on signal to 270°T and pgc, 270°psc. Average steam, 250; average revolutions 92.5.

                 G.E.T. PARSONS, Lieut.(jg) U.S. Navy.

4 — 8

Steaming as before on course 270°T, pgc, and psc, at standard speed 8 knots. 0615 Changed course to 295°T, and pgc, 300°psc. 0700 Sighted Entrance Buoy bearing 305°T, distance about 6 miles. 0720 Changed speed to 15 knots, steaming independently. 0724 Changed course to 310°T and pgc, 315°psc. 0727 Changed course to 280°T and pgc, 285°psc. 0730 Buoy #20 abeam to starboard, distance 1 mile. 0734 Changed course to 305°T and pgc, 310°psc. 0746 Entrance Channel Buoy "J" abeam to port, distance 75 yards. Steaming on various courses at various speeds conforming to channel. Average steam, 250; average revolutions, 93.0.

                 A.F. COHEN, Ensign, U.S. Navy.

8 — 12

Standing in Charleston Channel as before. 0800 Mustered the crew on stations, no absentees. 0820 Passed buoy #25 abeam to port, distant 200 yards. 0844 Moored to buoy C-1, Rebellion Roads, Charleston, S.C. Boiler #4 steaming for auxiliary purposes. 0925 Pursuant to Commanding Officer, U.S.S. BROOME fifth endorsement r16-4/00-A/DD210 of this date, Lieutenant G.W. Ashford, USN, was detached to return to Atlanta, Ga., for resumption of regular duties. Pursuant to Commanding Officer U.S.S. BROOME 2nd endorsement r16-4/DD210 of this date, RICHES, Paul B., 150 79 34, CSM(PA), F-4-D, FT, was transferred to Ga. Tech., temporary duty connection N.R.O.T.C. Cruise completed. Pursuant to Commanding Officer U.S.S. BROOME 3rd endorsement of this date, the following NROTC students of Ga. Tech. completed instruction and training and were detached this date: Frank W. Allgorn III, Noble B. Ayers, Otis A. Barge Jr, Paul E. Birdsall, Louis C. Bodenheimer, Richard C. Burlap, Tim Clapp, Robert L. Cliett Jr, John Stone L. Coppock, Albon O. Cowles Jr, Jack W. Darby, Edward Epstein Jr, Richard E. Forrest, Robert I. Biggs, Jr, Churchill P. Goree III, James A. Hodge, Maurice F. Hooper, Frank D. Jamison, Garland L. Kendrick, William H. Kilgore, Edgar F. Lindgren Jr, James H. Lockart, Walter B. Loncino, James M. Langley, Edward F. Oliver, Edward S. Parks Jr, Monroe L. Plaxico, Carl Reisman, George H. Schottler, Hunter W. Stewart, Shelton B. Sutton, James F. Trawick, Harold U. Van Arsdale, Robert Weatherford Jr, Frank A. Whitaker, Hugh E. Wright and James B. Young. 1030 Pursuant to Commanding Officer letter A/DD210 of this date, ABEL, Marion F., BM2c, USN, left the ship for patrol duty in Charleston, S.C.

                 R.S. McELROY Jr., Ensign, U.S. Navy.

12 — 16

Moored as before. 1205 USS DUPONT stood in, and anchored. 1315 Pursuant to Commanding Officer USS WYOMING 4th endorsement, AG18/P16-4/00 of this date, Lieutenant Jacob E. Cooper, USN, reported aboard for temporary duty in connection NR.O.T.C. Cruise. Pursuant to Commanding Officer U.S.S. WYOMING 2nd endorsement AG17/P16-4/MM of this date, BERNHARDT, T.B., 111 63 89, CGM(PA), F-4-D, FR, reported on board for temporary duty connection N.R.O.T.C. Cruise. Pursuant to Commanding Officer U.S.S. WYOMING 2nd endorsement of this date, the following N.R.O.T.C. students of Tulane University reported on board for instruction and training and transportation to New Orleans, La.: Edward A. Adey III, Andry, Richard C., Bruce Baird, Francis R. Barnard, Forbes Bastian, Wm. PL. Boulet, Charles A. Burleson Jr, Robert M. Cole, Nick C. Cromwell, Richard P. Cromwell, Henry C. Daubert Jr, Walter E. Douglas, Jr, Carey J. Ellis Jr, Charles W. Frank Jr, James M. Jennings Jr, Herbert J. McCampbell Jr, Albert B. McCoard Jr, Shepard F. Perrin, Virgil M. Wheeler Jr, Robert L. Boswell,

Approved: H.Y. DANNENBERG   Examined:
Lieutenant Commander, U.S. Navy,
Commanding.   A. MacIntyre,
                                  Lieutenant, U.S.N., Navigator.

(Original (ribbon) copy of this page to be sent to Bureau of Navigation monthly)

ADDITIONAL SHEET

U. S. S. ....BROOME (210)............................   Date .7 July..................... (10)

12 - 16 Contd.

John J. Desmond, Gelon H. Doswell, Richard C. Fitzgeralt, St.Marc J. Flotte, Alvin Gottschall, Osmond F. Green, David M. Kleck, Anthony E. Labarre, John F. Latham. Charles F. Maginnis, Wilson F. Minor, Wiley L. Mossy jr, Andrew L. Plauche, George W. Reese jr, George B. Riviere, Frederick H. Schmidt, Walter D. Shepard, Maurice M. Alexander jr, Wm. S. Howson, Pete A. McLeod, Conrad Meyer III, Cheri A. Miranne III, Edward D. Moseley, Thomas B. Parkerson jr, Raymond R. Perino, Malcolm S. Peters, Jinx Paterson, Paul O.H. Pigman, Ward C. Purdum, Lloyd J. Reuter, Louis L. Robein jr, Samuel W. Ryniker, John S. Walter, Henry E. Williams Jr, Vanzant, Joe C.

R.S. McELROY Jr., Ensign, U.S.Navy.

16 - 20.

1735 Pursuant to Commanding Officer letter QL/DD210 of this date, SLATER, M.C., MM1c, USN, left the ship for patrol duty in Charleston, S.C. 1823 KENNY, M.V., BM1c, USN, returned from three days leave.

R.S. McELROY Jr, Ensign, U.S.Navy.

20 - 24

2020 ABEL, M.F., BM2c, USN, returned aboard, having completed shore patrol duty in Charleston, S.C.

R.S. McELROY Jr, Ensign, U.S.Navy.

Approved: DANNENBERG
Lieutenant Commander, U.S.Navy,
Commanding.

Examined: A. MacIntyre,
Lieutenant, U. S. N., Navigator.

(This page to be sent to Bureau of Navigation monthly with Log sheets)

UNITED STATES SHIP _____ BROOME (DD210) _____ Thursday 5 JULY 11 **LOG OF THE** (40)
(Day) (Date) (Month)

ZONE DESCRIPTION Plus 6.   **REMARKS**

0—4
Enroute New Orleans, La., steaming singly on #3 and #4 boilers, at standard
speed 12 knots; steaming on course 309°T and pgc, 308°psc. Average steam,
250; average revolutions, 137.0.

A.F. COHEN, Ensign, U.S.Navy.

4—8
Steaming as before on course 309°T and pgc, 308°psc at standard speed
12 knots. 0538 Changed course to 294°T and pgc, 293°psc. 0610 Changed course
to 302°T, 303°pgc, 300°psc. 0614 Changed standard speed to 15 knots and
changed speed to 10 knots. 0620 Changed course to 310°T. 0621 Changed
course to 289°T, 290°pgc, 287°psc. 0625 Changed course to 282°T, 283°pgc,
281°psc. 0630 Sighted South Pass Rear Light bearing 280°T, distance 15 miles.
0704 Changed course to 269°T, 270°pgc, 261°psc. Sighted entrance buoy to
South Pass bearing 271°T, distance 6 miles. 0717 Changed course to 260°T
and pgc, 251°psc. 0733 Changed speed to 15 knots. 0751 Southwest pass
jetty light abeam to starboard, distance 75 yards, entered South Pass, steaming on various courses and speeds conforming to channel. Average steam, 250;
average revolutions, 130.2.

A. MacIntyre, Lieutenant, U.S.Navy.

8—12
Steaming on various courses at various speeds conforming to the middle
of South Pass, Mississippi River. 0800 mustered the crew on stations; no
absentees. 0846 Passed into main river. 1100 Passing Tropical Bend Light,
encountered heavy rain storm from WSW, visibility 1/2 mile, winds reaching
moderate gale force. 1125 wind abated to force 2; rain stopped. Made
daily inspection of magazines and smokeless powder samples; conditions normal. Average steam, 250; average revolutions, 164.2.

G.E.T. PARSONS, Lieut.(jg),U.S.Navy.

12—16
Steaming as before on various courses and speeds conforming to Mississippi
River channel. 1533 Moored port side to Canal Street Dock, New Orleans, La.
1540 Secured main engines and boiler #4. Average steam, 250; average revolutions, 153.8.

A.F. COHEN, Ensign, U.S.Navy.

16—20
1615 Pursuant to Commanding Officer U.S.S. BROOME sixth endorsement P16-4/
00-C/DD210 of this date, Lieutenant Jacob E. Cooper, USN, completed temporary
duty and was detached. Pursuant to Commanding Officer U.S.S. BROOME third
endorsement, P16-4/DD210 of this date, BERNHARDT, T.B., 111 63 89, CGM(PA),
F-4-D, FR, was transferred to Tulane University, temporary duty connection
N.R.O.T.C. cruise completed. Pursuant to Commanding Officer U.S.S. BROOME
Fourth Endorsement P16-4/QR4/DD210 of this date, the following N.R.O.T.C.
students from Tulane University, were detached, temporary duty connection
N.R.O.T.C. Cruise completed: ADEY, Edward A. III, ANDRY, Richard G., BAIRD,
Brice C., BARNARD, Francis R., BATSAIN, Forbes, COLE, Robert M., CROMWELL, Nick
C., CROMWELL, Richard P., DAUBERT, Henry C., DOUGLAS, Walter E. Jr, ELLIS,
Carey J. Jr, FRANK, Charles W. Jr, JENNINGS, James M. Jr, McCAMPBELL, Herbert
J. Jr, McCOARD, Albert B. Jr, PERRIN, Shepard F., WHEELER, Virgil M. Jr,
BUSWELL, Robert L., DESMOND, John J., DOSWELL, Ceion H., FITZGERALD, Richard
G., FLOTTE, St. Marc J., GOTTSCHALL, Alvin E., GREEN, Osmund F., KLECK, David M.,
LABARRE, Anthony E., LATHAM, John F., MAGINNIS, Charles F., MINOR, Wilson F.,
MOSSY, Willey L. Jr, PLAUCHE, Andrew L., REESE, George W. Jr, RIVIERE, George
B., SCHMIDT, Frederick H., SHEPARD, Walter D., ALEXANDER, M.M. Jr, HOWSON,
Wm. S., McLEOD, Pete A., MEYER, Conrad III, MIRANNE, Cheri A. III, MOSELEY,
Edward D., PARKERSON, Thomas B., PERINE, Raymond R., PETERS, Malcolm S.,

Approved:
J.Y. DANNENBERG
Lieutenant Commander, U.S. Navy,
Commanding.

Examined:
A. MacIntyre,
Lieutenant, U.S.N., Navigator.

(Original (ribbon) copy of this page to be sent to Bureau of Navigation monthly)

DECLASSIFIED
Authority NND803052
By _____ NARA, Date _____

ADDITIONAL SHEET

U. S. S. __BROOME (210)_____   Date __11 July_____, 1940

16 - 20 Contd

PETERSON, Jinx, PIGMAN, Paul O.H., PURDUM, Ward C., REUTER, Lloyd J., ROBEIN, Louis L. Jr, RYNIKER, Samuel W., WALKER, John S., WILLIAMS, Henry E. Jr, VAZANT, Joe C. 1638 JUTTNER, R.L., FC2c, STROUD, J.B., Sea2c, MORGAN, J.E., F2c, and STOKES, J.M., F2c, left the ship on 4 days leave. 1645 Received 40 lbs bread from Federooo Baking Co. Inspected as to quantity by Lieut.(jg) G.E.T. PARSONS, USN, and as to quality by THRIFT, V.R., PhM1c.

G.E.T. PARSONS, Lieut.(jg),U.S.Navy.

G.E.T. PARSONS, Lieut.(jg),U.S.Navy.

20 - 24
No remarks

Approved: J. J. DANNENBERG
Lieutenant Commander, U.S.Navy,
Commanding.

Examined: A. MacIntyre,
Lieutenant, U. S. N., Navigator.

(This page to be sent to Bureau of Navigation monthly with Log sheets)

November 1, 1994

Dear Anne,

I began my sophomore year at Tulane with a renewed interest in joining a fraternity. Several of them asked me to consider again and I finally decided to pledge Sigma Alpha Epsilon. Although SAE was one of the strongest fraternal orders nationally, it was rather weak at Tulane because of its inability to pledge enough candidates from New Orleans. At the time almost 80 percent of the student body was local and many of the out-of-town students were in either pre-med or medical school. At any rate I pledged SAE at the urging of Harry Davies, Henry Foss and John Miazza. The wheels were already turning in my head. My goal was to see that this chapter became the best on the campus. It ultimately reached this status a few years after I left school. Although the membership, as well as my pledge class, was small, there were some substantial guys in the chapter. My closest friend (and fellow pledge) turned out to be E. Carleton Guillot ("Carky"). Together we turned this group around. For most of our remaining college days we were inseparable. We double-dated many times. Carky introduced me to a number of girls from Louise McGehee's School, Sacred Heart and Newman High. Toward the end of our first year as SAEs we both became engrossed in fraternity activity. I'll never forget Carky and I sitting on the frat house front porch making plans to increase the membership, especially from New Orleans area schools. During the next two years we did just that. I like to think that Carky and I started it all to make SAE one of the strongest chapters on campus—and to my knowledge it remains so after these many years. We were a great team. He had the best-looking car on campus (when not many students had cars). It belonged to his father, but he was able to use it often. It was a new black Cadillac convertible with green leather upholstery and all the extra "toys" at that time. When you drove in it down the street, it turned everyone's head.

Some of the significant older SAE members that come to mind were Kenneth "Duke" Everts, Gene St. Martin, Andreas Mortensen, Claude Brown, Henry Foss, Lee Vanderpool, Harry Davies, Bobby Hendon and George Smoot. All of these guys were pre-med or medical students except Foss, Davies and Vanderpool. Harry Davies could play anything you wanted to hear on the piano. Henry Foss was always a challenge at the Ping-Pong table. Duke Everts was responsible for my passing the physical to get my commission in the Navy. Although I was in the Naval ROTC unit, I had a high pulse rate every time I took a physical. Duke gave me some sleeping tablets before I went in for the physical and this seemed to bring the rate down to normal. I was so grateful because I couldn't bear the thought of being turned down for a commission as Ensign in the Navy. Andy Mortensen took me out to the Audubon Golf Club and showed me how to play the game. I can only remember George Smoot as being very humorous when he was sober, and a wild man when he was drunk.

In my junior year, I was made SAE rush captain and Carky was my assistant. I was also treasurer and house manager for the chapter, although I didn't live in the frat house. In my senior year I was elected Eminent Archon (president) of the chapter, and Pan-Hellenic representative.

Carky and I went to the SAE Leadership School at the frat headquarters in Evanston,

Illinois, in the summer of 1941, but this trip will be described in a separate letter. That fall we had a very successful rush and pledged some great guys like Bob Catchings, Bill Chamblin, Jack Fagan, Cal Hadden, Forest Little, Ernie Roth and many others. At last we secured a nucleus of New Orleans boys. In my senior year we did even better by pledging Wally Diboll, Billy Kimble, Alan Turnbaugh, Ellis Work and others. The year following my graduation, we hit the jackpot and pledged guys like Henry LeMieux, Norvin Pellerin, Fred Muller and a host of other candidates from New Orleans. And we continued to get outstanding people from out of town like Bobby Boudreau, Ryan Sartor, Ed McGlasson, Tommy Farmer, Jerry Wellborn, etc.

During World War II the SAEs lost their frat house, which was leased. After the war I was advisor to the chapter for several years. I helped stimulate greater alumni interest and was influential in the purchase of the house at 1200 Broadway, which is still the SAE house today. I remember giving $500 to help buy the place and another $500 to install a kitchen. Those were the days when I was rich and single.

SAE had a number of distinguished alumni in New Orleans, but they weren't too active in assisting the chapter unless and until we were in dire straits. A few that I can remember were Ernest Lee and Paul Jahncke, Robert Wiegand, Ben Dart's father and uncle, Robert and Will Rudolf's father, Virginia Brodie's father, Dr. C. Gordon Johnson, Dr. John Pratt, Dean Leslie Buchan and Prof. Donald Derickson. Some others escape memory.

I really enjoyed fraternity life. Despite the unfortunate experience with the Delts, I had a burning desire to succeed and be a part of a group that became successful. Along with it came many pluses; you had camaraderie, you broadened your social life, you developed good long-lasting friendships, you learned how to get along with people of all kinds. If you held an office, you learned how to handle responsibility, how to manage and supervise others, how to develop and execute plans, how to stay within budget and make ends meet, etc.

During my time at Tulane I was also a member of the International Relations Club, the Taffrail Club, the Thirteen Club, and TURK, which, I think, stood for Tulane University Rooters Club. Can't remember exactly the purpose of these organizations or why I joined them. I'll say one thing: all that I've mentioned above, plus dating all the girls didn't help me very well academically, but I passed. Anyway, I guess I had a good time.

Have to stop.

Love you lots,
Dad

November 12, 1994

Dear Anne,

      In the summer of 1941, I became engrossed in fraternity activity including plans for rush week in September. Carky Guillot and I were selected by the SAEs to be Tulane chapter representatives at the annual SAE Leadership School at headquarters in Evanston, Illinois. This was an innovative endeavor to strengthen the order overall and was highly successful and, in fact, later emulated by other national fraternities. The purpose was to train members how to improve rushing techniques, better manage chapter finances, establish and implement house rules, improve scholarship and study habits, replace hazing with worthwhile endeavors and generally instruct everyone on how to better organize their chapters. As I recall, it lasted about a week and was mixed with lots of fun and fellowship. You were exposed to the cream of talented guys who were similarly selected by their chapters across the country. Carky and I decided to expand the trip to include some sightseeing elsewhere and to rush several prospective candidates in the process. We persuaded two very good prospects to take the trip with us. One was Cal Hadden from town and the other was Jack Sequin, my old close and best friend from Dallas, Texas. The four of us left New Orleans in Carky's 1930-something Ford convertible with a rumble seat. Think it was sometime in August. Along the way we tried to stay overnight in an SAE house as often as possible, since it wouldn't cost us anything. Believe the first night was in Memphis, Tennessee. We couldn't find the frat house at Southwestern University (now Rhodes) so we got a room at the local YMCA and they put us up on about the tenth floor with no air conditioning. While looking for this place in the car, we blew our horn too much and got stopped by a cop. Memphis had a law against excessive noise. We talked our way out of a ticket. I can also remember our coming back from dinner somewhere with several six packs of beer. It was very hot so we opened all the windows and proceeded to consume the beer. After drinking more than we should have, we dropped the empty cans out of the windows ten stories down to the alley below "to see what it would sound like." Thank goodness nobody complained.

      The second day we continued upriver in Arkansas toward St. Louis, Missouri. One of us (not I) for some reason had brought a BB gun along and we had to restrain him from shooting at certain targets while we were zooming down the highway. Later in the day we stopped in Blytheville, Arkansas, to visit Bill Chamblin, one of our prize rushees who came highly recommended. Both he and his parents were most impressed with our taking time to see them. He pledged SAE that fall. Bill was a very high caliber and popular guy at school. He was a terrific dancer and introduced the "Memphis Shuffle" to the Tulane campus. Had everybody trying to do it. In my last year at school he was elected the ideal Tulane student and Lana Hummel, one of the girls I dated, was selected as the ideal co-ed. Bill went on to medical school, Ochsner Clinic, and moved up east to practice. Anyway, back to the trip. We stayed a couple of days at the Washington University SAE house in St. Louis. While there I contacted Emerson Burnett, my old friend from seventh grade at Lusher School who moved back to the St. Louis area. Emerson took us all over town. Went out to an amusement area on the south side of Forest Park and took several rides on what was described as the most thrilling roller coaster in the United States. Pretty thrilling. One night we all went to a nightclub in Webster Groves and drank too much beer.

The day we left St. Louis we drove downtown on Main Street near Broadway (where Famous Barr and Stix, Baer and Fuller stores were located). We had previously bought sandwiches and bottles of milk, so we were eating all this stuff going down a very crowded Main Street. Somehow Cal Hadden dropped his milk bottle in the middle of the street and before we reached the end of the block, a policeman whistled for us to stop and waved at us to come back. He made Cal get out of the car and pick up all the pieces before traffic resumed. We were so lucky we weren't arrested because of this incident and because Carky made a U-turn to return to the scene.

The next night we arrived in Evanston very late because we had to wade our way through Chicago traffic. At that time there were no expressways. We obtained several rooms at the Northwestern University SAE house that faced Lake Michigan and was just six blocks from the SAE headquarters. While Carky and I attended the meetings at Leadership School, Cal and Jack Sequin had a great time sightseeing and doing all kinds of crazy things that put us in stitches every night hearing about them. Cal would do the nerviest things. Once we went downtown to the Loop and stopped in at the Dusenburg car agency, where Cal pretended he was going to buy one. He ended up insulting the salesmen and they practically threw us out of the place. The Leadership School folks managed to get dates for Carky and I one night. We went to the Edgewater Beach Hotel for dinner (the owners had also built the Edgewater Gulf Hotel on the Mississippi Coast) and later took the girls to the Aragon Ballroom to dance. Harry James' band was playing. The girls were dull, dull, dull. There were several characters renting rooms at the Northwestern University SAE house who were not attending Leadership School. One was Ambrose Schindler, an All-American football player from Southern Cal. Another was a graduate of Washington and Lee who had a terrific-looking new Cord (or Auburn) automobile and stayed intoxicated all the time we were there.

After leadership school, we decided to swing through Michigan and see what Detroit was like. On the way we stayed overnight at the University of Michigan SAE house at Ann Arbor. We were put in what apparently was a nice large room that extended out from the first floor. We couldn't imagine them giving us this room. Well, it rained very hard all night long and water dripped on us from so many places we couldn't find a dry spot for the beds. The next day our hosts had a big laugh over our difficulties. But they gave us a free breakfast. We then went on to Dearborn and visited the famous Ford Rotunda and took a tour through the Ford River Rouge assembly plant. It was fascinating. And to top it all off, David Dixon, my old friend from Sunday school and Fortier High, was our tour guide. He had taken this job for the summer. David later made a career in sales and sports promotion and was one of the key people in giving birth to the New Orleans Superdome. Later we made a quick pass through Detroit. Again, the traffic was awful—no expressways yet.

Our trip back south was uneventful because we drove maybe ten hours a day, just to get home, and we had run out of money. I vaguely remember staying overnight at the Sawanee SAE house (now University of the South). We took turns driving. Fortunately, we had no mechanical trouble with that old "Tin Lizzie."

Rush week began shortly after getting home. We pledged Cal Hadden and Bill Chamblin, but Jack Sequin decided to go to SMU.

Well, I've run out of steam.

Love you much,
Dad

November 21, 1994

Dear Anne,

Haven't told you much about my academic experience in the Tulane Engineering School. I may have mentioned this before, but I really wasn't cut out to be a professional engineer. However, I was aware of some interesting and worthwhile career opportunities in this field, and where it was helpful and perhaps essential to have an engineering background. So I selected the most general curriculum, mechanical engineering, and never switched majors. I wasn't so brilliant as to get top grades in every course. My goal was to at least understand whatever was being taught—grades were secondary, but important enough to be able to pass. One of my problems, though, was that I was involved in so many other activities outside of engineering that I didn't apply myself as much as I could have.

It seemed as though students in engineering were stereotyped as being too studious and rather dull. But this wasn't the case at all—we really enjoyed ourselves. We had more than our share of difficult courses, and long hours of laboratory work, usually from 1:00 to after 4:00 P.M. several times a week. But this was probably the reason why we developed a special camaraderie and overall had a pretty good time. Most of our classes were in Stanley Thomas Hall, an old building with very high ceilings. The top floor housed the School of Architecture. Now we thought these students were a special breed and perhaps a little weird. I think the only time we went up there was when we learned they had a life class in which the students did sketches from a nude female model. We looked in as observers.

Our chemistry class was in another building, a large amphitheatre-type room that held the whole freshman engineering class. Chemistry lecture was taught by Professor Moseley, a fascinating man. In addition to giving lectures on his main subject he would bring in outstanding people from industry to give guest lectures. One that sticks in my mind was Dr. Kettering who invented the automobile self-starter and among other things, had a lot to do with developing the first anti-knock compound in gasoline (tetraethyl lead). Every so often Moseley would give us a lecture completely unrelated to chemistry. To me the unforgettable one was when he asked you to look at your fellow student on the left and the right, and then he would state that the chances were either you or they wouldn't be around four years later. He continued to describe the process of selection. He said we were a very fortunate group because thus far we had survived the selection process. Of all the kids born when we were born, we managed to live. Many others didn't. Very many young children died of some disease or accident and we were selected to live. Of the survivors, many didn't finish grammar school or high school, but we did. Many of those who finished high school didn't or couldn't go to college, but we were the fortunate few who were "selected." And, looking into the future, only some of us would graduate from college. With World War II coming, only some of us would be selected to survive and come home with no scratches. Later in life, only some of us would be successful in our careers, in our family life and would gain a true sense of fulfillment. Therefore, we could treat our experience of life as a process of selection. Of the millions who start out in this world, only a relative few survive all the hardships and pitfalls to live a long and successful, truly happy life. Several years after Professor Moseley gave us this thought-provoking talk,

73

he committed suicide. Our chemistry lab class was headed by Dr. Crumpler, a very competent man. Among the many other interesting experiments, we learned how to generate rotten egg gas (hydrogen sulphide), which we sometimes put to devious use.

Another impressive professor was A. M. Hill, who would write a lot of valuable information on the blackboard with his right hand and almost at the same time erase it with his left hand before we could finish making notes. Hill had some weird ideas about things, one of which was that he didn't believe in life insurance anytime—it was "a complete waste of money." Still another very talented professor was John K. Mayer, who taught strength of materials and supervised much of our lab experiments in hydraulics and testing the strength of concrete beams. Then there was the somewhat absent-minded Professor Dunlap, who taught mechanics as I recall. And I can't leave out the honorable Professor Zurvigon (Mr. Z.) who taught several courses in electricity. I never could get interested in this stuff, especially in the lab, because I needed to see what he was talking about. So much of all this subject matter was over my head and, if it hadn't been for my good friends and classmates John Martinez, Howard Marx and Jim Jennings, I never would have made it. I couldn't understand what thermodynamics was all about until the night before the final exam when Howard Marx finally turned the light on in my head. Howard, Johnny, Jim and I did a lot of studying together.

One of the more interesting courses was surveying. We spent some time surveying the entire Tulane campus using the "DMD" method as I recall. It was fun and you were outdoors for a change using the latest surveying equipment. We were divided into groups of four or five, and since the architectural students took the course with us, their representative in our group was Arthur "Dirt" Davis, a very sharp guy and a real comedian. He had us laughing so much we could hardly keep our instruments in line. Davis went on to be very successful in his field with Buster Curtis. When we finally completed the survey, it was exciting to learn how close we came to the professional results.

Some other good friends of mine in mechanical engineering, and who survived to graduate in 1943, were Dick Logan, Pete McLeod, Tom Parkerson, Ray Perine, Will Rudolf and Sam Ryniker.

In my senior year I briefly got into campus politics and became campaign manager for Bob Grush, who ran for president of the engineering school. Bob was one of the few Tulane football players who dared take engineering. We won the election.

Well, that's all for now.

Love you and miss you,
Dad

November 27, 1994

Dear Anne,

　　Departing from college life for a bit, let me tell you about my interest in boats and sailing. When Dad first bought a Biloxi cat boat, I was in high school, and at the time I had too many other things on my mind to use it much. Besides, Dad liked to sail it or putter around with it almost every weekend. Mother would go with him occasionally, but she was very much afraid of the water and she couldn't swim. Dad loved to associate with everyone who had a boat of any kind out at the Southern Yacht Club pen. One nice thing about boat enthusiasts is that it really didn't make any difference whether you owned a skiff or a million dollar cruiser, everybody came down to the same level and fraternized. Everyone was always willing to accommodate anyone else needing assistance.

　　Our cat boat was one of those that the Slovak boat builders on back Biloxi Bay, Mississippi, would construct every year just to participate in an annual cat boat race in that area. After the race, whether the boat won or lost, they would throw it up on the beach somewhere and build another one for next year's race. It was one of those that Dad purchased for $100 (boat and sail). It was all wood, about twenty-six to twenty-nine feet in length with an eight-foot beam, had its mast in the very bow, one sail for a gaff rig and a huge wooden retractable centerboard. It was a heavy thing. When you stepped off the pier into this boat, it wouldn't budge very much. Anyway, after Dad taught me how to sail and handle it, I got enthusiastic. I also became more interested when I started to date girls. This was something different I could do to entertain them or possibly persuade them to have an interest in me. It was great fun to double- or triple-date and sail out into the lake in early evening, drop anchor a mile or so offshore and go swimming. Sometimes we brought snacks and cold drinks, but nothing alcoholic. This was something my parents made me promise not to do and I think I kept it most of the time. Besides I really didn't drink at that time—only an occasional beer.

　　I had many exciting experiences with that boat. Must have sailed it on Lake Ponchartrain a thousand times. Around New Orleans and the yacht club this type of boat was only good for pleasure sailing. The popular racing boats then were the Fish Class (owned by the club), the Lightning Class and the Star Class (the most popular, if you could afford one) sloops. Also there were a few Luders-16 Class boats and then the larger Gulf-One Class. I never participated in boat races. I had loads of friends who sailed with me like Jack Sequin, Edwin Stockmeyer, John Miazza, Steed McGee, Johnny Martinez, Jim Jennings, Carky Guillot, Sharpe Stanfield and Henry LeMieux and so many others, I can't remember. Once Johnny, Jim and I tried to sail across the lake to Mandeville, some twenty-seven miles away. We got halfway across and the wind died completely. We were stranded for hours and finally turned around and inched back to shore in the late evening. There were other times when I would get about a dozen guys to join me and we would pick a time when it was likely to squall. All of us were in our swimsuits. We'd go out and wait for a strong wind and heavy waves associated with a rain squall and see how close we could come to turning over without turning over. Of course we capsized most of the time and the coast guard (or Sam Gurvich) would have to come out and tow us in. It got so they knew who was crying for help and they wouldn't pay attention to us for an hour or so. All of this activity occurred before Lake Pontchartrain became polluted.

I had many dates for sailing, day or night. I think the first girl I took out was Betty Waggaman. She was gorgeous in a bathing suit or anything else. So was Lana Hummel. Others, as I recall, were Peggie Baker, Harriet Blish, Nancy Nunez and, later, Virginia Brodie, Norma Lewis and Rosemary Gugert. And then there were the Newcomb out-of-town girls like Pat Northway, Russey Barret, Gertrude (Gus) Chitty, Deanie Wallace, Dorothy Dell (DD) Johnson, Bitsy Lyons and Nia Hoffmeyer. Wish I could remember all the guys, in or out of the Southern Yacht Club, that had boat fever at the time I was active. Some were Cal Hadden and his brothers, Arthur Waters and family, Bob and Will Rudolf, Buster Curtis, Herbie O'Donnell, Gus Lorber, Buzzie Kelleen, Sam Ryniker, Buck Nolan, Billy Provensal, Norvin Pellerin and Fred Clerc. Also, the Duvic brothers and Dick, Connie and Janet Jones. Still others were older guys like Bache Whitlock, Louis Koerner and Harold Cornay. I also remember Earl Blouin, an older fellow, who seemed to win most of the races. At one time Garner Tullis had a magnificent oceangoing schooner. Wonder whatever happened to it.

When I returned from naval service in World War II, I sold the cat boat to Edwin Stockmeyer and bought half interest in a new Lightning Class sloop with John Miazza. We had Mr. Williams build it on the New Basin Canal across from the New Orleans Country Club. When it was almost completed, Williams went broke and John and I managed to appropriate and move it out to the lakefront in the old yacht pen behind West End Park. Just before it was completed, John's company transferred him to Long Island, New York, so I bought out his half.

About that time my father renewed his interest in boats and bought an old thirty-eight-foot, two-masted schooner. It was really too large for him to handle, but if I wasn't handy, he would attract a number of our friends to help him sail it. Mother would go with him occasionally but was still petrified of the water. I kept the Lightning even after I moved to Hattiesburg, Mississippi and later used it infrequently when Mother and I lived in New Orleans for several years. When we were transferred to Cleveland, Ohio, I sold the boat to someone who was a member of Southern Yacht Club and he did some racing with it. I didn't want to keep a boat on Lake Erie and have to pull it out of the water for almost half the year. Also Lake Erie was polluted and cold, so I switched my hobby to golf. I can still sail and have done it a few times over the years. Once you learn how to handle the wind you never forget how to sail. I always said that the next time I would have a boat it would be when I could afford to go down to the dock, clap my hands, and say, "OK, boys, I'm ready; let's go."

Must close.

Love you much,
Dad

December 7, 1994

Dear Anne,

Well, let's go back to my college days. What I am about to emphasize had nothing to do with academics. It was the social life, which was simply overwhelming! While the many aspects of social life didn't happen to everyone, they could have, and I'll have to admit they certainly affected me. I can't remember ever having a date in high school, but after I started at Tulane, I went wild! And at the expense of my school work.

Each school year began with the fraternity rush parties. It was hectic, whether you were rushing or being rushed. Right after a solid week of this activity, there were parties before, during and after the football games. Then the fraternity and sorority formal dances began—fall formals, winter formals, spring formals . . . During the year there were many informal sorority parties and Newcomb (girls) dormitory parties or tea dances (downstairs only, not upstairs). Then we had the class formals and school formals in the Tulane Gym, the annual Pan-Hellenic Formal, the Miami Triad Formal (named after your alma mater) and, of course, the annual Naval ROTC Formal Dance. From time to time you could slip into one of the medical school fraternity formals. In between all these functions were dances given by the high school sororities that were attended by many Tulane students, since most girls in high school were thrilled to be with the older, "more mature" college guys. In fact, during the Christmas holidays, which lasted about two weeks, there was a high school formal almost every night!

There were several excellent bands that played at all these dances. The most popular were Alexander's Ragtime Band and Al Streiman's Orchestra. These people could almost duplicate arrangements by the Dorsey Brothers, or Miller, James, Goodman, Artie Shaw or Duke Ellington. I can remember a trumpet player with Alexander who was really outstanding, and so handsome that the girls paid more attention to him than their partners. The way we danced at the time was so enjoyable. You couldn't get any closer to your partner on a slow one. Some of us jitterbugged a lot but I never could get the hang of it. Couldn't do the camelwalk either, but I could do the Memphis shuffle (that Bill Chamblin, my SAE brother, brought to the campus). These affairs were held at some wonderful places. My favorites were the old Southern Yacht Club, the New Orleans Country Club, or the Jung Hotel Roof. For reference, I am attaching a list of all the locations that I remember. In my last two years at Tulane, I had acquired a good-looking suit of tails. And for informal functions, I bought what I thought was a sharp-looking, light-blue checkered sports coat.

We had all kinds of dates: Coke dates, coffee dates, drugstore dates at K & B, library dates, bookstore dates, walking or skating-around-the-campus dates, beer dates at Bruno's on Maple Street or the College Inn on Carrollton Avenue, dates in Audubon Park (where we could drive around slowly or stop at one of several secluded spots). We had movie dates uptown at the Poplar, Mecca, Prytania or Tivoli Theatres, or downtown at the Saenger, Loew's State or Orpheum Theatres. I'll never forget having a movie date with Margeret Ann Trenchard on Sunday afternoon, December 7, 1941 (exactly fifty-three years ago today). As we were driving downtown on St. Charles Avenue, the news of Pearl Harbor came over the radio. We were absolutely stunned—it was unbelievable! We pulled over to the curb for a while to listen to everything. Seeing a movie was secondary, so we turned around and went back to her house and had Cokes in her kitchen, still listening to the radio reports.

Movie dates downtown could include stopping in at the Napoleon House or the Absinthe House in the French Quarter. After the dances which lasted until one or two in the morning, we might go down to the old Morning Call in the Quarter for coffee and powdered doughnuts. I always suspected their café au lait had a pinch of Hershey's chocolate in it. This combination really hit the spot. Sometimes we'd stop at Brocato's and get some delicious Italian ice cream—spumoni or cassata. Or we would go uptown to the Toddle House at Carrollton near St. Charles Avenue and have coffee or milk with a nice cold slice of chocolate pie that was covered with a layer of real whipped cream, or visit the "new" Camellia Grill across the street and have a thick and juicy dressed burger and something to wash it down.

Forgot to mention we also had dates to the football and basketball games. Also to the boxing or tennis matches. Boxing was still an intercollegiate sport when I was at Tulane. Their outdoor tennis courts were the most attractive I've ever seen—made from an orange-red Argentine clay.

We had dates to the school plays at Dixon Hall on the Newcomb College campus. And then there were dates for the annual Mardi Gras truck rides that followed the Rex Parade on Mardi Gras day. The fraternities would engage these huge, long flatbed trailers, decorate them, and everyone would don the same costume. Sometimes we would add a three-piece band. Getting ready for the big parade could be an ordeal with all the traffic involved, especially if it were cold—and it usually was.

I also forgot to mention that transportation was a problem while dating then, because not many students had cars at their disposal. We would often double-date or even triple-date. Of course the lucky people were the ones who didn't have to drive; they had the back seat all to themselves.

Then, AGG had dates on his sailboat, which I have mentioned before. And on top of all this activity during the school year, there were the debutante parties that some of us attended occasionally.

Many of the kids at school were pinned or went steady. But some, like yours truly, were footloose and fancy free and elected to be nice to everybody. Another convenient thing for the guys who were unattached was that they could go to the formals as a stag (single) and could dance with anyone they wished since the practice at that time was to allow cut-ins. Somehow the girls loved all of the cut-ins—the more the merrier.

So, you see, the social life in college was something else. How I managed to get through Engineering School without flunking out was miraculous. I'm sure I couldn't have done it without some last minute cramming and help from several of my more astute classmates. In addition to a stiff engineering school schedule, I had the Naval ROTC courses, which were no picnic. Somehow I survived!

Have to quit.

Love you,
Dad

Dance Locations in the 1930s and 1940s

Audubon Park Tea Room
American Legion Hall (French Quarter)
Bienville Hotel Roof (Lee Circle)
River Steamboats Admiral and President
Site of the Beverly Country Club (nightclub)
New Orleans Country Club
Lakewood Country Club (on the lakeside of Metairie Cemetery)
Old Southern Yacht Club
Jung Hotel Roof
Jung Hotel Ballroom
New Orleans Hotel Ballroom
LaLouisianne Restaurant
St. Charles Hotel Ballroom
Roosevelt Hotel Grand Ballroom (now the Fairmont)
Metairie Country Club Ballroom
Ponchartrain Hotel Ballroom
Tulane University Gym Floor
Naval ROTC Building, Main Floor
Louise McGehee School Hall
Josephine Louise House Tea Dance Area
Municipal Auditorium, Short Side
Old DeSoto Hotel Ballroom
Colonial Golf Club Ballroom

December 30, 1994

Dear Anne,

This will be the odds and ends letter—stuff that I hadn't related previously—covering different subjects and time frames. Just realized that it was one year ago when I started this kind of correspondence. It should be the last of those spanning a period in my life that I would describe as growing-up time in New Orleans.

Anyway—up at least into the thirties New Orleans still had its street hawkers, who peddled all kinds of things by shouting what they were there for, in an otherwise serene neighborhood. I've mentioned Charlie, the snowball man. Then there was the Good Humor man that sold chocolate-coated ice cream bars on sticks like the original Eskimo Pies. Then the character who came by on a mule-driven calliope wagon selling Roman or cotton candy. There was a wide assortment of fruit and vegetable peddlers in their horse or mule-driven wagons. In the fall you would see the chimney sweepers dressed in black with a top hat and carrying a bag of sticks and long handled brushes. They were kind of scary to the youngsters, especially when they glared at you and their shrieks pierced the air. Once in a while an organ grinder would come by with his monkey. At that time the city still had mule-driven garbage wagons. The workers always made lots of noise with the metal garbage or trash cans and were pretty sloppy most of the time. And the prevailing odor wasn't very pleasant. Also, up until the time we could afford refrigerators, there were men who delivered ice several times a week. It was fun to watch how they quickly chiseled into a large block of ice to get down to the size that would fit in your ice box. The milkman always came before we got up. I also remember that two companies seemed to dominate the laundry business—Chalmette, with their red trucks and the other one, whose name escapes me, with their white trucks.

Growth was so prolific in New Orleans that many kinds of trees would grow up to sixty feet high in about twenty years or less. In the twenties and thirties, it seemed like nearly all of Carrollton was lined with a fast-growing camphor tree that I understand was imported from Asia. They lasted until we had a freeze when the temperature stayed below thirty-two degrees Fahrenheit for two or three days. When all of these trees died, the neighborhoods looked so naked. Other trees were planted and we had shady streets again in just a few years.

Now, back to college days. I've mentioned too often about not learning enough at Tulane. However, the engineering school curriculum did provide me with an excellent background for the type of work I encountered in my business career, namely, sales and marketing of petroleum products and, later, chemicals. I think I succeeded in at least understanding most of the subject matter in school even though my grades were just fair. And perhaps, just as important, I learned how to reason, how to get along with people better, how to cope with adversity, how to handle responsibilities and even how to begin to develop a social and political awareness. I have memories of many wonderful songs and tunes from college days. I could recall a hundred or so, but the ones that still stick in my mind are "My Reverie," "Deep Purple," "Little Brown Jug," "String of Pearls," "Frenesi," "Harlem Nocturne" and "A Nightingale Sang in Berkley Square." There were so many others. As you know I still retain a nice collection of the music of that era on about five hundred record albums. Someday I hope to upgrade the "best of the best" on tapes or CDs.

In addition to having good friends in school or in the fraternities, I developed other friendships within the Tulane Naval ROTC Unit. People like Johnny Desmond, Wilson Minor, Bill Lutes, Julian Brignac, Malcolm Peters, Charley Frank, Allen Lill, Howard McAfee and others. Of course, many of my other friends in school were also in the naval unit. This organization naturally increased in importance and prestige on campus the further we got into World War II. The war was beginning to prey on everyone's mind during my last two years at school. It was a foregone conclusion that every able-bodied young man, in or out of ROTC, would most likely go on active duty somewhere in the armed forces. A number of the students ahead of me were killed or wounded in some theatre of action. I can recall at least a dozen of the guys in our Naval Unit who were killed or disabled during the war. I have mentioned before about being so impressed with the ability of Lieutenant Cooper, one of the unit instructors who accompanied us on the *Wyoming* cruise. He went on to command a destroyer, saw lots of action and ultimately became a four-striper (Captain USN). Another fine instructor was Lt. Streuby Drumm who was transferred to duty at BuPers in Washington, D.C. He made a special effort to see that I was reassigned to another destroyer after I was declared in excess of complement on my first ship. This story will come later. Then there was Lieutenant Wintle, who was transferred from the unit to a cruiser in the South Pacific. He died when his ship was sunk near Guadalcanal. The morning after the bombing of Pearl Harbor, I remember going into Lieutenant Eves' office at the unit. He had been recently transferred from his ship at Pearl. There were tears coming down his face—his ship was sunk and many of his crew had perished. In later years, Eves came back to be commandant of the Tulane Naval Unit.

I haven't said much about your grandmother's (my mother's) family. She was Thelma Austin Gosman, one of five children of John Franklin and Maud Mack Gosman. John Gosman and family came from Bethlehem, Pennsylvania. His sister, Elizabeth, married Fred Dupuy, a plantation owner from West Baton Rouge Parish. His sister, Emily, married William Campbell Anderson, an engineer in New Orleans. Their daughter was reared in the Gosman home and grew up to marry Wilmer Johnson of the Johnson Iron Works (and later the Todd-Johnson shipyards on the West Bank of the Mississippi River). Grandmother Maud Mack Gosman's parent's families (the Mcknights and the Austins) came from Ireland. Understand Mcknight was changed to Mack in the crossing. Maud Mack had two sisters, Lily and Catherine. Grandfather John Gosman was with the New Orleans Public Service, Inc. and died at an early age. My mother had one brother, Frank, and three sisters, Maud, Clare and Genevieve. My Aunt Maud was a devout Catholic, never married, and had a wonderful attitude on life. She was truly a saint. My mother and father met when they were with the New Orleans *Times-Picayune*. Among other things, Mother could paint pictures, compose poetry and loved to play bridge. In fact, her bridge club remained active for over sixty years, and they continued to play auction rather than contract bridge.

During my last year in college the younger guys in my neighborhood on Pine Street convened what seemed like every night in front of J. C. Randall's house on the corner of Pine and Green Streets. They would come from all over Carrollton on their bikes and shoot the bull for hours. I guess they met at J.C.'s house because he was popular with the guys his age. Some of his buddies, as I recall, were Billy Arbogast, Dick Rothermel, Billy Balmer, Allen Favrot,

Sidney Pugh, Allen Oden, Louis Burkes, and "Inky" Ingargiola. Anyway, J.C. joined the Marine Corps and was killed at Iwo Jima. Yours truly was in that area most of the time on his destroyer.

I was always an avid fan of the Tulane football team. They played their home games in the old Tulane Stadium (later the Sugar Bowl Stadium) on Willow Street just a few blocks from my house. When I couldn't go to the games I would park cars in my driveway for twenty-five cents apiece. When I was there, Tulane was a national power in football under Coach Red Dawson. I used to watch them practice often. I remember making friends with Jack Tittle, a lineman from Marshall, Texas. Once, when I was watching practice, Jack came over to the fence where his family was standing next to me, and he introduced me to his parents and his younger brother, Y.A., who later became an outstanding quarterback for LSU and several NFL teams. The backbone of the team consisted of Paul Kruger, Pete Mandich and Tommy O'Boyle, all recruited from a high school in Gary, Indiana. Others were Carl Dailey, Fred Cassibry, Harry Hayes and Bubba Ely, but the star running back was Bobby Kellogg. At the home games on Saturdays the crowd would cheer when the team came out of the stadium corner, but the loudest cheer came from all the kids standing in the end zone when "Jitterbug" Kellogg came out last and somewhat detached from the rest of the squad. He would turn and wave at the kids and they would go nuts.

For years Tulane always had an outstanding tennis squad coached by Emmit Paré. They probably won the Southeastern Conference championship a dozen times. They always seemed to have a super player, beginning with Frankie Parker, then Cliff and Ernie Sutter, then Guy Cheng, Billy McGehee, Roy Bartlett, Lou Schopfer, Earl Bartlett, Jack Tuero, Ham Richardson and many others. I have mentioned those beautiful Argentine clay courts and the neat-looking stands that were next to the old Tulane gym and surrounded by a nice, dark-green fence lined on the inside with a tall stand of bamboo.

The golf team played and practiced on the Audubon Park course. We had a few good players when I was there, like Vincent D'Antoni, the NCAA champion, and Harry Deas.

Can't forget to give you a brief history about sister (your aunt) Jane. She left Newcomb College when she was a junior and joined Pan-American World Airways as a stewardess. Her career with Pan-Am covered about forty years. She flew to practically every country in the world except Russia. She was eventually promoted to management positions in the Pacific Alaska Division at Pan-Am, where, in the flight service department, she was involved in recruiting, hiring, crew briefing, scheduling, personnel supervising and administrative responsibilities. She may have been the most senior female in the Division at one time. Aunt Jane retired and is an active Pan-Am alum.

I tried to be nice to all the girls when I was going to college. I remember dating Betty Waggaman, Lana Hummel, Harriet Blish, Sugar Williams, Peggie Baker, Nancy Nunez, Pat Northway, Margaret Ann Trenchard, etc. There were so many girls I just enjoyed dancing or talking with (and I'll have to admit also caught the gleam in my eye), like Dottie Eaves, Marian Dear, Dodo Kellogg, Jackie Labry, Mary Cutting, Tookie Byrne, Lulu McCutcheon, Mona Aldigé, Betty Morphy, Marion Sandoz, Catherine Burns, Catherine Verlander, Nadine Steinmayer, Evelyn Stolaroff, Nonie Perrilliat, Glenny Wiegand, Lillian Hammond, Jackie Mayhew, Jackie LeRoi, Beverly Bisso, etc., and even older girls like Didi Woolfolk, Corinne Waterman, Peggy Fenno and Nathalie Owings. Now, I realize all this certainly sounds like I'm bragging, but that's not the purpose. I was just so fortunate to have known and been associated with so many wonderful girls during my college years—that's all.

Well, the time came for graduation (May 1, 1943). I received my BE in Mechanical Engineering degree, my commission as Ensign, USNR and my orders all on the same day and left town the next day. I can remember during my last week at home having a date with Betty Waggaman to go roller skating. Also, dates with Nancy Nunez and Mary Ann Delacroix.

So it was off to the wars. I had no qualms about going on active duty or getting into combat. Never gave a thought to what might happen to me. That was the chance we all took. But like old Professor Moseley said, somehow I was "selected to survive." Thus my growing up, at least in New Orleans, came to an end.

Must stop. Miss you lots.

Love you so much,
Dad

Part IV

The Navy Years

January 20, 1995

Dear Anne,

Before I received my commission as Ensign, USNR, from the Tulane Naval ROTC, we were asked to indicate what type of sea duty we would prefer (not that we would get what we requested because usually you didn't, but it was always possible). I had heard that the smaller the ship, the more responsibility you were given. This was true and this was just what I wanted. Also learned that the Navy was building a large number of destroyers, so I put in for destroyer duty, new construction, Pacific, preferably Seattle, Washington. I was going off to the wars and wanted to be as far away from home as possible. Didn't want to be tempted to run home and didn't care for any doting family stuff. Received my commission as well as my orders on the day I was graduated. I opened up my orders and wouldn't you know, I got a destroyer under new construction at Mobile, Alabama, of all places—the closest location to home—only 165 miles away!

Well, I packed all of my gear and took a Greyhound bus to Mobile. I reported to the U.S. Navy Supervisor of Shipbuilding at the Gulf Shipbuilding Corporation yard at Chickasaw, Alabama, a few miles up the Mobile River from town. I was assigned to the contingent of personnel who were to be the crew for the USS *David W. Taylor*, DD 551. I was housed in a BOQ (Bachelor Officers Quarters) just outside the shipyard. It so happened that I was the first officer to report for this duty. Well, the first thing I wanted to do was see my ship. I went down to the yard where there were several destroyers as well as minesweepers, all under construction. The future *David W. Taylor* was practically a skeleton. It turned out that it took almost a year to complete its construction and fitting out. Everything and everybody moved so slowly. It seemed like the yard had hired just about every pea-picker from three states to work on building these ships. This yard actually took over three years to complete five destroyers. In contrast, the Bath Iron Works yard at Bath, Maine, was turning out a destroyer every month. Anyway, I got settled in the BOQ and became acquainted with the officers of the USS *Capps*, DD 550, which was due for completion before the *Taylor*—sometime in August. I had no one to tell me what to do yet so I buried myself in all the manuals of the equipment in the fire rooms and engine rooms (I knew I would be assigned to the engineering department). Also pored over every blueprint imaginable. This ship was one of the Fletcher Class destroyers, which displaced 2,100 tons. It was about 325 feet long with a thirty-eight-foot beam, had four boilers generating superheated steam to turn over two 60,000-shaft horsepower turbines (therefore had twin screws). The normal complement in personnel was twenty-three officers and 300 or so enlisted men. For firepower we had five five-inch guns; five rapid-firing twin 40-mm guns and a dozen 20-mm machine guns. The destroyer was equipped to launch eight torpedoes and had a half dozen racks for launching depth charges. I may not be accurate with this info, but it's close. Also had the latest fire-director equipment, radar, sonar, and navigation equipment. Well, to busy myself every day I began to trace all the lines on the ship, like steam lines, water lines, drain lines, fuel lines, power lines, etc. By the time all officers and crew were assembled and organized and the ship was commissioned, I knew everything there was to know about that engineering plant.

I became well acquainted with most of the officers attached to the USS *Capps*. Will never forget their skipper, Commander Trippensee, who was later transferred to another ship and then died in combat. The officers I was closest to were Lieutenant DeBardeleben (from Birmingham), Ensign Green (from St. Louis), Ensign Dewey (from Detroit), and Ensign Thompson (from Florence, Alabama). In time other officers came in on assignment to my ship. Those I became more acquainted with were the skipper, Commander W. H. Johnsen, a regular naval officer from Iowa (who had never seen an ocean until he went to Annapolis); the Exec. Lt. C. A. Marinke (from Pittsburgh); Lt. Hutchins, the Gunnery Officer; Lt. Zenas B. Deer, Engineer Officer (from Corpus Christi, Texas) to whom I reported as assistant; Lt. Joe Mike Tully; Ens. Julian K. Gilbert (from Cleveland), who was my BOQ roommate; Ens. Oleair (from Elyria, Ohio); Ens. Brittingham; and Ens. Vince Colan, a mustang who was First Lieutenant (head of the deck force).

We had a small dining area in the BOQ. All meals were cooked by stewards mates who were in the enlisted quarters next door. Only a portion of the enlisted men stayed in our area; the balance were housed at Blakely Island. Captain Trippensee made me the mess treasurer, i.e., I handled the collection of all funds (subsistence) to pay for the food. I didn't mind, in fact, I enjoyed taking care of expenses and handling the money. When we finally moved aboard the *Taylor* and later caught up with the *Capps* in the Pacific, I gave everyone a refund, which was appreciated.

The shipyard had to have over a thousand people working on all phases of construction. In addition there was a large group of Navy people from Bu Ships to oversee and approve everything that was done. To stimulate interest and maintain a high level of morale, the shipyard management had organized a softball league. Teams were formed from the ship fitters, pipe fitters, electricians, crane operators, welders, foremen, etc. When I arrived there was lots of competition between the teams from these groups. So, after a while, we went to the league organizers and asked if the naval officers could enter a team. They all laughed at us and said we couldn't play the caliber of ball they played. They really thought we weren't good enough but finally agreed to let us start. By the end of the summer we were at the top of the league in the standings and gained the respect of everyone in the yard. I played first base. Captain Trippensee was our pitcher (and he was very sharp). Green, Dewey and Oleair were also on the team. Couldn't remember anyone else but we had lots of fun playing several times a week until we left in the fall.

We also initiated a little social activity at the BOQ and had several parties before we left. Had an excellent record player in our quarters. The stewards mates would have that thing going all the time and had the volume up as high as it would go. They played several pieces constantly, like Benny Goodman's "Six Flats Unfurnished," Tommy Dorsey's "Boogie Woogie" and "We'll Get It," also Ellington's "A Train."

Not long after I arrived in Mobile for duty, we received an invitation to a formal dance given by a group of very sweet and lovely girls at the Mobile Country Club. It was here that I met Jamie Crawford and we hit it off very well. I continued to date her throughout the summer and on up until the time she left to go back to Randolph-Macon College in Lynchburg, Virginia. Jamie made my stay in Mobile most enjoyable. She introduced me to all of her friends, like Jean and Jane Sapp, their brother Phil, whom I later met out in the Pacific, Jean Smith (of the bakery family) and many others. She had me over for dinner several times with her family at their home in Ashland Place. I would rent a car every time I had a date with her. The popular places around Mobile at the time were The Battle House, the Rose Room at the Admiral Semmes Hotel, Constantine's downtown for an excellent meal, and a few so-called nightclubs like the Airport Inn, the Plaza and The Spot. Jamie took me to other parties in Mobile and over to Point Clear, Alabama, and several other places on the eastern shore of Mobile Bay. It was my first exposure to the Grand Hotel and surrounding area. I was most impressed. In fact, it was one of the reasons Point Clear was selected as a place to retire. It hasn't changed much—marvelous countryside, nothing glitzy, "resorty" or commercial—just a laid-back sub-urban atmosphere with lots of things to do and accessible to all kinds of stores and services.

In August of '43 Vince Colan and I were sent to Damage Control School in downtown Philadelphia, Pennsylvania, and we stayed at the Copley-Plaza Hotel. School was in the Girard Trust Bank Building. Had some great times with dates going to the Rathskeller and to the Bellevue-Stratford Bar. Also marvelous food at the original Bookbinders restaurant down near the waterfront. I remember the current record hit was Bing Crosby singing, "Sunday, Monday or Always." I made a quick trip to see Aunt Glenn in Harrisburg, Pennsylvania. Also made a trip over the weekend to New Haven, Connecticut, to see Johnny Martinez, a close college friend, who was at Yale in an Air Force training program.

The shipyard at Chickasaw didn't have a "Rosie the Riveter," but there was (only) one female working on those ships in that mass of humanity by the name of Lightning Keller. She was very conscientious and dedicated to her job and was also good-looking and had a cute personality. While she withstood all the obscenities and wisecracks from the yard workers she was actually protected by the head of the electrician's union. In fact, she lived with his family. Anyway, after Jamie went off to school, the guys in the BOQ bet that I couldn't get a date with her. To make a long story short, I was successful and they had to pay me off. Actually, she was a really nice girl from out in the country near Flomaton, Alabama. I just couldn't understand what drove her to working in that shipyard. Guess it was the money. Anyway, she had guts.

We finally put the USS *David W. Taylor* in commission in Mobile on September 18, 1943. A few days later we made a quick run over to New Orleans to pick up torpedoes at Belle Chasse, Louisiana. I didn't have a chance to go home, but I called. Just before we left for this trip, two other officers reported aboard, Lieutenant Stromberg and Lieutenant Sayers. They had been at BuPers in Washington and used some connections to get sea duty on the *D. W. Taylor*. The trouble was we already had a full complement of officers and no room for any more, which put our skipper, Commander Johnsen, in a bind. So he wired BuPers for further instructions and their response was to bump the two most junior ensigns off the ship and one of them was AGG. This was the second big disappointment in my early life. I was crushed because (1) I had learned all the intricacies of the engineering department machinery, (2) I could go anywhere on that ship blindfolded and (3) I had cultivated many warm friendships with the officers and men, especially Captain Johnsen. Well, I had to take my lumps and move on. I was detached from the *Taylor* the day before it left for sea trials. I was transferred to New Destroyer Commissioning School at the Norfolk, Virginia Naval Base. To me this was an insult after spending six months watching and overseeing a tin can under construction and putting it in commission!

The first thing I did upon arriving at Norfolk was to contact Streuby Drumm, my old naval science instructor at Tulane who was in BuPers. A few days later I was assigned to the

Mertz Detail NOB Norfolk, Virginia. The *Mertz* was also a Fletcher Class 2100-ton destroyer exactly like the *Taylor* and under construction at Bath Iron Works, Bath, Maine. I owed my placement on the *Mertz* to Capt. Streuby Drumm. Here was another fork in the road of my life where I spent about thirty months of sea duty aboard the USS *Mertz* instead of wherever the *Taylor* would have taken me.

While organizing the training of some of the crew for the *Mertz* at the Norfolk Base, I had some great times at the Grand Old Officers Club on the base. I corresponded with Jamie Crawford, who was at Randolph-Macon, in Lynchburg, not too far away. She asked me to spend a weekend there so I could take her to their big school formal dance. It was a coincidence to see Ann Springer there from New Orleans. I took piano lessons with Ann. Her date was Stanhope Hopkins, her boyfriend, whom she later married.

Shortly after returning to Norfolk, I came down with the mumps, of all things, and had to spend six days in the naval hospital. Couldn't imagine how I got this stuff. I was beside myself in the hospital and gave all the nurses fits because I couldn't stand missing anything on duty and certainly didn't want to run the risk of getting booted off another ship from this setback. Anyway, they kept me in bed where I should have been and finally released me when it was safe to get up.

Not long afterward I received orders to report to the U.S. Navy Supervisor of Shipbuilding, Bath Ironworks, Bath, Maine, for assignment to the *Mertz*. I couldn't wait to get up there, so I went over to the naval air station adjacent to the base and learned that I could get a free ride to Boston the next morning as a passenger in one of a squadron of torpedo bombers. They strapped me in the torpedo bay underneath, which gave me an excellent view of the terrain we covered. And since they weren't in a hurry, they flew at low altitude and followed the coastline all the way up to Boston. What a wonderful experience. Never saw so many majestic homes and estates along the coast. I transferred from plane to train in Boston and arrived in Bath around 11:00 P.M.

Well, this is getting far too lengthy. Take care.

Love you so much,
Dad

January 30, 1995

Dear Anne,

Upon arriving in Bath, Maine, close to midnight, I was surprised to see Tom Barry waiting for me in the station. The *Mertz* exec, Lt. Cdr. J. P. Andrea, heard of my coming and asked Tom to pick me up. It was cold and snowing and Tom had had a few somewhere and was feeling no pain. Gosh, the things you remember. In a few days I blended in well with the officers and men assigned to the *Mertz* detail. The Bath Iron Works shipyard was very well organized and everyone was so industrious—quite different from that laid-back yard in Chickasaw, Alabama. I was assigned as first assistant to the Engineer Officer, Lt. Henry Odell Russell, a terrific guy (more about him later). Had no trouble with the power plant and other equipment. It was exactly the same as the *Taylor's*. We made several short trips down the Kennebec River toward the ocean and back to check out some of the gear. What surprised me was the rise and fall of the tides in this part of the country. Seemed like they changed as much as fifteen feet, which is a heck of a lot.

After only being with the *Mertz* a week, we pulled out of Bath on November 19, 1943, and steamed down to the Boston Navy Yard where the ship was formally commissioned, USS *Mertz* DD 691. We took on torpedoes, supplies, ammunition, food, etc. Boston was a great town for liberty and shore leave. I should explain it was called shore leave for officers and liberty for the enlisted men. I'm guessing we were here several days before leaving for our shakedown cruise and sea trials. While it was (a damp) cold and light snow was falling most of the time, we frequented the night spots like the bars at the Copley Plaza and Statler Hotels. Also the Bradford Skyroom, the Latin Quarter, Mayfield, the Cave Room at Stubens, and the Officers Club at 12 Arlington. The best place to eat was Pieroni's; the lobsters were delicious and huge. The hit songs at the time were Jimmy Dorsey's "Star Eyes" and "Tangerine" with Helen O'Connell and Bob Eberle doing the vocals. I remember we organized a terrific dinner party for all the officers and their wives at the Copley Plaza Hotel before leaving for good the next day. Sometime during the evening each officer was asked to say a few words. When my turn came I was a little high and so I said what was on my mind. Can't remember but whatever I said, it brought down the house and everyone thought I was the hit of the party. Good first impressions always help.

Well, off we went to Bermuda along with four other new destroyers, USS *Melvin, McDermott, Newcomb* and *Uhlman*. Once at sea our skipper, Commander W. S. Estabrook USN, changed his colors from being a quiet reserved person to a character that was worse than Captain Queeg in *The Caine Mutiny*. While a very competent naval officer and ship handler, he trusted no one and came down hard on everybody on that ship. During our shakedown, which lasted about thirty-five days, everyone stood watch on watch. This means standing a watch (performing some duty) for four hours and off four hours, and then back on watch again for four hours. This continued all day and night the whole time we were at sea. And every time we had a drill or exercise of some kind all hands had to get up and participate for the length of the exercise. The rationale was to get us to learn all of our duties aboard ship as quickly as possible, but it was killing most of the officers, and especially the crew. In addition to trying to become a worthwhile unit of the U.S. Fleet, all landlubbers, which were most of the personnel, had to get use to the rough seas, the rolling, pitching, yawing, etc., of this ship in probably the deepest portion of all the world's oceans. Another unusual effect of the sea, particularly in this area, were the swells. This is a condition where even if there was no wind or whitecaps, the water surface would bob or swell up and down at great lengths and anything that floated went up and down with it. The swells around Bermuda were so great that you could see a mountain of water several hundred yards away that was literally higher than any part of your ship, and seconds later the ship was on top of a mountain of water overlooking the valleys around us. At times when you steamed through this kind of sea at any high speed, if you caught the next "mountain" at the right moment, the bow would either look suspended in air or it would catch an immense quantity of water that covered the entire bow almost up to the bridge deck. Somehow, we all endured.

We had a two-day reprieve from all this on Bermuda Island. We couldn't dock at Hamilton, the largest town, we so we dropped anchor out in the bay. Bermuda was (and still is) a fascinating place. Only about twenty miles long, but a good portion of it curls around the bay, so if you stretched the land mass out straight, it would be about thirty miles in length. Bermuda was a veritable toyland from the sea. All of the houses and buildings are made of stucco or some ceramic material and painted in all kinds of pastel colors with red, gray, or white tile roofs. There wasn't much to do ashore except to buy cashmere sweaters or have drinks at their two night spots, the Ace of Clubs Bar and the Twenty-one Club—also the Officers Club. The British gave the U.S. Navy full use of the island and its facilities during World War II. On the last liberty one of our crew, who had too much to drink, fell off our motor whaleboat as it returned to the ship and drowned. And, unfortunately, our chief boatswain's mate apparently became so despondent that he hung himself. He tied a rope on the wheel of the main deck forward hatch, put the other end around his neck and jumped into the hatch area. These incidents were very embarrassing to Captain Estabrook who was in hot water anyway throughout our shakedown cruise. Shortly before we departed from Bermuda we were given a stiff inspection by a regular navy, full captain—never forgot his name, Captain Madiera. We spent half a day and most of the night cleaning ourselves and the ship for the inspection. Everyone had lined up on top side in our full dress blue uniforms. This crusty old officer walked in front of Estabrook to review all personnel. Every time he saw an enlisted man with some length of service he would ask him to stick out his arm to show his service hash marks. Every stripe on the coat sleeve represented four years service. When some of our chiefs revealed four or more hashmarks (stripes), Madiera would give him a half smile, grunt an approval and then say "Very good—as you were," meaning he could bring his arm back to his side—and show no emotion in doing all this. Captain Madiera was "unhappy" with the condition of our ship and its crew. Actually, we suspected he gave hell to all the new ships just to keep them in line, to work harder and remain vigilant. Madiera called all officers including the skipper down to the (officer's) wardroom and gave us all a tongue lashing. Then he told Estabrook in front of us that he was ashamed of the despicable condition of the ship and all personnel. He turned toward Lt. Commander Andrea, our Executive Officer (who was also a true blue Annapolis graduate), and said "Are you sure you are a Naval Academy man?" This mortified Andrea as well as our skipper.

Anyway, after Madiera left, Captain Estabrook called us into the wardroom again and gave Andrea and all the officers holy hell and finally said, "I'm tired of being the son of a bitch on this ship," and promptly retired to his stateroom. Estabrook took this whole situation personally.

Well, we finally returned to Boston, somewhat more seasoned than when we left. I forgot to mention that during that shakedown we conducted numerous trials, drills, and exercises with the other new ships. One trial was to make a full power run, i.e., to see how fast we could go with all four boilers and our two steam turbines running at full capacity. We registered thirty-nine knots (that's over forty miles per hour). The *Mertz* never went any faster during its entire service in commission.

With about four days in Boston, Bill Sanders, Bob Sims and I went to New York City to cut up and/or relax. Also spent a day in Providence, Rhode Island, but can't remember why. Before leaving Boston for duty in the Pacific we had a cocktail party in our wardroom for the family members and friends of all officers. Somehow I met a very nice girl at another function in Boston. She was a student at Wellesley, and I remember her name was Norma. Anyway she accepted my invitation to come to our cocktail party. Everyone was impressed with my date, especially our doctor, Tommy Thompson, who was married but still had a roving eye. He talked to Norma a little too much, to his wife's chagrin. So I guess he caught hell later on.

Well, we finally received orders to report for active duty with the Pacific Fleet. We steamed down to Norfolk NOB to take on more provisions, fuel, ammo, food, etc. On January 25, 1944, we left Norfolk for the Canal Zone (Panama) with the USS *Roe* and USS *Eichenberger,* convoying the USS *Clay* (supply ship) and a French warship by the name of *Athos.* Only things of significance were to see the water turn from dark blue to a luminescent turquoise and observe an endless number of flying fish jumping out of the crests of the waves. We steamed down past the Bahamas and saw the Miami Beach lights at night and later barely saw a little of eastern Cuba and western Haiti as we sailed through the Windward Passage.

It was quite an experience going through the Panama Canal. Passed by Colón on the Caribbean side, then through the Gatun Locks, then over Gatun Lake and through more locks to Balboa and Panama City on the Pacific side. We waved at many natives who walked in the locks area. Lots of kids somehow came down to watch our ships. I was surprised to see many who didn't look altogether native. One of my old machinists mates, Cunningham, MM1C, who had been on duty there several times said, "Mr. Gottschall, you see all these kids—I bet half of them are mine." We gave one-third of the crew liberty for one night in Panama City. About all they could do was frequent the bars and try to stay away from the blue-moon queens. These were girls who would tempt the sailors to buy them drinks. Blue moons weren't alcoholic, probably pink lemonade, but the sailor paid a high price for it as well as his own drink. The last man to come aboard before we departed the next morning was another one of my senior machinist mates by the name of Hartman. About an hour before we left, we got several of our guys on MP duty to run back to town and look for Hartman. He had passed out in one of the bars, like Kelley's Ritz Bar, so they carried him back to the ship. We needed him—he was a good man when he was sober.

We steamed up the Pacific Coast and had faint glimpses of Costa Rica, Guatemala and Mexico. Saw only mountains in the distance from time to time. On the way we had a machinery casualty. Our after-turbo generator developed a serious steam leak and we were forced to go to the San Diego Naval Repair Base instead of heading directly for Pearl Harbor, which meant at least a few more days in the states before we left for the wars. Everyone took advantage of our stay in San Diego. Actually, this caused us to miss the beginning of the U.S. military offensive against Japan, i.e., the invasion of Majuro in the Marshall Islands. Our armed forces were successful only after a high cost in human life and casualties. But we weren't there, yet.

Anyway, the San Diego night spots at the time were the Grant Hotel Lounge downtown, Pacific Square, a ballroom that hosted big name bands; and some nightclubs like The Tops, the Busted Bulkhead, Sherman's, The Hole in the Wall, LaJolla, and The Cove. Lt. John Anderson was our supply officer and paymaster. He, Odell Russell and I bunked together in the same stateroom. Andy was a wonderful friend and a delight to be with. He had a distinct New England accent. During our stay in San Diego he "fell in love" with some girl and corresponded with her for the next two years. The popular songs then were "My Ideal" and "Sweet Eloise."

We finally got our generator repaired and departed from San Diego on February 23, 1944. Arrived at Pearl Harbor Naval Base near Honolulu, Hawaii, and reported to ComDesPac and Cominch, Pacific. Shortly after arriving we were ordered to escort the carrier, USS *Intrepid* back to San Francisco along with the USS *Capps, Wintle* and two DEs (destroyer escorts). We moored next to the *Capps,* which was the first ship built down at Mobile. I made my one and only visit to the *Capps* and surprised all of my officer friends with an unexpected dividend from being mess treasurer back at the BOQ in Chickasaw, Alabama. When we got under way to go to San Francisco, the *Intrepid* developed serious rudder problems so we all returned to Pearl Harbor and missed a chance to cut up in San Francisco. The *Mertz* didn't actually return to Pearl. We were ordered to lay off the harbor entrance for five days before getting word to come in and refuel. There was some word that a Japanese sub was snooping around, but we couldn't locate it. On March 6, 1944, we left Pearl again convoying another carrier, the USS *Essex,* for about 200 miles until it joined other ships and we returned to Pearl. We went in and out of Pearl for several days undergoing various training exercises with other ships. Then finally left the Pearl Harbor area with the USS *Melvin* and convoyed the USS *Sperry,* a supply and repair ship, to Majuro in the Marshall Islands. This was our first venture into an area of active combat. At the time the Marines were conducting mop-up operations on these islands. Meanwhile, our skipper was getting more ornery and our normally good-natured executive officer was getting close to a nervous breakdown trying to please him.

Well, sweetheart, my hand is getting tired.

Love you much,
Dad

February 12, 1995

Dear Anne,

Continuing from last letter regarding our entering the combat zone, the mop-up operations in the Marshalls didn't involve occupying all of the islands held by the Japanese. As long as they couldn't be sustained with supplies they were militarily ineffective and left to "wither on the vine." One of these islands was Jaluit. The *Mertz* was ordered to patrol around this island twenty-four hours a day. Intelligence advised that there was a Jap sub in its little harbor and it was necessary to keep it there for the time being or sink it, if it tried to head out to sea. This mission involved only our ship—we relieved another tin can that was circling Jaluit. We were advised not to come within about 3,000 yards of the beach, because the Japs had shore batteries that could fire at that range. One night on the midwatch (12:00 to 4:00 A.M.) our Mr. Gardiner had the (officer of the) deck duty on the bridge as well as the conn, i.e., he was in charge when the skipper sacked out. I suppose he got bored and curious, so he steered within 3,000 yards to have a better look at things. When we got in range, the Japs opened fire on us and we immediately turned tail. Nothing hit us, but we learned the hard way that the enemy was on that island. The next morning the skipper was told we were fired on but they didn't tell him we went inside the 3,000 yards. We didn't know it, but a few days later the sub made a run for it and succeeded in eluding us so we were ordered back to the main fleet staging area off Majuro and near Tarawa.

On March 22, 1944, we left Majuro as part of the U.S. Fifth Fleet with 103 warships. This group was known as a fast carrier force. On the way we crossed the equator. All aboard who had not experienced this before were initiated by going through a little hazing and having our heads shaved *smooth*. Then we paid our respects to King Neptune (our Chief Bastings, CWT, in a god-awful costume). Thereafter, I maintained a very short crew cut. I wasn't going anywhere and there were no girls to impress. From time to time, between inspections, the sailors would grow all kinds of mustaches and beards. I didn't try, because I probably had the lightest beard on the ship. The purpose of this fleet movement south and west was to conduct a raid on the islands of Palau, Yap and Woleai. This consisted of our carrier-based aircraft bombing Jap positions as well as some shore bombardment. On the night of May 31, we were subjected to a Jap air attack but encountered no damage. The next day we found and finally sank a Jap transport ship. Our marksmanship wasn't very good. At General Quarters, my post was below in the after-engine room so I couldn't see anything, but the story we got was amusing. This was our first encounter with a real target. Our five-inch shells finally hit portions of the ship and the Jap crew started jumping off into the water. In trying to sink it our shells began to splash in the surrounding water—so much so that the Jap crew decided it was best to swim back and get aboard. We finally destroyed it.

While all this was happening our old Chief Machinists Mate (CMM) Gregoire, who had a general quarters station on deck, was heard to say, "Mr. Andrea, give me a four-man working party and I'll carry those goddamn shells over to the right place faster than that."

Anyway, the overall raid was successful although we lost a few planes. A couple of years ago *National Geographic* had an article about the lakes on these islands and showed pictures of how beautifully clear and serene they were—including shots of several U.S. fighter planes at the bottom of one of the lakes. Brought back memories. We returned to the Marshalls staging area and moored at Kwajalein Atoll.

On April 10, 1944, we left Majuro with a carrier for Espíritu Santo in the New Hebrides Islands and arrived in an attractive little harbor just big enough to moor our two ships. One little thing you would detect when approaching any of the islands in the South Pacific was that you could smell the vegetation before you could sight land. When we came close to the carrier upon entering the Espíritu Santo harbor, I had the chance to wave at Theo Harvey, one of my Tulane ROTC classmates who was on the carrier. There was just a small navy repair base here, but it did have an Officers Club, the only thing not off-limits in the area. We had one night of shore leave and I was in the lucky 25 percent of officers who rated going. However, we couldn't stay ashore longer than a few hours. The club was open for snacks and drinks from 4:00 to 7:00 P.M.. Well, six of us arrived there when the bar opened and proceeded to drink almost anything alcoholic. The club was at the top of a small hill and, except for the front gate, was surrounded by a thick six-foot hedge. We continued to drink and bitch and joke, etc., for a couple of hours. Unfortunately, I had too much and somehow, after we got on the subject of football, I proceeded to tell everyone how good a scat back I was playing sandlot ball and got out in front of our table to illustrate how I moved. Well, my good buddies who were also fairly drunk, got tired of my raving about football, picked me up and threw me over that hedge. I rolled down in the soft grass about fifty feet, climbed back up, squeezed through a small opening in the hedge and returned to finish my story on football. They threw me over the hedge again. I finally got back inside and, after a few more drinks, the bell sounded that the bar was closing and we had to leave. I was so full of booze I could hardly walk. When we got down to the foot of the hill, I passed out. I was loaded into a jeep, poured into our whaleboat at the dock and when we got back to the ship, I was hoisted aboard in a cargo net. When I woke up the next day I couldn't remember anything after the first time I was thrown over the hedge. Everybody got a kick out of my performance except our Executive Officer, Andrea, who, thank God, didn't tell the skipper. That was one of the few times AGG had too much to drink and misbehaved. I've been stone drunk about four times in my life and this was one of them. They never caught me in this condition again.

Anyway, we returned to Majuro—then departed for Pearl Harbor on May 2, 1944. For the entire month of May we went in and out of Pearl almost every day. Purpose was to participate in gunnery and shore bombardment exercises, south of Maui and Lanai and west of the big island of Hawaii. We practiced hitting targets on Kahoolawe, a small deserted island with no trees or growth of any kind. The Navy had used this island for target practice for years. It must be half full of lead and steel. Once in a while the mist around there would clear and you could see the majestic island of Hawaii in the distance looking like a huge mountain in the sea. When we got closer, we could see the pineapple and sugar cane plantations that went up the side of this gorgeous land mass, at times into the clouds. Truly a beautiful sight.

We were able to get ashore on Oahu at Pearl or Honolulu for only a few hours at a time. One day Odell Russell, Bill Sanders, John Anderson and I went over to the Royal Hawaiian Hotel, an elegant, elaborate structure of pink stucco surrounded by an abundance of bamboo, tropical flowers, plants and trees. We took a short dip in the ocean in front of the hotel. It wasn't much fun, because there's really not much of a beach. You had to wear tennis shoes to keep from cutting your feet on the coral rock. It was here that Russell took pictures of us, some of which I think you may have seen, Anne. I was so very thin—looked like I was starving.

On May 31, we left Pearl Harbor with a large assortment of ships including most of our destroyer squadron (54-Div 105) and the battleships *California, Maryland, Tennessee* and *Colorado*. Also three APOs (troop ships) and others and headed for Roi Kwajalein Atoll in the Marshalls and arrived on June 8.

About this time our first executive officer, Lt. Commander J. P. Andrea, was transferred to another destroyer to take command. He was so happy to finally have a ship of his own and to get away from Estabrook. Wish I could remember the destroyer he commanded (think the USS *Spence*) because about a year later his ship and two other tin cans capsized in a violent typhoon. He went down with his ship. The story we heard was that of all their personnel (about 325), only five men survived! And only did so by catching a loose life raft and getting under it so they could breathe through the perforated platform, because the rain was so dense there was little room for air. What a tragedy!

Anyway, Andrea was succeeded by our senior full lieutenant, John Hays Gardiner, a dedicated naval officer and a true gentleman. John had a distinguished background, which I will describe later. After the war, Bob Sims and I visited his family and had dinner at their home in Pride's Crossing, Massachusetts.

And on this note, I must stop.

All my love,
Dad

February 18, 1995

Dear Anne,

The next thing of any significance was leaving the Marshalls with a large fire support task force as part of the invasion of several islands in the Marianas Group, namely Saipan, Tinian and Guam. The first action was on Saipan, just north of the other two, all of which were well fortified by the Japanese. On the night before the invasion of Saipan would commence, we had an unusual machinery casualty (this description was used when something serious went wrong with machinery in our power plant). Our main condenser in the forward engine room sprung a leak. This meant that relatively unpure salty cooling water could seep into this steam condenser and foul up our ability to convert our clean condensate (water) back into steam, which ran our main turbines and turned over our starboard propeller. Therefore, we had to secure this plant completely and operate only one screw (propeller). This was like losing an engine on a twin-engine airplane. Of all the times for this to happen, it had to be the night before we were going to participate in our first active combat. And besides, we had to get this thing fixed or our ship would certainly be vulnerable to what lay ahead.

We could barely maintain desired fleet speed with one propeller but we managed. Most of our engine room personnel, including Odell Russell and myself, stayed up all night with the problem. We had to take off the huge main condenser header, paint all the condenser tube ends (about a hundred of them) with soapy water, then blow air into the condensate side to see if we saw any bubbles, which indicated the source of the leaks. We finally found three leaks and welded those tubes shut, and then put everything back together again by 0400 (4:00 A.M.) the next morning. By that time the whole fire support group of our invasion force had to slow down anyway as we approached the island target area.

There were no fireworks yet anywhere. The "smoking lamp" was out over the entire fleet (meaning no lights anywhere). Invasions were always planned to begin on moonless nights. This particular night was not only without a moon, but the sea became very calm with almost no wave action or swells. (That's why this ocean is called the Pacific.) It was a scary feeling to know that soon the fireworks would start. There would be a tremendous amount of shore bombardment of the landing beaches and later on that morning (of June 14, 1944) thousands of our Army and Marines would speed toward the beaches in all kinds of landing craft, and many would die or be severely wounded. Well, when it finally happened, you didn't think too much about this part of it. You were focused on doing your particular job and there wasn't much time to worry about the horrors of war. Our branch of the naval force had it easy. We didn't have to go ashore and we didn't have to fly close over the combat area to receive any anti-aircraft fire. Our main function was (1) to fire our guns at targets on the beach and (2) to protect ourselves and other larger ships from enemy aircraft or submarines.

From a distance Saipan looked like a long mountain range in the sea. As I recall the Army went up the east side and the Marines landed and went up the west side of the island. We were on the side where the Marines landed. A few days after our troops established beachheads and secured the southern portion of Saipan, the *Mertz* was ordered to escort the *Norman Scott,* another destroyer in our squadron, back to the Marshalls. The *Scott* had been torpedoed and skip bombed by a Jap plane which incidentally crossed our bow in the process. Although badly damaged, the *Scott* could move on her own power.

We arrived at the naval base at Eniwetok on June 23 and promptly returned to Saipan on June 29, 1944. We were then associated with a task group on July 3 that consisted of five CVEs (small carriers) and a squadron of destroyers (DesRom56) and began raiding operations on Saipan. Also participated in lots of shore bombardment. We would do figure eights from about 5,000 yards out and would fire at targets directed by aircraft pilots or ground troops moving up the west side of Saipan. While my general quarters station was down in the after engine room during all this activity, I managed to sneak up on top side (deck) a few times. On occasions we'd get so close you could see our troops and tanks moving up the coast and the Japs in slow retreat. They would rather die than surrender so progress by our forces was very slow and painful. Here we were watching a battle from a relatively safe vantage point on a ship that had a clean place to sleep, three meals a day and showers to stay fresh while those poor guys on the beach went through hell. The Navy was also lucky in this campaign because the Jap fleet had encountered Admiral Spruance's fast carrier force, whose aircraft downed forty-five Jap planes in the first raid and ninety-eight planes in a second raid plus bombed a number of their land-based airfields. Also our subs sank two of their carriers and caused the Japanese Fleet to retreat. Therefore we won the air war which made our invasion easier. We lost thirty of our aircraft. The enemy lost 346 aircraft total and two carriers. This skirmish was called "The Great Marianas Turkey Shoot." As a result, the Japanese were only able to send a few planes to bomb our Saipan invasion forces. There was little or no enemy sub action although we had thought we would get a lot in this situation.

On June 16, 1944, we departed from Saipan again with the destroyers, *Conyngham*, *Longshaw,* and *Callahan* and two CVEs for Eniwetok. On July 20 we left Eniwetok for Guam with twelve AKs, five DDs, and two CVEs arriving on July 22, 1944. The next day we were ordered to operate with a CVE task group in support of the invasion of Tinian, which is south of Saipan in the Marianas. Won't go into details. Same combat experience as at Saipan. The *Mertz* was unusually lucky again and came through this campaign with no scratches. On August 3, 1944, we went up to Saipan, which was now in our hands except for the northern tip of the island at Marpi Point, where remnants of Jap troops were hidden in caves on the cliffs that jutted out into the ocean. Every day it seemed a few more Japs would try to kill themselves by jumping off the 100-foot cliffs into the rocks and/or surf below. If they survived, they would still refuse to be picked up in the water.

I should tell you of an unusual experience on our last day at Saipan. Our forces had secured most of the island, all but maybe the northern 25 percent, which still contained many pockets of Japanese holed up in underground bunkers or tunnels, etc. By this time a fleet post office was established ashore and most of the mail to all personnel was routed through this location. Periodically, we would send an officer assisted by a yeoman (our mailman), a signalman and a boat engineer over to the beach to deliver and pick up our mail. The officer was always someone from our communications department. Anyway I bugged John Gardiner, our executive officer, to let me go ashore with the men this last day in Saipan. He reluctantly agreed but cautioned that we were on call to leave the area that night or sooner so to be sure not to waste any time.

The *Mertz* was anchored about five thousand yards out along with fifty or more other ships of all kinds. So the four of us set off in our motor whaleboat for the shore. About halfway to the dock I looked back and saw that one of the destroyers was sending signals by searchlight. (You could see them even during the day.) I asked our signalman to interpret the communication. He couldn't make sure of it and said it wasn't coming from the *Mertz* anyway. The other guys felt certain it wasn't also. So we tied up at a portable dock, walked over to the nearest makeshift road, hailed an army truck that took us up north about three miles to the post office. While our mailman and I were collecting the mail, the other two men disappeared and it took about an hour to locate them. They didn't tell me where they went or what they did until after we got back to the whaleboat. They had found some dead Japs that had not as yet been disposed of, took some of their belongings and even pulled out some of their gold teeth! I was livid and told them what I thought of anyone doing this. Anyway, we couldn't catch a ride back to the dock so we walked as fast as possible. I was getting nervous about taking this much time. We passed a sugar mill that undoubtedly was destroyed by air attacks and also passed by a stockade surrounded by barbed wire that housed a number of Saipan natives and their families. They were sort of half Polynesian and half Oriental and they looked as though they were in terrible shape. They were confined almost like wild animals, but under the circumstances, our military people hadn't time to do any better, and they were never sure whether they were good guys or bad guys. Anyway, we finally got back to our boat and returned to our mooring area at top speed. The only trouble was we couldn't find our ship. It wasn't anywhere near the ships that were anchored on either side of us. Finally and luckily we found it in the distance. It had pulled up anchor and was standing by to get underway as soon as we returned.

Well, it turned out that the *Mertz* was the ship that was signaling us to return when we were en route to the shore. We had received orders to depart with the fleet at sundown and had to take over our screening position, etc. Our skipper, Captain Estabrook was beside himself. He had given Gardiner hell for letting us go in the first place. And Gardiner was upset and disappointed as well. Anyway, we finally got into position in time and plowed through the sea at flank speed to return to the Marshalls. Later in the evening, I went up to the bridge and found Estabrook slumped in his captain's seat on the outside of the bridge deck. He was glaring ahead and chewing his lower lip as he often did when he was unhappy. I apologized for what happened and explained why we didn't return sooner. He never answered me or even looked at me. So I went below feeling terrible and so sorry that I had let John Gardiner down. I apologized to him and he understood the situation. He was a gentleman, a wonderful naval officer. Everyone else thought it was amusing. At least they got their mail. In time the skipper forgot about it, mainly because he didn't really inconvenience the task group commander. That was the only time he ever got upset with me. He was often upset with most of the other officers, but I'll relate some of those stories later. Captain Queeg (in *The Caine Mutiny*) had nothing on Estabrook.

Have to go.

Love you much,
Dad

P.S. Well, I have to tell you one more story. When we returned to the Marshalls, the USS *Mertz* and Captain Estabrook in particular, was awarded a Bronze Star medal for our superior performance in shore bombardment at Saipan. We were delighted except for one of my machinist mates—Robert Vincent Fields III—a real screwball. He swore that if Estabrook received an award of any kind, he would do something drastic. Sure enough, on the day our squadron commander came aboard, we were all lined up in our dress whites on the forecastle. He marched smartly up the deck, said a few words of praise to us and then pinned the Bronze Star medal on Estabrook's chest. As soon as he did this, old Fields broke ranks, ran up and did a swan dive off the bow of our ship. Needless to say all pandemonium broke loose. We had to launch our boat and retrieve Fields, who was floating in the water and laughing his head off. Estabrook confined him to our brig, which was one of our storerooms, for several days, and then busted him from First Class to Third Class Machinist Mate. This was a sharp loss in pay and entered into his personnel record, but he didn't care. Said it was worth it.

February 24, 1995

Dear Anne,

On August 10, 1944, we arrived at Eniwetok Base in the Marshalls with destroyers *McGowan, Wadleigh* and two AKs, and prepared for a nine-day tender availability, which meant having a chance to make all necessary repairs aboard ship, to replenish stores, ammo and other provisions, and also to give some degree of relaxation for the crew, such as it was. Naval operations in the Pacific were much different than on the Atlantic side. The Pacific area was so huge that when you returned from combat for a rest, there was no place for the personnel to go for R and R (rest and relaxation). If available, a small section of one of those "sandbars" in the middle of the ocean was used to let the enlisted men go ashore for a few hours to walk around on some land and get rid of their sea legs. They were also given two cans of (usually warm) beer, and that was liberty. The officers didn't get much, if any, shore leave except to chaperon the men on their liberty and keep them from misbehaving.

On August 19, 1944, we left Eniwetok for Makin Island in the Gilberts group with Squad Dog 54 minus the *Norman Scott,* which was still under repair, and also with destroyers, *Sigourney, Aulick* and *Conyngham.* Stayed around Makin just long enough to rendezvous with a convoy and departed for Guadalcanal to join the U.S. Third Fleet, under the command of Admiral Halsey. I forgot to mention that during the Saipan, etc. campaigns we were part of the U.S. Fifth Fleet under the command of either Admiral Spruance or Mitscher. Anyway, the U.S. Third and Seventh Fleets were the naval contingents of an overall military force of Army, Navy and Marine Corps under the command of the famous Gen. Douglas MacArthur. He had vowed to retake the Philippines after the Japanese forced him to give them up at the beginning of the war in the Pacific.

Between August 24 and September 8, we patrolled and operated in the Guadalcanal area around such locations as Tulagi Harbor, Lunga Point, Florida Island, Purvis Bay, Savo Island and Cape Esperance, all in what was known as the British Solomon Islands. Nothing much happened except we went over the spot that was called Iron Bottom Bay where about a year earlier there was a naval battle between U.S. and Jap forces and several of our cruisers and destroyers were sunk. So were some Japanese ships. Somewhere on the bottom were Lt. Jack Wintle, my former naval science instructor at Tulane and Herbie McCampbell, a classmate, who went down with one of the cruisers. This was at the time when the U.S. Marines and the Japs had some bloody fights on Guadalcanal.

On a lighter note, about this time we received our latest supply of V-disc records that were forwarded periodically to all stations and ships at sea. Never will forget three pieces that we played over and over again: Harry James's band with either Kitty Kallen or Joni Janes singing "It Seems I've Heard That Song Before" and "I'm Beginning to See the Light" and an Australian hit called "Waltzing Matilda."

Anyway, on September 8, we left with a fast carrier task force of the Third Fleet for an invasion of several islands in the Palau group where we had launched raids the previous spring. The islands we had in mind were Angaur and Pelelieu, even though we led the Japs to believe we were going to land elsewhere. We had the same combat experience as in the Saipan and Tinian campaigns so there's no need to be repetitious. We luckily came through again without any damage. The only things noteworthy were this time we saw a few dead Japs in the water, and we tried to capture a Jap pilot whose plane was shot down by a ship ahead of us, but he killed himself before we could take him prisoner. We completed this operation successfully in just a few days and returned to Manus in the Admiralty Islands on September 28, 1944.

Manus was an established base with a very well protected harbor for many ships. It was a sizable island compared to those atolls where we replenished our supplies previously. I went ashore a couple of times. Visited the Officers Club for just a few hours, like from 4:00 until 7:00 P.M.. We all wore our khaki uniforms with no coat and open collars since it was unbearably hot and humid. The second time I went to the club there must have been several hundred officers there from all branches of the service. They even had an orchestra in back of the bar playing many of the popular tunes of the day. Once, when they began to play "Begin the Beguine," one of the officers got up on top of his table and sang the words. He had a marvelous voice—very touching—so when he finished everyone got up and cheered. I'm almost sure this was the place where I bumped into Lee Vanderpool, one of my SAE fraternity brothers, also Dick Marschall (whose sister married Bob Cosgrove, my next door neighbor) and Phil Sapp, Jean and Jane Sapp's brother from Mobile. Made you feel good to see somebody from home.

Also at Manus one day I accompanied our gunnery officer over to a huge cargo ship to make arrangements to take on ammunition. The name of the ship escapes me, but it had all kinds of explosives aboard. The reason for mentioning this is that the next time we came back to Manus, this ship was gone and we learned that a few days after we left Manus this vessel caught fire somehow and then exploded into smithereens. Just about all personnel were lost, maybe 500. They said the noise was deafening and it completely disappeared from view. What a tragedy. And to think that I was aboard the week before!

Well, on October 10, 1944, we left Manus with a large combined military force of Army, Navy and Marines. Our objective was the big one. We were going to recapture the Philippine Islands. Our first goal was to occupy Leyte, a sizable mass of land in the middle of this island group just inside Leyte Gulf behind Samar. On or about October 20, 1944, we landed and began to neutralize Leyte without too much difficulty, but the big show was probably the largest battle in naval history. The Japanese High Command knew they were losing the war and therefore decided to make a daring and desperate attack on our naval forces in and around the Philippines. They divided the remainder of their entire fleet into several groups and made a three-pronged attack on our fleet and supporting units. One Japanese task force under Admiral Ozawa came down from Japan to the northern side of all the Philippines; another group under Admiral Kurita came from Singapore through San Bernardino Straits in north central portion of the islands; and the third group under Admiral Nishimura from Borneo and Admiral Shima from Formosa came into Leyte Gulf through Surigao Straits. We had a formidable array of our navy in Leyte Gulf—can't remember all of the names but perhaps seven or eight battleships, a dozen light and heavy cruisers, maybe fifty destroyers, all kinds of landing craft, PT boats, supply and troop ships, etc., including the USS *Mertz*. Since the landings on Leyte were going well, we were ordered to do figure eights off Dinagat Island where our radar could sight any enemy ships coming through the Surigao Straits to the south or the middle Jap task force that could come from the north along the east coast of Samar. Anyway, we all got word on the evening of October 23 that many Jap ships (BBs, CHs, CLs and DDs) were coming through Surigao Straits at top speed. We slowed them down slightly when two squadrons of PT boats sneaked in and fired everything (torpedoes) they had, but did little damage. The Japs kept coming and unbelievably almost in single file. Our squadron was ordered to refuel and make a torpedo run at them by crossing the entrance of the straits into Leyte Gulf. Unfortunately or fortunately, the *Mertz* was the last to get refueled because of a Jap air attack, so all of our squadron (minus the *Mertz*) as well as another squadron crossed the straits in single file at flank speed and launched every torpedo they had at their ships. (We were asked to return to our post making figure eights off Dinagat.) Our destroyers got several good hits and either sunk or disabled the first four or five of their craft entering the Gulf, but the stupid Japs kept coming one after the other. We lost one out of our two squadrons of destroyers making the torpedo runs—the USS *Grant* was sunk after receiving heavy damage. The problem the Jap Navy had was that only their lead ship could do any firing. They played into our hands very conveniently since our ships were lined up perpendicular to their force and we could throw everything we had into their leading ships. In naval terms this maneuver is called "crossing the T," where you are at the top of the T and the other guy is forced to be at the bottom of the T. We were told that you could see the Jap ships on radar as a series of blips coming toward you and as they moved within range the closest blip would disappear (meaning it was sunk or close to sinking). This whole thing was happening in the middle of a moonless night. Well, we decimated the Japanese forces by early morning, around 3:00 A.M. on October 24th. The few ships that survived turned around and fled. Damage to this branch of their fleet was devastating. They must have lost over ten thousand men. We lost only the destroyer *Grant* in this sector of the battle from our surface Navy but there was also damage from the few Jap aircraft that came over the next day. They had a new tactic. Their pilots were ordered to dive into our ships along with their bombs so they couldn't miss and committed suicide in the process. They were the kamikazes and they were deadly. We continued to patrol the area off Dinagat the next day with the *McNair* and a PT boat squadron. In the afternoon, a Jap Zero (airplane) came in to us low over the water. I was in the after-engine room at the time. We first heard our five-inch guns firing away, then our forty-millimeter guns began to fire and finally, when our twenty-millimeter machine guns starting pumping away, you knew someone was close and something was going to happen. Then there was an explosion on our starboard side—the Jap plane had disintegrated about 200 yards away. A few pieces of the aircraft landed on our deck. We fought off several other kamikazes later in the day, but couldn't shoot them down. Meanwhile, the other Japanese task force coming through the Philippines north of us knocked off three of our escort carriers and some destroyers (CVL *Princeton;* CVEs *St. Lo* and *Gambier Bay;* DEs *Johnson, Noel* and *Samuel Roberts*) but when some of our aircraft hit and sank a large Jap cruiser and damaged a battleship in this group earlier plus some valiant fighting by the DE *Johnson* and their courageous skipper, they turned around. If this hadn't occurred, this task force had plans to come down the east coast of Samar from the north and enter Leyte Gulf at the same time their southern force was coming out of Surigao Straits. This could have been a disaster for the U.S. forces and their support groups, and the little old *Mertz* was going to be the first ship they would sight had they arrived. Luck was with us again!

On October 2, 1944, we left Leyte Gulf, Philippine Islands, with Squad Dog 54 and the destroyer *Hale* for Hollandia, Dutch New Guinea and arrived on October 30, 1944. Hollandia was a harbor occupied by some of our forces while we were on another campaign to the north of this area. The harbor was surrounded by mammoth tropical trees—eucalyptus, teak, mahogany and some ebony. Never saw such large trees or such dense growth so near the beach.

This is enough for now.

Love you much,
Dad

March 6, 1995

Dear Anne,

    My naval experience with the Japanese in World War II can get boring, but this was all I did for almost two years, so please bear with me. On November 9, 1944, we left Hollandia with Squad Dog 54 and about twenty-five AKs (ships that carried all kinds of provisions and troops) and steamed west to Leyte Gulf, Philippine Islands. Our job was to convoy and provide protection against enemy aircraft and/or submarines. As we neared these islands, we were attacked by a single Jap torpedo bomber that just missed an AK aft of us. We finally shot it down. Arrived in Leyte on November 14, unloaded and departed under sporadic air attacks. These enemy plans would come out of nowhere. This would disturb the whole naval support group because you didn't know which ship the kamikaze would dive on. There didn't seem to be any coordination on the part of these attacks. These were no large groups of enemy aircraft as we had previously encountered. Every few hours a single "bogey" would come over and try to dive on some unlucky ship, sometimes successful, but most of the time not. Thank goodness! It almost seemed like many of the kamikazes didn't have their hearts in crashing into us. But you never knew the outcome until you either shot them down, scared them away or got hit. They all were probably land based near Manila. In the Philippine Islands campaign they gradually became more of a nuisance.

    Well, we departed Leyte Gulf and arrived back in Manus on November 20. Left Manus again with six CVEs and nine DDs and arrived at a new staging area in the Palau Islands on November 30. Then left promptly to avoid an air raid by a considerable number of Zeros from a Jap carrier group. We proceeded to Leyte, but had to turn back to Palau to avoid a severe typhoon (an Asian hurricane). We should have stayed at Palau anyway, because the typhoon caused the Japs to cancel their air raids. We had a very rough time getting back to Palau. Never saw heavier seas. You were supposed to ride out these storms with the wind coming from your port quarter, but that didn't mitigate anything. Under these conditions you could rarely afford to go out on deck. If you were off watch, you just strapped yourself to your bunk. I never really got seasick, but I did get dizzy and the only thing to alleviate the dizziness was to lay down and shut your eyes. Everything loose or partially loose on the ship moved. If you sat in your stateroom chair to do anything, it would slide from one side of the room to the other. If you were at your desk, you had to hold on to something solid with one hand while trying to do anything with the other. After a while this experience would get you angry and you would start to use foul language even with no one around to hear. This existence was both ridiculous and humorous. Every once in a while you would hear the crashing of plates in the crew's mess compartment or the officers' wardroom. The chairs in the wardroom slid all over the place, if they weren't hooked to the dining table. Trying to enjoy a meal was almost impossible. But there were always some "old salts" who behaved like nothing was wrong and would say, "So what are you bitching about?" You wondered how you could stand it hour after hour, day after day, but you did. The best place on ship in bad weather was on the lower level of the engine spaces, or in the (emergency) after-steering compartment just ahead of the propellers, or better still, way up in the ship's director cabin above the bridge. This unit was as stable as our gyroscope and remained level no matter how much the ship bobbed and weaved. Only the gunnery personnel on watch could stay up there. Anyway, it was during this terrible storm that three of our destroyers and two DEs capsized and nearly everyone was lost. Our former exec., Lt. Commander Andrea, was the captain of one of those tin cans, (the USS *Spence*), and he went down with his ship. We all felt so sad and sorry for John Andrea. He tried so hard to be a good naval officer, and when he finally got a command, this had to happen

On December 10, 1944, we left Kossol Roads, our Palau Island staging area for the invasion of Mindoro, Philippine Islands, one of the largest of all these islands. We were one of about twenty-four destroyers screening three battleships, two light cruisers and six carrier escorts in this attack task group. On December 15, we passed through Surigao Straits and participated in the occupation of Mindoro. This time we were under constant air attack. The *Mertz* shot down one plane and damaged several others; the whole task group destroyed ninety-seven Jap planes. The destroyer *Harriden,* just ahead of us, had her stack blown off with lots of casualties. Two suicide bombers just missed one of our CVEs, the *Savo Island.* After the usual fighting that goes on in this type of campaign, (which I won't bother you with), we returned from the Sulu Sea through Surigao Straits back to the base at Palau. On December 26, we left with three DDs and the battleships *Mississippi* and *New Mexico* for Leyte and arrived on December 28 at San Pedro Bay off Tacloban, Leyte. One New Year's Eve, December 31, 1944–January 1, 1945, we were subjected to another air attack. On January 2, we moved over from San Pedro Bay with three DDs and six LSMs for Ormac Bay, Leyte. On January 3, we returned to San Pedro Bay to pick up some LSMs and convoyed them to Dulag, Philippine Islands.

Whenever we moored or anchored at different spots along the Leyte Coast (even under air attacks) the Philippine natives would come out from nowhere in their long boats laden with all kinds of artifacts to sell to the sailors. They were under orders not to do this, but they came anyway. Had so much junk and trinkets that you'd think we were tourists. They were clever though. Would usually have a beautiful girl sitting in the bow of the boat wearing a brightly colored thinly clad sarong. She was there just to look at, never to touch. These young girls always had very long, fine black hair, combed just right. The sailors may have bought some of their stuff but they'd spend most of the time looking or flirting with the girl. When their boats got too close, the officer of the deck would have to shoo them away. Here we were in the middle of a war and these simple Filipino natives were trying to make a buck selling trinkets and using their daughters to help stimulate sales.

On January 5, 1945, we departed from San Pedro Bay with fifty LSTs, ten AKs, three DDs and six PCs for Lingayen Gulf, Luzon, Philippines. This was the big and final push to kick the Japanese out of the Philippines. Took the route through Surigao Straits and west to Mindoro where we refueled on the ninth. Along the way you could see land on either side of this waterway. Sometimes we got pretty close. It was very mountainous, but the weirdest looking terrain I had ever seen, almost scary. Just didn't look real. Anyway, we arrived in Lingayen Gulf on the eleventh with reinforcements in the occupation of Luzon. The recapture of this land mass and the capital, Manila, were met with little resistance by the Japs. Only remnants of their army had remained. But this didn't stop the kamikazes. On the twelfth, we were attacked by four suicide dive bombers. We turned away two of them with our excellent fire. Other ships weren't as lucky. Some kamikazes were successful in crashing into an AK, a destroyer escort and the APD34. On the thirteenth we did figure eights at the entrance to Lingayen Gulf and then left that evening with two DDs and two APDs to return to San Pedro Bay, Leyte. On the nineteenth, we headed for Ulithi Atoll to report to the U.S. Fifth Fleet again and to participate in any future fast carrier operations. Arrived at Ulithi in the Caroline Islands on the twenty-second. This atoll was made into the major staging area for the Fifth Fleet. We had four days alongside the USS *Dixie,* a destroyer tender, to make necessary repairs and replenish provisions. This was the time one of my wisdom teeth started hurting, so I visited a dentist on the *Dixie.* He felt that all of my wisdom teeth needed to come out. In fact, he found a fifth one. So he proceeded to inject me with Novocaine, except he gave me too much. I passed out and fell on the deck. He lifted me back into the chair, slapped my checks, apologized and then pulled out all five wisdom teeth. I was in agony for a week. In time, everything healed.

We reported to Fast Carrier Task Force 58.5, under the command of either Admiral Spruance or Admiral Mitscher. On February 10, 1945, we left Ulithi with 58.5 consisting of the heavy carriers *Enterprise* and *Saratoga,* the new light BB *Alaska,* cruisers *Baltimore* and *Flint* and two other squadrons of destroyers (nine to a squadron). This group headed for air raids on Tokyo, Japan, in support of the invasion of Iwo Jima in the Volcano Islands. While we had, by this time, established B-29 bases at Saipan and Tinian, the targets on Japan were still so far away we began to lose too many of our bombers attempting to return to base either damaged or low on fuel. Thus we had to take Iwo Jima for use as an intermediate base for our B-29s.

On February 16–17, 1945, we steamed up to Japan and made heavy air raids on Tokyo and the surrounding industry about one hundred miles away. At this point the Japanese had relatively little surface Navy left to fight us, but what they did have was always dangerous, because they became more reckless and suicidal and could still put any of our surface Navy in jeopardy. They still had lots of submarines to give us fits. And they continued to operate a fairly large number of aircraft, mostly land based, all of which were assigned to kamikaze duty.

From February 19 until March 10, 1945, we provided air support to the marines landing at Iwo Jima. We finally took this island, but only after very heavy casualties. We lost over 7,000 men and the Japs lost about 23,000 men before it was all over. Perhaps it was worth it, but at a terrible cost.

It was about this time when our skipper, Cdr. W. S. Estabrook, was transferred back to the states, to the U.S. Naval Academy (of all places). We aren't sure how this transfer came about, but it wasn't long after the first of the year when he had to complete and submit fitness reports on all of his officers. Such reports were the captain's opinion of your ability, perform-ance, promotability, behavior, etc., and were made a permanent entry in your service record as a naval officer. Well, to make a long story short, we had twenty-two officers on the *Mertz* under Estabrook and he gave unsatisfactory fitness reports to more than half of them. (I wasn't one.) The reports went to our squadron commander for review and concurrence before being forwarded to the Bureau of Naval Personnel in Washington, D.C. When our squad commander reviewed them, they were promptly returned to Estabrook for resubmission. We understood through the grapevine that the squadron commander told Estabrook that if he had that many unsatisfactory officers under his command then perhaps something was wrong with their captain. Anyway, not long afterwards old Estabrook was transferred. I say "old" when he was no more than around thirty-five at the time. Most of his officers were from thirty all the way down to AGG, the youngest at age twenty-two. Estabrook was so weather-beaten that he looked like a man of fifty most of the time. Lots of sea duty will do this. On the day of his departure, we all shook his hand and wished him the best. When he went down the sea ladder to the captain's gig the poor guy was almost in tears. As the boat went around our bow he stood up and saluted his ship. I may tell some other stories about this man later. He was truly another Queeg.

Estabrook's successor was Commander W. S. Maddox, another academy man, with an entirely different personality. He couldn't believe our ship was so neat, clean and orderly, from the bridge all the way down to the bilges (bottom of the engine spaces). He was also impressed with how well the officers and the enlisted men knew their duties and how smartly and professionally we carried out orders. In spite of what we may have disliked about Estabrook, he left everything "in ship shape." Maddox soon realized that we were all so uptight that he gave very few orders and let us use our own judgement most of the time. He decided that the *Mertz* could almost run by itself. Maddox was a very different, unusual naval officer—competent, personable, very intelligent, diplomatic and, best of all, had a good sense of humor. These characteristics eventually washed off on us and everyone began to relax and enjoy themselves more. He was an exceptional bridge player. He would get up games among the officers as often as he could. When in port or in a staging area long enough, he would ask the other skippers that played to come over to our wardroom for a game. If he couldn't get a foursome, he would ask one of us to fill in. I never played bridge very well, but once he asked me to substitute. I hid my ignorance by getting good cards most of the time. Then once, during the evening, after completing a hand, he would ask that we leave all the tricks as they were and say, "Let's see if I can still do this." He would turn over the first card of every trick (both his and the opponents) and then identify the other three cards in the trick before he saw them. Wow!

Have to go, again.

Love you much,
Dad

March 15, 1995

Dear Anne,

On March 12, 1945, we arrived back at Ulithi Atoll, Caroline Islands, to replenish provisions, ammo, refuel and get a few repairs from the destroyer tender, *Cascade*. Had no time for any liberty (among the palm trees). The powers that be in the navy were working everybody's tails off. The strategy from this point on was to keep hitting the Japs as often as possible in hope they would give up and we all could go home. But this didn't happen so quickly.

Left Ulithi on March 14, 1945, with a sizable fast carrier strike force consisting of heavy carriers *Enterprise, Intrepid* and *Yorktown*, heavy battleships *Wisconsin* and *Missouri*, light BBs *Alaska* and *Guam,* cruisers *Flint, San Diego, St. Louis,* most of my Destroyer Squadron 54 and two other squadrons of DDs. Objective was to conduct some air raids on the Japanese mainland and to support the occupation of Okinawa. This type of fast carrier strike force took up a large amount of space in the sea. The carriers, being the most vulnerable to any attack, were in the center of the force, either in line, if two, in a triangle, if three, or in the shape of a diamond, if four. They were surrounded by a ring of battleships and cruisers, and these in turn were encircled by a larger ring of as many as three squadrons of destroyers—in most cases about twenty-four. Can't remember exactly but this array of ships was probably 10,000 yards or more in diameter. We had to have this much space because the turning circles of carriers and battleships were large, also because often we were on a zigzag course (changing every ten to fifteen minutes) to confuse enemy submarines. In the process of changing course (direction), either from zigzagging or to put us into the wind to ease carrier aircraft takeoff, all the destroyers really had to scamper. Most task force commanders wanted every destroyer to have the same bearing off the same larger ship. Then sometimes the force commander would change his mind and want the screen of destroyers to rotate several positions ahead or behind. There were times when things could get hectic, especially at night, with all the lights out. Every so often a destroyer would just miss getting rammed by one of the larger ships. I forget now but we also had to do special maneuvers when the task force came under enemy air attack. The Japs knew of our likely formations. Sometimes they came over in groups and tried to destroy a single target, primarily a carrier. Other times they would spread out and come in alone and low over the water between ships so we were forced to almost fire at each other trying to knock the plane down. One of the destroyers in my squadron was hit in the engine spaces by friendly fire. It was put out of commission with heavy casualties, but didn't sink.

Our communications officer, Roswell Galbraith, kept a copy of some of the radio communications between ships and aircraft while we were in these task force groups. They were very funny to hear the first time (fifty years ago). Maybe not today. Every ship or unit in the force had a call name for identification—some of them crazy. Anyway, a few of these communications (that weren't so raunchy) are as follows:

"Ripper, this is Russia [Admiral Halsey]. What are you doing?"
"Russia, this is Ripper. Did I understand you to say you wanted the Ripper Division sent north?"
"Ripper, this is Russia—Keee—Rist yes, get 'em going!"

110

"Was that a Jap plane, Kate?"
"No, that was a Jill, I'm sure."
"Well, whatever it was, it's a Zero now."

"Hello, Coldstream. Are you the ship bearing 180-12 [180 degrees—12,000 yards]? Over."
"Hello, Russia, this is Coldstream. Negative."
"Hello, Schooner, this is Russia. Is that you bearing 180-12. Over."
"Russia, this is Schooner. I don't know. Over."
"Schooner, Russia. Are you kidding? Over."
"Russia, Schooner. Negative. My gyro is out. Don't know where I am."
"Kodak [task group], this is Russia. Schooner goes to the lost sheep circle. Out."

"Joker from Hoboken IV. Am I correct in assuming you go to Station 15?"
"Joker, Affirmative. Out."
"Joker from Hoboken IV. Then are you going to station 15. Over?"
"This is Joker. Affirmative. Out."
"Joker, Hoboken IV. What took you so long to assume station? Over."
"Joker, faulty plot [navigator made a mistake]. Out."
"Hello, Joker, this is Hoboken IV. In the future I suggest that when you see other ships
    proceeding toward stations, you tag along with them. It's not a case of everybody being
    out of step but Joe. Out."

"Geese on northerly course, identify yourselves."
"Honk, honk."
"Roger. Out."

"Hello, Ripper, this is Russia. Clear all Charlie Able Peters [close air patrol] from the area.
    Let 'em come in [the returning fighter aircraft land]."

"Hello, Luxury 4. I have four hours pumping of ballast on board. Request instructions."
"This is Luxury 4. Pump!"

"Someone just passed my bow. Over."
"That was me. Out."

"Hello El Toro, this is MacBeth. My bogey [enemy plane] was a phoney. Ouch!"

"Hello, Kodak [fast carrier force], this is Russia [Admiral Halsey]. Secure all the fans, the
    shit's going to fly any minute."

"Russia, this is Armada. Bogey bearing 225-5. Over."
"Hello, Armada. This is Russia. I evaluate your bogey as an albatross. Out."
"Russia, this is Armada. If it wouldn't be a violation of security regulations, what is an
    albatross? I can't find it in the Call Name List or PacCall instructions."
"Helloooo, Armada, this is Russia. An albatross is a bird with a wing span of twelve feet,
    just covered all over with feathers. Out."

"Hello, Russia, this is Ruffian. We put a suicider in our hip pocket. Out."

"Pilot report to Russia. That Kamikaze stopped talking at zero nine two-eight. He was white with meatballs on his wings."

"Hello Russia, this is Green One. Splash one Betty [enemy plane]. Tally Ho!"

"Rowdy, this is Pelican. Bogey bearing zero five zero-sixteen and closing."
"Pelican, Rowdy. Don't pay attention to him. The guy behind him is the guy with the gizmo—the guy with the little tin fish [torpedo]."
"Rowdy, this is Pelican. Two bits on the guy with the little tin fish."

"Unknown station, this is Russia. Who was that who just crossed my bow?"
(No answer.)

"Hello, Ripper, this is Russia. Are you moving up to your new station?"
"Russia, this is Ripper. Affirmative Posit! [He's already there!]"
"Ripper, this is Russia. Roger. Out."
"Russia, Ripper out."

"Russia, this is Chatterbox. I have aboard one damaged Jap. Looks like he will live. There are two more in the water. How many do you want?"
"Chatterbox, Russia. All of them, if it's not too much trouble."

"Hello, Russia, this is Werewolf. I've just rammed a destroyer. Believe it's Gimlet. Sorry! Out."
"Hello, Gimlet, hello, Gimlet, this is Russia. Are you all right?"
(Long pause.)
"Hello, Russia, this is Gimlet. Negative!"

"Plane to base. Do you still see that bogie on your screen?"
"Base to plane. Negative."
"Plane to base. You're goddam right. I just shot him down."

"Culpepper, this is Sandbox. Can you give me any reason why you can't keep on station? Over."
"Sandbox, this is Culpepper. Negative. Wilco. Out."

"Hello, Groupies, this is Leader One. Will you hold reveille on your signalmen?"

We had an NH system that we called Nancy Hanks. It was an infra red cover put on our searchlights, so we could communicate by searchlight day or night, but you couldn't see the signal flashes until you put on infra red goggles. Here are some cute transmissions:

"Nancy will take you now."
"Too wet out for Nancy."
"Nancy's busy."

112

"Nancy's got a date."
"Nancy's slip is showing."
"Nancy has a customer."
(And a few that were worse than these)

Another thing that occurred on long jaunts was refueling at sea. This was a risky undertaking in rough weather. Small ships like destroyers would come alongside, say, a battleship to obtain fuel and we would be bobbing around like a cork while the BB was sailing along smoothly through the water. The BB crew would throw us a light leader line that led to a heavy Manila line and finally a large eight-inch black rubber hose, which we connected to our fuel lines. The ships couldn't get too far apart or the hose would snap and spill Bunker C fuel oil all over the place. Nor did you want to get so close you might scratch the BB's hull and ruin ours. Bunker C was a heavy sticky fraction of crude oil and had a strong sulfurlike odor. As assistant engineer officer, I had to keep in touch with my "oil king," who was in charge of loading all fuel tanks forward and aft. We had to know how much each tank could take and how much to sluice from one partially full tank to an adjacent empty tank. When it was over we made a quick calculation as to how much we took and let our skipper and the ship loading us know exactly how much we received. We had very few mishaps. Most of our men were on the ball.

We would also get an occasional surprise from the loading ship. Sometimes they would give us about fifty gallons of really good vanilla ice cream, which was a delicacy to everyone on a tin can. Once, when we were taking on ice cream, somebody made a mistake—the line popped and the dessert we were looking forward to fell in the drink (water) and sank immediately. And they couldn't give us any more. Never heard so much cussing and foul language. Sometimes, they would swing over several crates of fresh oranges. They were always tasty. And sometimes these larger ships had mail for us, which everyone looked forward to.

In a fast carrier force you had the opportunity to watch dozens of aircraft take off every morning for scouting purposes or for raids. In a day you could see more than a hundred planes take off one at a time. Once in a while there would be a miscue and the aircraft would crash into the sea. This happened more often when planes were returning from raids either damaged or low on fuel. We picked up pilots all the time, which was another duty for DDs. We picked up the same pilot twice. Lucky guy, 'cause you did not always find them alive.

Well, this is enough for now. Take care.

Love you, sweetheart,
Dad

March 19, 1995

Dear Anne,

Let me run through the chronology of events during the next several months without too much comment:

March 17–20, 1945

Made raids on Southern Japan again.
Carrier USS *Franklin* hit, badly damaged. Helped pick up some survivors.
Shot down three planes, one of them heading for us about 1,000 yards away.

March 20–25

Made raids on Okinawa.
Took turns manning a radar picket line around our forces landing on the beach. Every ship on picket duty subject to kamikaze attack. Another destroyer and the *Mertz* were assigned this duty, but our orders were canceled at the last minute and they sent two other tin cans in our place. The next day we heard that both of these ships were hit by kamikazes—lucky *Mertz*! By the end of this campaign, the U.S. Navy (and British Navy) lost thirty-six ships. 350 were damaged and about 5,000 sailors were killed.

March 25–30

Conducted more raids on southern Japan and the Rykuyu Islands.

April 1

Our carrier planes sink three Jap destroyers, two DEs and one cargo ship.

April 4

Mertz and *Monssen* with CAP (cover) of twelve planes go in close to the beach to wait for damaged aircraft returning from air strikes.
Located and sank two Jap mines.

April 5

Sank three more mines, later sank four more mines.

April 6

Nips make raid on us with 155 planes. They sink three or four of our tin cans. Our force shoots down 116 planes total for the day. Our heavy carrier USS *Hancock* hit. Things are getting rough.

April 7

Our carrier aircraft locate and bomb Japanese task force, sink one battleship, two carriers, and three or four destroyers.
Japs raid us in the afternoon, our CAP knock out thirty-five planes total. Surface ships get six planes.

April 9

Mertz attacks and sinks a Japanese sub with depth charges. Sent our boats out to pick evidence that floated to the surface.

April 11

Another Jap air attack. Battleship *Wisconsin* just missed getting hit.

April 12

Conducted night air attack from our carriers. Used flares for aircraft guidance. Most of these night fighters were Marine Air Corps *Corsair* F-4Us with inverted "gull" wings.

April 14–16

Another Jap air attack. Our task group shoots down fifty-six planes on morning of the sixteenth.

April 17

Japs conduct a night attack on us. The guys on our bridge sound like they are going nuts.

April 18

Helped sink another Jap submarine. Picked up several pairs of human lungs as positive evidence. Our doctor, Tommy Thompson, thought this was most interesting. You'd think he had caught some rare fish.

April 19

Exploded mine a short distance off our port beam.

April 20

Another Jap air attack. No casualties.

April 28

Another Jap air attack. Destroyers *Haggard* and *Hazelwood* hit in our group. Our task force shoots down a total of eighty-seven planes in one day! These guys are just plain crazy. They don't care if they die, as long as they try to take you with them.

May 2

Destroyers *Morrison* and *Luce* are sunk. Thirty-three Jap planes shot down during the day.

May 7

Another Jap air attack. Heavy carrier USS *Bunker Hill* badly hit.

May 10

Destroyers *Hadley* and *Evans* shoot down four planes each. We're getting pretty good. We are always picking up our pilots. Sometimes we don't know which one to save first.

May 14

After sixty days at sea we finally pulled into Ulithi Atoll for a rest. This time we insisted that all of the crew get a half day on the beach. They could do anything they wished for about six hours. Gave each man two cans of (hot) beer. Another officer and I were sent along to see that they behaved. These sailors had everything figured out. Some would buy the beer rations of several others and proceeded to get drunk. Others were intent on making money—lots of money. I came upon a large crowd of guys from several ships. In the middle of the crowd was a game of chance. They used the base of a large sawed-off palm tree for a table. On the table they placed a piece of canvas painted with the various combinations of numbers you would see on a pair of dice, i.e. anything from two ones (snake eyes) to two sixes. On the canvas were squares reflecting every combination of numbers that would come up when the dice were thrown, like ‖XXX│2│3│4│5│6│7│8│9│10│11│12│XXX‖ Also painted in each square were

116

the odds you would get, if the thrown dice total matched the number painted on the canvas. These wild, half-drunk sailors would put all kinds of money in every square. Before the dice were rolled each square was loaded with dough. After the dice were rolled, the winner or winners got their money back plus the odds. But all of the money in the other 10 squares was swept with a hand broom into a gunny sack. This game would go on for as long the operators were permitted to stay ashore. At the end of the afternoon they returned to their ship with literally thousands of dollars in profit.

Although gambling was prohibited aboard ship, you couldn't stop some of the crew from playing poker around their bunks or somewhere on the fantail. Some kids lost their shirts. Others made a fortune. Most of the guys who were well-heeled would lend money to those who were hard up on the basis of "Six for Five." The borrower had to pay back six dollars for every five dollars borrowed—that's 20 percent interest.

Well, back to work. On May 24, left Ulithi with a fast carrier task force for raids on Okinawa, which wasn't an easy place to occupy It was no small island, in fact, quite large compared to many others. In that campaign the Navy took heavy losses from kamikazes. The Army and Marines also suffered heavy casualties before Okinawa was contained.

June 2–3

Raided Hyushu, Japan.

June 4

Got hit again by a severe typhoon. This time an unusual thing happened. The bow of the cruiser USS *Pittsburgh* was knocked off, about the first fifty feet. Fortunately, the right watertight doors and hatches were shut and she managed to return to base and ultimately back to the states.

June 8–9

Raided Kyushu, Okinawa and Sakishima.

June 10

Bombarded Daito Shima.

June 14

Returned this time to San Pedro Bay, Leyte, Philippines, for replenishing and a rest. Went ashore a couple of times to a makeshift officers club and had a few drinks. Met several of my Tulane ROTC classmates—Sam Ryniker, Dick Logan, Manuel Duvic and several others. It was heartwarming to see and to be with them for a while. I'm sure the feeling was mutual.

One of my best machinist mates jumped ship while we were at San Pedro and was missing for three days. He finally returned after staying with a Filipino family up in the hills. He had had a perfect record and had never misbehaved before, so his punishment was relatively light, but he was the envy of everyone else aboard.

July 1

Left San Pedro Bay with a fast carrier force for Japan.

July 10

Raided the Tokyo area on Honshu. Our aircraft destroyed 96 planes and damaged 137 others on the ground. Lost seven of ours. Hit all targets.

July 13

Received orders to return to the states for our long delayed overhaul. Happy Day! An overhaul was supposed to have occurred after twelve months at sea, but our task force commander felt we were essential for further combat duty. Even after getting our orders, he kept us for several more weeks.

July 14

Raided Hokkaido, Japan. Picked up a Corsair pilot.
Bombarded the southern coast of Hokkaido and conducted air raids on same.

July 16

Raided Hokkaido again. Bombarded a huge steel works. This was accomplished by battleships *Iowa, Missouri* and *Wisconsin* plus cruisers *Dayton* and *Atlanta* and screened by Destroyer Squadron 54 (including the *Mertz*) plus the destroyer *Frank Knox*. The tin cans would position themselves in a line between the target area and the line of larger ships in order to protect them from possible submarine attack. The bombardment was conducted at night with the heavier ships firing sixteen-inch projectiles almost continuously for what seemed like hours. Usually every fourth or fifth shell was what was called a star shell. Contained no explosive but burned some kind of white powder so you could see these streaking things sailing over you and headed toward the targets. In a way it was a marvelous display of fireworks, but certainly devastating to those in the target area. The noise was deafening.

July 17

Raided Honshu again to the north. In fact raided the whole east coast. At 2315 (11:15 P.M.) came within eight miles of Honshu (only forty-five miles from Tokyo) and bombarded lots of industrial targets. This time we screened the BBs *Iowa, Missouri, Wisconsin* and the British battleship, HMS *King George V.* Assisting us were two "limey" (British) tin cans and DesRon 54. I should say what was left of our squadron (other DDs replaced those that were incapacitated). Destroyer Squadron 54 normally consisted of the USS *Remey, Wadleigh, Norman Scott, Mertz, Monssen, McNair, McGowan, McDermott* and the *Melvin.* During our tour of duty in the Pacific every ship in our squadron was damaged to some extent except the *Mertz.* One hit a mine, one took a torpedo, two were hit by kamikazes, one hit by friendly fire, one lost its entire superstructure and two were sprayed by machine gun bullets. The *Mertz* never got a scratch, but we had lots of close calls.

July 18

Raided the Tokyo area again. Our squadron alternated between being part of a screen for the fast carrier forces and screening the BBs that bombarded the Japanese coastline. All of this activity was in conjunction with the B-29 raids coming from Saipan and Tinian.

July 23–24

Raided the Kure Naval Base and targets on the Japanese Inland Sea.

July 28–29

Raided Honshu, particularly the Tokyo area.

August 2–3, 1945

Air strikes on Kyushu and Korea were canceled to avoid another typhoon.

August 8–9

Air strikes on central and northern Honshu. Subjected to a Jap air attack just when we were beginning to think they had no planes left. Shot down six that came over our formation.

August 10

USS *Mertz* was detached from Task Force 38 and proceeded to join Task Unit 92 of the U.S. Sixth Fleet under Adm. Jack Fletcher. Even though we had orders to return to the states, the shortest way was by the great circle route from the Japanese coast to Adak, Alaska, and then down to the Mare Island Navy Yard at San Francisco. Admiral Fletcher's unit was headed back to Adak and wanted to take advantage of our experience to conduct a few more raids so we had to join them.

Have to stop. Hope this wasn't too boring.

Love you much,
Dad

March 31, 1995

Dear Anne,

I should interrupt the Mertz itinerary-saga to tell you more about our first skipper, W. S. Estabrook, Commander USN. Most products of the U.S. Naval Academy are singular people, but as always there are a few exceptions. I've mentioned before that he was worse than Captain Queeg in *The Caine Mutiny*. At least we thought he was. As I look back on our experience with him you had to feel sorry for the guy. He couldn't have been more than thirty-five then, and that's less than half my age today! He was well trained, very intelligent and knew all the naval regulations by heart, but apparently never really knew how to get along with people. Basically, he lacked confidence in himself (and shouldn't have) and, because of this trait, he had little confidence and trust in those whom he supervised. The first sign of his personality came about on our shakedown cruise to Bermuda—how he handled the inspection critique of Captain Madeira. Next came the handling of our chief boatswains mate's suicide. Then he began to treat his executive officer, Jim Andrea, like a dog and almost drove him to a nervous breakdown by making him personally responsible for everything that went wrong on the ship. When his whipping boy was transferred, he started to lay it on thick with his department heads. I could tell many stories about how he treated them, but here are just a few.

Lieutenant Gladding was our Communications Officer, a rather chubby, affable fellow. Estabrook gave him fits in seeing that he personally delivered any important message that came over our wireless or through our decoding machine. Once he was so disappointed with how Gladding conveyed a message that he made him stand, facing the wall in the corner of our wardroom for thirty minutes before he could sit down to eat with the rest of us.

Lieutenant Gaustaferro was our Gunnery Officer, a very sharp articulate man, who was constantly chewed out by Estabrook for not doing the right thing on our firing exercises. Once Gus was ordered to report to Estabrook's sea cabin. He knocked on the door several times and there was no reply. He called to the captain—no reply. He finally opened the door, went in and asked Esty what he wanted. Esty ordered him out of the room because Gus hadn't properly requested permission to come in. Gus had to go outside three times and try again. Finally, Esty

120

told Gus that the proper statement to make was, "Captain, this is Gaustaferro, request permission to come in?"

Lieutenant Russell was our Chief Engineer Officer. Since Esty was a former engineer officer himself, he gave Russ hell all the time about his men on watch below not taking steps to reduce smoke coming from our stacks. Esty was also a former navigator and knew a great deal about the various constellations in the sky. He made Russ design and install his favorite constellation (made up of tiny lights) above his bed in his sea cabin so that when Esty turned on a switch he could see the arrangement overhead in his darkened cabin.

Lieutenant Gardiner, our First Lieutenant and later Executive Officer, was an outstanding individual with a great deal of experience aboard other ships (which made him well qualified to succeed Jim Andrea as exec.). He was too intelligent and too much of a gentleman to be intimidated by Estabrook. Esty would yell and scream at him, but John took it and would always give the skipper a cold stare—never saying anything unless he had to. Esty never could ruffle John Gardiner.

Estabrook completely ignored all of the enlisted men except my senior Chief Machinists Mate, Eduard Gregoire, a twenty-five-year man in the regular Navy. When Esty couldn't get the answers he wanted from any officer, he would ask Gregoire, who always treated him with the utmost respect, but thought he was a first class s.o.b. and a disgrace to the Navy.

A few good points about Estabrook. He was an outstanding ship handler. He had a keen sense of direction in the middle of the ocean with no reference points. Had an uncanny ability to know where his ship was with respect to anything and where any object was with respect to his ship. He had an unusual ability to dock or moor a vessel in any kind of wind, rain, tide, rough sea or otherwise inclement weather. And he prided himself on his competence.

He stuck to the book on naval regulations, time-honored procedures, etiquette, etc. No one could begin a meal that he planned to have with us in the wardroom until he started first. Everyone stood at attention until he was seated at the head of the table, with the executive officer at his right, the ship's doctor on his left and everyone in descending order of rank filling out the rest of the table. Two sittings were necessary for every meal, the first one for those going on watch and the second for those coming off watch. So some of the officers had a "breather" if they didn't have to eat with the skipper.

Estabrook had several peculiar mannerisms. He was always chewing on his lower lip or picking on his lip fever blisters or rubbing the mole on his face. He smoked, but no one else smoked until after he pulled out a cigarette. On active maneuvers, which required destroyers to jump around in a task force, he stayed in his sea cabin behind the bridge and had standing orders to be awakened if the slightest unusual thing happened. He would stay on the bridge or in his sea cabin for days. Often had meals by himself in his sea cabin. The only time I ever saw him use his stateroom below was when we docked or moored in port. Any officer who stood OOD (Officer of the Deck) duty caught hell frequently from Estabrook. None could do anything right in his estimation. I can't recall him complimenting any officer even it was well deserved.

We had all kinds of communication devices on board ship. There was the general PA (public address) system for all hands that originated either on the bridge or the quarterdeck. We had numerous lJV phone systems between all stations as long as someone manned earphones and speakers. And then we had voice tubes. Below are some memorable 1JV phone communications:

"Fantail, this is the bridge. Ask Mr. Harding how much longer it will be to secure all lines."

"Mr. Harding, how longer will you be?"

"Tell them about ten minutes and every time they ask you again, tell them ten minutes."

"Aye aye, sir. Bridge, this is the Fantail. It will be ten minutes and every time you ask it will be ten minutes."

"Bridge aye. Captain, ten minutes and every time you ask them, it will be ten minutes. . . . "

"Fantail, Bridge. Mr. Harding lay up to the bridge immediately."

"Forward Engine Room, this is the captain. Let me speak to the chief on watch."

"Bridge, this is Forward Engine Room. Gregoire on duty, sir."

"Gregoire, this is the captain speaking. Stop all engines! When you are ready to proceed without making smoke, let me know!"

(Five minutes later.) "Captain, this is Gregoire. We are ready to proceed without making smoke."

Quotes from Captain Estabrook:

"Even this goddamn cigarette lighter has no respect for me." (And he throws it over the side.)

"Send for Mr. Gladding. He's fouled up my message again!"

"Mr. Russell, get up to the bridge SAP!"

"Mr. Russell, your department and organization are on the rocks!"

"Will you tell the executive officer to come to dinner immediately!"

"You are not interested in your job! You are thoroughly incompetent!"

"Navigator, has this been plotted yet? Stop everything and do it now! . . . What do you mean it's right where your thumb is?"

"I wish to God you had a little more naval discipline before they sent you out here!"

"I am *not* pleased!"

"*You* have *dropped* the ball!"

"I am thoroughly unhappy about this whole thing!"

"There will be a meeting of all officers in the wardroom immediately!"

"*Do* you understand?"

"*You* are ruining my career!"

"Why? Why? Why?"

"I'm tired of being the son of a bitch on this ship!"

"Mr. Gardiner, if you don't get on the ball and do your job, I'm going to come down this voice tube and get you."

"Mr. Brown, you are about as useful as a wastepaper basket on this bridge!"

Captain Estabrook: "Mr. Drennen, do you respect me?"

Drennen: "Why, yes sir."

Estabrook: "Get that look off your face. I want you to skintillate!"

Drennen: "Yes sir, Captain. Whatever."

Estabrook: "Mr. Drennen, what do I always tell you when you mess up?"

Drennen: "Call my relief, sir."

Estabrook: "What else?"

Drennen: "Leave the bridge, sir."

Estabrook: "What else?"
Drennen: "Go down to my room and count rivets, sir."

"Mr. Russell, Bridge. The captain wants to know how much longer you'll take to complete
    taking on fuel?"
"How much to go?"
"How much have we taken?"
"How much forward?"
"How much aft?"
"How much longer now?"
"Mr. Russell, the captain wants you up to the bridge, immediately."

"Mr. Gottschall. Which boilers are on the line?"
"What's the superheat [temperature], Ass Chief?"
"Where's your fuel report?"
"How much fresh water have we got?"

Lieutenant Guastaferro after a hell of a bawling out by Estabrook: "Routine."

Well, that's enough about old Estabrook except for one more story. We understood he
left the Naval Academy post for the command of a tanker. Then returned to the academy to be
the Executive Officer of Bancroft Hall, the living quarters for the entire student body of
midshipmen. Not long afterwards a story came out in the *Atlantic Monthly* magazine by an
ex-midshipman who had resigned because he couldn't stand the intimidation by a certain
officer in the faculty organization—one W. S. Estabrook, Captain, USN.

Most of my active duty in the Navy was aboard the USS *Mertz* DD691, from about
November 1943 until around July 1946. Most of the time was at sea on the other side of the
world. I managed to write Mother and Dad about once a month. There wasn't much I could
tell, because all outgoing letters were censored by an officer with censorship duty. And, of
course, you couldn't reveal where you were specifically or what you were doing. The censor
officer read your letters, sealed them and put his censorship stamp on them before mailing.
Consequently the letters had to be pretty dull except to assure the recipient that you were still
alive when they were written. Mail to all naval personnel was sent to the Atlantic Fleet or
Pacific Fleet P.O. for forwarding to the last ship or station to which you were assigned. I now
find that Mother saved all my letters and later gave them to Aunt Jane who turned them over
to me only last year. Some of the stuff was so childish and embarrassing, reflecting my loss in
what I could say. Anyway, I haven't thrown them away. I also wrote to Jane once in a while,
because I knew Mother passed on my letters to her. Also corresponded with several girlfriends—it was a pleasure to get their replies. Again, I couldn't tell them much, so I tried to
be amusing—and hoped they thought so. Some girls I would like to have written were getting
married to somebody. I wrote occasionally to my good friends, Jim Jennings, Johnny Martinez
and Carky Guillot. And I wrote frequently to my very best friend, Jack Sequin, all the way up
until the time when my last letter to him was returned with a message stenciled on the envelope
stating, "Unable to deliver—missing in action." It was a sad day.

Well enough for now. Will continue with my tour of duty on the USS *Mertz* next time.

All my love,
Dad

April 13, 1995

Dear Anne,

During the Iwo Jima and Okinawa campaigns (March, April, May of 1945) we were at general quarters so often that instead of running back and forth to our battle stations, we inaugurated Condition One Easy, which meant we would stand near our stations for as long as we were in this standby GQ situation. Sometimes for most of every twenty-four hours. Under these circumstances I didn't stay below in the after-engine room, but remained on the main deck near the engine room hatch. This was also the area occupied by one of our deck officers. Lt. Robert Gilmer Pihl, USN, a mustang (former enlisted man). For many an hour we would straddle a deck locker and play cards, mainly Gambler's Solitaire. This was a game where one party would sell the other the cards for fifty-two dollars. We would alternate these positions every game. Without going into detail about how this game is played, at one time "Boats" Pihl owed me over $500. Every time I insisted he settle up, his comeback was always, "Gootch, don't worry, I'll pay you, but the way things are going, you won't be around to enjoy it." Finally, after many more days of playing this stupid game, he got even with me and we quit. We had lots of fun kidding each other and it was a good way to pass the time and forget about possible eventualities.

I could write pages about my assessment of each officer on the *Mertz,* most of whom I lived with for two years or more. Let me try to condense my impressions of each or perhaps what I remember most about each:

William S. Estabrook—his cold blue eyes, his chapped lips, his leathery face with expressions of fear, sadness, pain or anger.

James P. Andrea—his sincerity, his false air of happiness, his confused look over a plotting board.

Everett B. Gladding—his clipboard of papers, the pencil in his mouth, his punctuality, his knack of remembering, which nearly always saved his ass.

Joseph F. Guastaferro—his alertness, his enthusiasm, his quick responses, his speeches at firing practice, his coolness.

John Hays Gardiner—his drawn mouth, his raised eyebrows, his persistent questioning, his appreciation of a good joke, his fairness. I was most impressed with this man who was our Executive Officer most of the time aboard the *Mertz*. It so happened that John was a Groton/Harvard graduate from a so-called blue-blooded family in New England. His grandfather was once the governor of Maine; understood part of his family owned Gardiner's Island at the east end of Long Island, New York. John's side of the family came from Gardiner, Maine and resided on an estate near Pride's Crossing, Massachusetts. Although he was just a reserve officer, his experience on boats and on previous naval ships made him well qualified to succeed Jim Andrea as exec. He was too intelligent and too much of a gentleman and a diplomat to be intimidated by Estabrook. Esty would always yell and scream at him, but John just took it and stared back at the skipper, who could never get him upset.

Dr. Howard T. Thompson—his "battle dress," his abundant conversation (B.S.), his roving eye, his selfishness.

Richard Lazenby—his frightened look.

Roswell Niles Galbraith—his lazy smile, his tenderness, the bags under his eyes.

James M. Drennen—his face before breakfast, his banter, his comebacks.

Roger Bozzone—his complexion, his velvet voice, his small brown eyes.

Henry Odell Russell—his good nature, his "dumb" look, his curly hair, his self-confidence, his technical competence.

Lester L. Gutshall—his mustache, his knack for not being around when the fireworks began.

Robert T. Sims—his head side cocked, his baggy pants, his droopy eyelids.

John R. Anderson—his New England accent, his energy, his walk.

Thomas J. Barry—his giggle, his short answers, his obscurity, his tardiness in relieving the watch, his love for the mattress.

William J. Sanders—his simplicity, his conscientiousness, his earnestness, his good nature, his wit.

William Berthold—his face in rough weather, the helmet on his big head, his contribution to the war effort (almost nil).

Howard Dwight Hahn—his calculations.

Robert C. Harding—his pipe smoking, his bushy mane.

Donald P. Curtis—his quiet manner.

E. M. Shafer—his bureaucratic views.

William B. Huckabee—his red face, his snicker, his rapid profanity.

U. E. Ritchey—his size, his football yarns.

William S. Maddox—his smiling face, his hearty laugh, his red glasses, his bridge game, his composure.

William George Abbott—his quiet intelligence.

Udel K. Rosenberg—his seasickness, his perseverance.

Robert S. Brown—his 1JV phone conversations.

William G. Jones—his assessment of the gals, his tic.

Henry Meador—his navigational interpretations.

Leslie Maurer/J. A. Benham/William Lyons/Dr. C. Manry—no distinctions I can recall.

Continuing with the USS *Mertz* action in the Pacific theatre:

August 11, 1945

Joined Task Unit 92 of the U.S. Sixth Fleet, which consisted of cruisers *Richmond* and *Concord,* plus the remainder of DesRon 54 and a couple of other tin cans not in our squadron. We raided the Paramashiro Islands north of Hokaiddo, Japan. Bombarded targets on the beaches and sank three armed trawlers.

The weather got stormier the farther north we proceeded toward the Aleutians. One night we lost a mess cook who was dumping garbage off the fantail. We responded as quickly as possible and were assisted by other ships, but couldn't find him. We made only one pass at the possible area, because the water temperature was thirty-eight degrees and he wouldn't have lasted longer than a few minutes. These accidents will happen in a rough sea.

August 14

Arrived at Great Sitkun Island, Sand Bay, in the Aleutian Chain and took on fuel. While there our skipper, Commander W. S. Maddox, was quickly summoned to the island headquarters. He came back in a jeep, all smiles and waving his arms—at 1308 (1:08 P.M.), August 14, 1945, the Japanese had surrendered, the war with Japan was over! This was tremendous news for us, because our squadron was to depart the next day for Mare Island Naval Base, San Francisco area, and we would probably be the first increment of active combat naval ships to return to the states. Later in the day we were ordered to moor over in Kitkun Bay, Adak, and on August 15 we moved over to Sweepers Cove, Adak, Alaska. That evening our skipper was called to a high level meeting at Sixth Fleet headquarters, Adak. This time he returned with a gloomy look on his face. He got on our PA system and announced that our orders to San Francisco were canceled and we were to standby in the Adak area until army and support troops were mobilized. We were to be part of a naval force to escort these units to Japan to occupy part of the Japanese mainland. This was very demoralizing to everyone in the crew who had spent almost two years on active combat duty west of the Marshall Islands. Anyway, we took it—that's all you can do.

Not everyone was immune to the stress and strain of an extended period at sea with little or no R&R. One of my men faked losing his mind and was found sound asleep in the captain's sea cabin. We had no choice, but to transfer him. Another truly lost it—he became very melancholy, wouldn't get out of his bunk, wouldn't eat, even relieved himself in his bunk. He had to be transferred to the nearest hospital.

Still another man gave me a difficult time in port (I forgot where) when I was standing the OOD midwatch (from 12:00 'til 4:00 A.M.). We were moored in a harbor somewhere. My messenger had gone to get a cup of coffee and I was alone. All of a sudden a seaman approached me in his dress blues with his gear slung over his shoulder. He said, "Sir, call the whaleboat, I'm going home, my Mother wants me." I tried to reason with him, even asked if he could wait till morning. When I couldn't satisfy him, he said he was going to see the skipper. He dropped his bag and dashed off in the direction of the captain's stateroom. I went after him in close pursuit. We both slid down a ladder to a passageway leading to the captain's room. I made a flying tackle and brought him down in front of the skipper's door. Other people in CIC heard the scuffle and helped me contain the poor guy. The next day he had to be transferred to the nearest hospital ship.

I neglected to mention that sometime in and around Adak, John Gardiner, our exec., was relieved by John Benham, a senior officer from another ship. Also, Henry Odell Russell, our Chief Engineer Officer, was ordered to go back to the states and prepare a list of machinery alterations to the *Mertz* whenever we would return to the Mare Island Naval Base. As a result, I was promoted to Chief Engineer Officer. While I could handle the job, the responsibility for properly operating a 60,000-shaft HP power plant and supervising two other officers and eighty enlisted men felt heavy on my shoulders. I had just celebrated my twenty-third birthday.

Prior to leaving Adak with the occupation force we had several opportunities to go ashore. One of my close friends at school, Edwin Stockmeyer, had written me that his brother, Carl, was stationed at Adak in naval intelligence. I looked him up and we had a great time one evening at one of the two officers clubs on the base. Had a very good dinner and too many drinks. We were joined by another Tulane grad and classmate of Carl's, Stenning Murphy. Adak had very little vegetation, no trees and a rocky terrain. In racing back to the dock in Carl's jeep, I thought I would lose my cookies going up and down those hills and around the curves. Was very light-headed at the time and thought I would float away.

I had an unfortunate experience the other time I went ashore. Was in a party of five officers including Doc Thompson, Bob Sims, Bob Harding and Galbraith. We went up the hill from our boat dock to the main officers club, a huge building with all kinds of facilities. This was a special night at the club to celebrate our victory over Japan. There must have been 500 officers there from all branches of the service. They had a large band behind the ballroom floor playing all the hit tunes of the day. But no dancing, no women. We grabbed a nice table next to the dance floor. After three or four drinks, we all began to feel no pain. All of a sudden a party of four sat down at another table across this huge dance floor—two couples—two naval air corps officers with two Red Cross nurses. After a while they got up to dance and had 500 pairs of eyes on them. I focused on one of the officers and realized he was Al Bodney who lived around the corner from me in New Orleans. I couldn't believe it. So I straightened up and walked over to meet them. Al was just as surprised as I—and delighted. He introduced me to his date and the other couple, insisted that I have a drink, then his date asked me if I would like to dance. This was okay with Al and we proceeded to dance all over the ballroom floor. I hadn't been this close to a female in about two years. I completely forgot my manners and neglected to bring her over to meet my shipmates, which turned out to be a terrible mistake. When I returned to my table, everyone understood except Doc Thompson, who was livid. Thompson was married, but always had his eyes on the opposite sex and we suspected he was a womanizer anyway. Well, Doc did nothing but glare at me and mumble all kinds of obscenities. And by that time he had downed about seven or eight drinks. Well, it was time to go, and we all put on our heavy overcoats and wobbled into the cold air and struggled down that steep hill to the pier where our boats would pick us up. Even though I knew Doc was mad at me I elected to tell him a fib—that I had made a date with the Red Cross nurse. We walked out this long pier and stopped where our boat would arrive. As soon as I turned away from Doc to look for our boat, I found myself flying through the air down into the cold water. I quickly realized the Doc had pushed me. I never went underwater because my overcoat spread out like an umbrella. I turned around and swam back to the pier and found a line dangling down nearby. I was also helped by everyone but Doc Thompson. As soon as I got my bearings I lunged for Doc, hoping to push him over the side, but was restrained. Our boat came in and took us back to the ship. Couldn't wait to get my clothes off and take a hot shower. Roswell Galbriath told the skipper what had happened and he put the Doc in hack for twenty-four hours, i.e., he was restricted to his room. Fortunately two days later Doc Thompson's relief came aboard and he departed for the states. He left the same time John Gardiner and Odell Russell were leaving. I never saw Doc Thompson again. It was an unfortunate situation that was partially my fault. I didn't help matters by getting under his skin. Maybe it was because we both had too much to drink. Everyone aboard ship sympathized with me and blamed the Doc for his conduct. Anyway, life had to go on. This was another one of AGG's learning experiences.

August 31

Left Adak, Alaska, with a huge army occupation force—dozens of troop and supply ships escorted by most of Adm. Jack Fletcher's Sixth Fleet, including cruisers USS *Salt Lake City, Pensacola, Chester, Richmond* and *Concord;* also DesRon 54 minus the *Norman Scott* and *Wadleigh;* also destroyers *Hood, Bearss, Izard, A. W. Grant, Hughes, Anderson;* also special support ships USS *Zeal,* USS *Panamint* ACG 15 and many others.

September 8th

Arrived at entrance to Taugaru Straits. Escorted by a Japanese DE through the straights into Mitsu Bay and anchored in Ominato Harbor in Northern Honshu, Japan.

September 9

Japanese surrendered Northern Honshu and Hokkaido. The *Mertz* moved over to anchor at the mouth of inner Ominato Harbor to observe the remaining units of the Japanese Imperial Fleet. Naval personnel were not allowed onshore.

September 12 to 13

Patrolled and did figure eights in Mitsu Bay—investigated all Jap ships moving from Aomori to Hokadate.

September 18

Received orders to head back to San Francisco for overhaul. Departed with USS *Remey, Monssen* and three CVE's for Pearl Harbor.

September 20

Arrived Pearl Harbor Naval Base, fueled and took on provisions.

September 22

Departed Pearl with USS *Remey* and *Monssen.*

October 1

Arrived Navy yard, Mare Island, for scheduled overhaul. It was truly heartwarming to pass under the great Golden Gate Bridge at San Francisco.

The balance of my service in the Navy will be described in future letters. However, not long after our return to the West Coast, I sat down one night in my stateroom and recorded a few impressions of my tour of duty aboard the USS *Mertz* before they disappeared from memory as follows:

- Well, it's all over, or almost over—we've done so much since we started—it seems like a dream—
- Remember how it was so messy, so uncomfortable, so inconvenient—how nerve racking—but in spite of everything, it was still a thrill—what a game we played—a string of chances and somehow we won out every time—and because we always pulled through, we never fully realized the danger present or the risks involved. Now, that it's over with no scratches, it was an experience we wouldn't have traded for anything—
- Remember this ship—this hulk of metal, which at times you despised so much and yet it was the only thing that meant security—
- Remember how rough it got—how dizzy you felt—not always sick, just dizzy, numb—didn't want to think—couldn't—just wanted to lie down with your arm over your head—and you rocked from side to side, then up and down, up and down, then side to side—until somehow it finally subsided—
- Remember how quiet it was at times—how bright the nights were—how the water spanked against the bow and formed either white foam at night or ripples of green or blue on either side in the daylight—remember how the bow seemed to be chasing the dolphins just a few feet away—
- Remember how sultry and hot it could get—remember the stench of hot beer on those ridiculous island liberty parties—remember the smell of vegetation when you got close to land, but couldn't see it yet—
- Remember those odors from the vent fans humming on deck-the smell from the potato locker—the aroma from the galley—the singing of all the machinery in the engine spaces—the whine from the main turbines—the B.O. from the crew's quarters—the pungent smell of Bunker C fuel oil—
- Remember the midwatches on the bridge—the flashlights—the plotting board in CIC (Combat Information Center)—the repeated throbbing of the sonar gear—the quick bursts of language on the radios—
- Remember Condition One Easy—how long we waited—the ring of the GQ bell—the red lights—remember the noise from the aircraft, ours and theirs—remember how quick things happened and you didn't have time to think of the consequences—

But now it's all over—it's been over.
Have to stop.

Love you much,
Dad

April 21, 1995

Dear Anne,

Before continuing with my activity in getting the USS *Mertz* through an overhaul at Mare Island, let me give you a few more quotes and conversations that I recorded earlier at sea. Most seemed humorous at the time, but if they aren't to you, please bear with me. I selected those that contained the least obscene language. The others will be buried in secrecy forever.

Lieutenant Guastaferro (after being humiliated again by the old skipper):
"Jesus Christ, I hate that man!"

"Come on, Barry, let's go up and drive awhile."

Lieutenant Harding: "Now's the time for all good men to go to sleep with a swell-looking blond."

Lieutenant Maurer: "Now, when I was on the *Mckean*, we did it differently, we—"

Lieutenant Lazenby: "Oh, golly day! We're out of position!"

Lieutenant H. O. Russell: "Where's my hat?"

Lieutenant Gladding (otherwise known as Whaletail, Happy Buttom, Glad Ass):
"Will someone please pass the peanut butter?"

"Battle happy, that's what I am, battle happy!"

Lieutenant (j.g.) Anderson (from Maine):
"You're a haught ticket, you ah."
"You ain't just a'kiddin."
"Man O'man."
"Jeepers Creepers."
"Oh, hell yes."
"She's a sha(r)p cookie."
"Now, how about that."
"I'll be a sad, sad apple."
"I'm going to punch you right in the friggin' belly!"
"How do you like the way——-."
"Friggin pigs, that what you ah!"
"Pass the p'dadas."
"I got five dollas you caun't."
"Who's gaught my sauks?"
"God, what happened to the whata (water)?"

Lieutenant (j.g.) Lyons: "Hello, Ruby; goodbye, Jane."

Ensign Meador:
    "Well, there was this here girl, you know—no kidding, you know—"

    "Captain, our position is . . . just . . . about . . . *here*" (putting his thumb on the chart).

Lieutenant (j.g.) Sanders at breakfast before another GQ:
    "Nothing could possibly happen to us today. This can't be a man's last meal!"

    "Oh, oh—call the pharmacist mate, Gottschall's going to blush."

    "Wow! Hey, Gootch, let's go over to the beach and bounce."

Ensign Berthold (otherwise known as The Oid and ComSackPac):
    "Hey, Houghton, got some more of this stuff?"

    "Nuts to GQ, pass the chocolate sauce." (Third helping)

Lt. (Doc) Thompson (taking out a man's appendix on the wardroom table in rough weather): "Does it hurt?"
Seaman Brinkley: "Oh, you know it do."

    Lt. (Doc) Thompson:
    "Is the captain ever coming down, Hunter—I'm starved."

    "An egg is an organism with a shell around it."

    "One time I delivered this baby, picked him up by his feet and slapped his hind end, and the bloody thing almost went sailing out the window."

    "Once I was trying to blow up this cadaver's lungs and somebody slapped his chest. I got stuff in my mouth that had been inside that stiff for two years."

    "The other intern said 'Forward pass' and I caught the kid six inches from the floor."

    "At the operating table, I looked into the top of this nurse's gown and said, 'My, what pretty feet you have.' "

    "Drennen and his shaving cream produce a chemical reaction."

    "Did you see Drennen blowing good cigar smoke down the voice tube to combat?"

1MC (PA system) communications:
    "Now, Hartman, lay down to the supply officer's stateroom to pay your ship's service bill."

    "All hands, man your battle stations for dawn alert—Ding Ding Ding Ding Ding Ding."

    At 0245 (2:45 A.M.): "Now all hands, repeat all hands, rise and shine, roll out and hit the deck to unload stores."

Lieutenant Jones remarks:
    "Boing."
    "Whupp."

Lieutenant (j.g.) Pihl (otherwise known as Boats):
    Coming up to Russell, "Hey, Chief, how about a little professional advice?"

    "Now quiet down there, or I'll frap you between the running lights."

    "Jesus, what a piece o' gear that is."

    "She had false teeth and dirty skivvies."

    Of Estabrook: "Christ, what a dull tool!"

    "Every time I go into the head, Russell's making a dummy run on the port throne."

    "Boy, she's got Affirm two-blocked at both yard arms."

    "Come on, shove off!"

Commander W. S. Maddox:
    (Docking the ship): "Nudge him over, Jim."
    "Yes, I know that."
    "Throw that goddam line off. Throw it off."
    "Light on the Remy."
    "Come on, Remy, haul ass!"
    "Gimme another range and bearing on the Melvin."

Lieutenant Drennen:
    "Speak respectfully of these eggs—they've been in the Navy longer than you have."

    "Now, you take a quart of vanilla ice cream, mix it up with some rum, see, and while you're stirring it all up, blow a little cigar smoke in it, then stir it all up some more, keep stirring it up, then taste it, and boy, now you've got something!"

1MC (PA System) communications as per W. S. Estabrook's instructions: "Now the third section lay down to the crew's forward messing compartment for breakfast."

1JP phone communication: "Control, this is four-five mount—Audia requests permission to go to the head."

Lt. Commander James Andrea, our first executive officer under Estabrook:
    "This is a standing order. These orders must be carried out!"

    "It's the policy of the ship that——"

    "Look in your standard organization book!"

    (Talking to signalman): "Don't you know that hat's against regulations—you can't wear that!"
    Signalman Servideo: "You kiddin?"

    Shore leave discussion—Lt. Commander James Andrea, presiding:

Officer: "May I have permission to leave the ship, sir?"
Andrea: "Have you caught up on all your work?"
Officer: "Yes sir."
Andrea: "What about your course?"
Officer: "Up to date, sir."
Andrea: "Are you in the shore leave section?"
Officer: "Yes sir."
Andrea: "Well, now only 25 percent may go, you know. Where's Guastaferro? . . . Gus, how many officers have left the ship already? Six! That's one too many! Why wasn't I informed about this?"
Officer: "May I leave, sir?"
Andrea: "Leave! By Jesus, no! Too many officers have abused my orders already."
Officer: "Yes, sir."
Andrea: "Ho hum—hey, Doc, how about taking in the sights tonight, eh? I've been so busy with ship's work, I haven't taken time off for ages, but I don't mind—you know, on my last ship we——"

Signalman Servideo:
    "An error he makes, Hah!"

    "Here, have a cigarette, Mr. Gottschall. I almost made a rate this month."

    (Servideo again at GQ with tommy gun): "When that next plane comes in, I'll cut down that SOB."

Seaman Hirsch at first real GQ: "This is it! This is it! Hot shrapnel falling all about me!"

First seaman: "So you're from Tennessee, too—which part?"

Second seaman: "Cleveland, it's close to Tullahoma."

First seaman: "Cleveland, huh—say did you know a little bitch named Lucy McGee? Boy, she really was—"

Second seaman: "Know her? I married her!"

First seaman: "Oh!"

The last of a number of enlisted man with the same request one morning back in a staging area: "Mr. Gottschall, I'd like to put in for a transfer."

Gottschall: "I'm sorry Smith, we just can't afford to lose you now."

Gottschall, turning to Chief Gregoire after he left: "Gosh, Gregoire, why don't you put in for a transfer?"

Gregoire: "No, not me, Mr. Gottschall. I want to stick around and see what happens next on this son-if-a-bitch."

Chief stewards mate in port: "Good morning, good morning, good morning, it's quarter to eight, Mr. Bozzone. Last call for breakfast."

Chief Masterson (who is still living in New Paltz, New York): "The line to the bosun's locker forms to the right."

Chief Davis: "What's the dope, Mr. Gottschall?"

Standard request after a wardroom meal with Him present: "May I be excused, Captain?"

Wardroom breakfast routine:

Officer: "Jones, what do we have for breakfast?"

Jones: "Eggs and bacon, suh."

Officer: "Have we got any cereal?"

Jones: "Yes suh, we got cereal."

Officer: "What kind?"

Jones: "Ah don't know."

Officer: "Bring me some eggs, then."

Jones: "We ain't got none—we got corn fritters."

Officer: "Oh hell, just a cup of coffee then."

Jones: "Coffee?"

Officer: "Yes, coffee and some toast."

Jones: "Toast, suh?"

Officer: "Yes!"

Jones (in wardroom answering phone from the bridge):
> Buzz.
> "Hello, Wardroom."
> "Who?"
> "Ah can't hear you."
> "Ah don't know."
> "He might be."
> "Ah don't know that either."
> "This is Jones."
> Click.

Lt. J. F. Guastaferro at gunnery exercises:

"All hands, man your battle stations. All guns, remove your muzzle covers. Report when manned and ready to fire in all respects. Gun 3, why aren't you manned and ready? Harper, report to the gunnery officer's storeroom immediately after this exercise. Put your firing keys in automatic, parallax in automatic. Gun 5, your parallax in automatic? All guns ready sector. The firing tonight will be at a surface target. All guns will fire five rounds of AA common except Gun 3, which will fire starshells. Plot, you got that? Put Gun 3 in starshell computer. All guns make sure of proper fuse settings. All guns train out on target bearing two six zero. Gun 2, you on two six zero? Get on target, Gun 1! What's the matter with you? Swing to *port side,* Gun 4! Firing will be controlled at the director. Word to load will be given by control. All guns stations! What's the problem, Gun 4? What! Chief Gunners Mate Moore report to Gun 4 pronto! He's there? Everything okay? Good! How's she doing, plot? All guns . . . stand by . . . load . . . fire, fire, fire—kick it out, Gun 2—fire Gun 1! Gun 1, train out to zero nine zero—kick it out, Gun 1. . . ."

"Uh, yes sir, Captain—no sir . . . I know, but . . . report to the bridge? . . . Aye, aye sir—all guns ready surface replace your muzzle covers—set the regular condition watch, Watch 3 on watch. All guns put your powder cans in—yes, sir . . . be right down."

Poem composed by MM2c. Frank Hayden, forward engine room watch:

To the Man on the Lower Level

The heart of this ship is down below
That's a fact, but just few of us know
Down here sits a man on his rump
Watching and guarding the main feed pump.
His job seems to be quite a bore
But he's doing his part to win the war
He's not the man behind the gun
But he gets cut in on John's Well Done

The following are some of the *less* horny, *less* foul-mouthed remarks made from time to time by Chief Machinist Mate, Eduard J. Gregoire, USN (twenty-five years of service in 1943). They would even be funnier if you heard him stuttering the way he did:

"Is you is or is you ain't my baby?"

"Yeah, it's one of those Hamashita Class BBs."

"Lemme tell ya, this stuff's good for coughs, colds, sore holes, and pimples on the kazaza. Guaranteed not to rip, tear, shrink or roll up your back like a window shade."

(On shore bombardment): "Mr. Andrea, give me a four man working party and I'll carry those goddamn shells over there faster than that."

"It isn't the idea of dying. It's the fact that you're dead for such a goddamn long time."

"Turn to—remember Pearl Harbor."

(After a meal): "Hey, how long have we been on this life raft, anyway?"

"He who does not shine the heels of his shoes does not wipe his pooper."

(Of Estabrook): "He's a hard man, that man is."

"You can keep your action, I want to get out of this Navy without any unauthorized holes."

"Ooooh, hell yes."

"Good ship, happy crew, today is Sunday, turn to!"

"No, Mr. Gottschall, I don't want a transfer, no sir. I want to stick around and see what happens next on this son of a bitch."

"Christ, what food, just like my mother used to make when she was drunk."

"It's murder, that's what it is."

"Geez, his eyes shone like two pissholes in the snow."

"Man, it's black as a well digger's ass down here."

"We're always two jumps ahead of the sheriff."

"Goddamn admirals and ComDesPac, don't give a shit if we ever get back."

"I take a shower before every invasion, whether I need it or not."

"The only difference between this ship and any other ship is that we're always *fouled* up—but lucky, but lucky."

"When we started firing at that goddamn ship, everything got so hot in the water that the crew climbed back aboard."

(Of Doc Thompson): "Look at Cyanide, loaded up like a Peruvian jackass heading for the high Andes. Those kamikazes are going to use him for a bull's eye."

"That pyromaniac is going to wear out his loading machine."

"Hogan's goat has nothing on us."

"The Navy doesn't pay you for what you know or what you do. They pay you for the goddamn inconvenience they put you to."

"There are two kinds of bastards—a tenement raised bastard, and a unauthorized bastard, which is one born in a cornfield or a pasture somewhere."

"God save the King, they say—yeah, well, God had better save that son-of-a-bitch, cause the goddamn British Limy Navy can't."

"C-C-Captain, this is Gregoire, f-f-forward engine room, we are ready t-t-to proceed without m-m-making smoke."

Poem composed by Lt. Roswell Niles Galbraith, Assistant Communications Officer:

Now I can't remember digits and no longer get the figits
When the meatball boys come over angels high

Weekday names escape me while old memories plague me
Of the years when love and fun were always nigh

Now, I view each burning plane with casual disdain
And the General Quarters gong makes little sound

I'm tired of bending ear to predictions of the year
When the ship will hoist to truck her homeward bound

It is all so symptomatic of my being Asiatic
And a veteran I am without a doubt

But you can bet your bottom dollar
When the bars come off my collar
I shall never discuss what war is all about

Well, I had to get all this stuff off my chest somehow. Will continue with my naval career history in next letter.

Thinking of you always.

Love,
Dad

April 27, 1995

Dear Anne,

On October 1, 1945, we pulled into the Mare Island Navy Yard at Vallejo, California, on the upper end of San Francisco Bay. This was a time of mixed emotions and getting used to being back in the good old USA. With the war over we were all eager to have a good time and make up for the loss of such, after having been at sea for almost two years. But we still had serious responsibilities to get the *Mertz* squared away. Mine was mainly the engineering department, which probably had the most work to be accomplished. Our power plant had been overworked and in need of many repairs and/or alterations. We also had to replenish any and all spare parts that we had used. Initially this overhaul period was to put everything on the ship back in working order so it could continue to be of active service to the Navy. However, after a while we learned that the *Mertz* was scheduled to be decommissioned, mothballed and put in standby status in the Nineteenth Reserve Fleet at San Diego, California. This would occur after all repair work was completed at Mare Island, since the Navy wanted all ships in this category to be easily reactivated, if need be.

The separation from naval service of both reserve officers and enlisted men had begun during our overhaul period. Unfortunately, it happened too fast. We began to lose many of our key personnel and received very few replacements with any experience. This situation was very frustrating to those who wanted to get things done, and it got worse each succeeding week. Our skipper, Commander Maddox, was transferred to another ship. John Gardiner, who had lots of separation points, was released from service. So was Odell Russell, after submitting recommendations for the repair work in our department. Gardiner's successor, Lt. Commander John Benham was also separated. A Lieutenant White came over as our skipper from the USS *Remey*. Lots of confusion. What was really frustrating was to see the rapid collapse of a formidable fighting machine (our entire Navy) into nothing close to its former effectiveness.

Anyway, all of the repair and organization problems were balanced somewhat with the opportunity to go ashore almost every night for some R & R. The problem here was that we overdid it. We went wild. I can remember getting into our dress blues every day about 4:30 P.M., and catching a bus from Mare Island to downtown San Francisco. This was the only means of transportation and it took about an hour to get there. We'd go first to some bar in one of the better hotels, have a few, then eat some marvelous food somewhere, then back to the bars or cocktail lounges again, often called the "passion pits." We'd stay in town until 2:00 or 3:00 in the morning, return on that slow bus to the Navy Yard by 4:00 A.M., have only two or three hours sleep, and get up promptly at 7:30 A.M. to carry out the many duties the next day. Around 4:30 P.M., we'd go through the same routine as before and continue this pace for three or four nights in a row before we got tired. I'll never know how we had that much stamina, but somehow we did. Guess we had lots of pent up energy—and we were young.

We were at the Navy Yard for about two months. Can't remember every night out but here are a few highlights:

We were invited to a formal dance in a downtown Oakland hotel, given by their Junior League or something similar. There was a cocktail hour, a buffet dinner and later dancing with as many as sixty of Oakland's fairest. During the evening, I tried to dance with a cute brunette wearing a neat purple velvet gown. Every time I tried to dance with her, somebody else would cut in. After several attempts, I danced with her long enough to ask if she would like to sit out and talk. She readily agreed. Still many of the other officers muscled in on our conversation. Well, I asked her if I could take her home after the dance and to my surprise she accepted. So we took a taxi all the way out to an eastern suburb of Oakland. In due course I asked her for a date and she said she'd love to—in fact, she said, why don't I take her to another dance at the Oakland Country Club. She even got dates for two other officers on my ship. We had a wonderful time at the club, which was on a hill overlooking the bay across from San Francisco. The band played all the popular tunes at the time, like "A Kiss Goodnight," "We'll Be Close as Pages in a Book," "Kiss Me Once—It's Been a Long, Long Time" and "Spring Will Be a Little Late This Year." You know, I've been pretty good on names but I forget hers. She was a marvelous ballroom dancer. After we moved down to San Diego, she and two of her girlfriends came down to Los Angeles and met us for a night on the town.

Another time ashore Bill Sanders, Bob Sims and I went into San Francisco and had dinner in the elegant dining room of the old Palace Hotel. A Navy captain (four-striper) sat down at a table nearby with three very attractive girls. We spent most of the meal eyeing and talking about them. Then the unbelievable happened. This captain came over to our table, introduced himself and wanted to know if we had any plans that evening because his daughter and her two friends didn't have anything to do, and since we seemed like nice guys, he thought we could show them a good time! Well, we all had a wonderful evening. Incidently, the Palace Hotel, among other things, was famous for where Pres. Warren G. Harding died many years previously.

Still on another occasion we started the evening at either the Fairmont Hotel or the Top of the Mark Hopkins bar. Anyway, Bill Jones, Roger Bozzone and I met three girls, who were Kappa Kappa Gammas from University of California, Berkeley, and we all had a lot of fun. We didn't believe who they said they were until they showed us their sorority pins and their bluebooks from Cal-Berkeley.

We left the San Francisco area on November 30, 1945. The trip down to San Diego was delightful—no more drills or exercises, no more general quarters. During the trip, I elected to take a nap on the wardroom sofa. This was the only time I dared to do it, and my good buddies took a picture of me snoozing away. Occasionally you could see the California coastline in the distance and we also saw a school of whales. Passed by the famous Santa Catalina Island. Arrived at our destination late December 1. San Diego has a long, slender compact harbor which leads to the naval base. Downtown San Diego faces the Coronado Peninsula. We moored alongside the USS *Remey* and *Monssen,* which were also to be mothballed. No sooner had we settled down when we began to lose more of our experienced people. This created all kinds of problems, but I would rather dwell on the fun we had in San Diego. This area had an ideal climate. From December '45 through May '46 we never had a cloudy day. The temperature was always in the sixties and seventies.

I remember taking a little time over the Christmas holidays to go back to New Orleans to see Mom and Dad, the first time since I left home in May of 1943. While it was heartwarming to see the folks, it all felt so weird being back home. Things weren't the same and I couldn't put my finger on it. It was sad to hear from family and friends I bumped into about other friends who died or were injured in some theatre of action in the war. I had dates with several old girlfriends like Lana Hummel and Peggie Baker—all the others were either married or living elsewhere. I went back to Mobile to see Jamie Crawford. Attended a dance with her at the Admiral Semmes Hotel and saw some of the officers who were stationed at the shipyard when I left the USS *David W. Taylor.* Couldn't believe they were still there all this time. I returned to the West Coast to find things more disorganized than ever in putting the *Mertz* in mothballs. More officers and men had been separated. And the few replacements were no help.

Have to stop, sweetheart

Love you much,
Dad

May 12, 1995

Dear Anne,

While in San Diego we were continually beset with all kinds of problems in preparing the USS *Mertz* for inactive status. This was particularly frustrating for those of us who had spent some time on the ship and were so used to getting things done well whenever it was required. We worked hard at trying to fulfill our responsibilities during the weekdays and then tried to forget them in the evenings and especially on the weekends. We got out of town as much as possible, either running down to Tijuana, Mexico or up the coast to Los Angeles, Laguna Beach or Newport, or even up to the mountain area inland. Most of the weekends were spent in and around Los Angeles. All of these places had their watering holes, passion pits, or whatever you wanted to call them. In San Diego proper they had The Little Club Bar at the Grant Hotel, the bar at the Coronado Hotel, The Tops, The Paris Inn, Sherman's, the Pacific Square dancehall, Eddie's or The Hole in the Wall—and there was always the Officers Club. In Los Angeles there were so many I'll just mention those places associated with some stories.

Most of the time we would rent cars to go anywhere out of town. When we went to Los Angeles, we would often stay overnight at what was a bachelor officers quarters near Hollywood. This convenient one story building had a reception room/lobby in front with nice living room furniture and a battery of telephones. Behind was a large dormitory with lockers and double-decker cots. In the rear were some nice showers, etc. This was our "base of operations" in Los Angeles. The facilities were apparently for officers only; there may have been a five-dollars-per-night charge for everything. Some of the weekends in Los Angeles that I can recall were as follows:

The girl I met in Oakland came down with two friends and we went out on the town. Took them to Slapsie Maxie's, a popular nightclub operated by Max Rosenbloom, a small-time actor and former prize fighter. They had a great floor show featuring comedian Ben Blue, Keenan Wynn and The Leonard Brothers who sang an unusually funny rendition of "Sonny Boy." I still remember the lyrics.

Another time we took some dates to the Coconut Grove in Hollywood for dinner and danced to Freddy Martin's band.

Still another time we took some girls to the Hollywood Palladium, a popular dance hall in the area where Stan Kenton was playing and June Christy was singing the vocals.

Also went nightclubbing with H. O. Russell, our former chief engineer officer (who was from Los Angeles), his wife, Helen, and her sister. Had a very enjoyable evening swapping stories about our tour of duty on the *Mertz*. Had our picture taken at this club. Still have it.

Another time we went to a nightclub near Hollywood and saw a weird new jazz combo consisting of Dizzy Gillespie, Charley Parker and Slim Gaillard, who would come out with the craziest sayings like eating bourbon and avocado seed juice sandwiches.

Sometimes we would stay overnight at a place called the Swedish Bathhouse. This was where you checked in at the back door and slept in a dormitory-type room. No matter how late you got in the night before, they would sound an alarm and wake you up at 7:00 A.M. Then they would herd all the guys stark naked down a long hall at the end of which was a large room containing a swimming pool with no sides to it. So we either jumped or were pushed in. The water was frigid! After you swam to the other end, they gave you these large towels and led you into a dining area where you were served a huge breakfast by some buxom Scandinavian girls. Afterwards you could go back to your quarters, shower, clean up, dress and take off for another day of excitement. What an experience. And we never got too tired.

Another time I met John Martinez, my old college chum, in Los Angeles. He was stationed at some Air Force Base in Arizona. We rented a car and went somewhere for dinner. Later I drove John around Beverly Hills and almost had a serious accident. Another car darted out into our street and we came just short of hitting each other. The driver of the other car was Van Johnson who behaved like he had a few.

Once we attended a huge cocktail party/dinner dance given by Edward Everett Horton at this mansion somewhere in the Sacramento Valley. There were at least fifty young, attractive hostesses to help us have a good time. Everett Horton wasn't there, but his mother was. She held court in one of the large drawing rooms. Her hobby was reading palms. So I bit and had her tell me my fortune. Much of it was what you wanted to hear, but she did concern me when she said that sometime in mid-life, I would have a serious illness. Of course that never happened, but I contended that she didn't give me a good reading because she read my right palm and I was left-handed. Anyway the whole affair was enjoyable. I think we dated some of the girls on other occasions. They were all nice girls. A nice girl in those days was one that you wouldn't dare, or she wouldn't permit you, to go beyond a kiss goodnight.

I went to Los Angeles with different officers who were still with the *Mertz*, mostly Bill Sanders, Bob Sims, Bill Jones, Bill Abbott or Roger Bozzone, who were all "rich" and single at the time. We were rather extravagant in some ways—thought nothing at renting a car or taking a taxi anywhere.

Also had an unusual experience coming back from Los Angeles one Sunday night. Believe it was Sims, Jones, Abbott and I. Bill Abbott was originally from Wilton, New Hampshire. His uncle was William George Abbott, the famous director/playwright, who passed away recently at the age of ninety-something. Bill had an older brother who sang very well—so well in fact that his goal was making it in the movies. So he went out to Hollywood before the war, was screen tested, etc. They liked his voice, but the problem was he sang too much like Bing Crosby. Before returning east he and Crosby became good friends. Anyway, as we were going through Del Mar, California, Bill suggested that we look for Crosby's summer place there that Bill's brother had often visited. After some searching we found it up on a hill overlooking the ocean. Some lights were on in the place so we decided to see who was home. A housekeeper came to the door and said nobody was there, but when Bill said his brother had been a good friend of Crosby, the housekeeper enthusiastically invited us in, served us cocktails and showed us photo albums with pictures of Crosby and Bill's brother singing together. After some delicious snacks, we thanked him and departed for San Diego.

Another time on our way back to San Diego, Bob Sims had to stop to make a phone call. It was at some kind of short-order cafe that had a nickelodeon. He came running out to the car to urge us to come in and hear a new song that was on the machine. We went in and played the record two or three times before leaving. It was Betty Hutton singing "There's a doctor living in our town/There's a lawyer and an Indian too/Neither doctor, lawyer or Indian chief could love you any more than I do (etc.)." We all thought it was a cute novelty song and it turned out to be a hit. The things one can remember—after fifty-some-odd years.

We made several trips to Tijuana, Mexico, which was only a few miles south of San Diego. The one I recall was when we went down there to the local racetrack. Had a great time betting, but found that the best chance to win was to bet on the jockey. All of the horses were puny—and almost the same jockeys were used in every race. Later, we went south from Tijuana to Rosarita Beach where there was an elegant old Spanish-style stucco inn behind an attractive courtyard. The other side of it faced the ocean. The dining area was outside near the water. We sat under a brilliant starry sky that night and were entertained by a group of troubadours while we had some marvelous Mexican food.

One more story and I'll quit. We became good friends with two officers on the USS *Monssen* which was always moored next to us. They were Trevor Rees-Jones from Dallas and the great Lou Locke from Philadelphia. Lou somehow had his own car. So one weekend we all piled into his wheels and headed inland for Cuyamaca Lake, way up in the mountains behind San Diego. We stopped somewhere and bought liquor and several cases of beer. I think the month was March. Anyway, his car didn't have much power and we had to go up slowly in first or second gear. After a while we all got thirsty and broke out the beer. It took forever to reach our destination and it seemed uphill all the way. The longer it took, the more we drank and we were all shouting, "Going up, going up, all the time." It also got colder the higher we went and we weren't prepared for this. Consequently, more drinking. When we arrived at the lake there was snow still on the ground. After locating the cabin that we rented, we moved in and then started building a huge snow man. It didn't take long for some girls to come by and they invited us for a cookout on the deck behind their cabin. Had the juiciest hamburgers and more beer. The girls were up there to ski and let us use their skis for a little while—until we all wiped out. Had a great weekend. We coasted almost all the way back to San Diego.

Okay, now I must stop—hope this isn't too boring.

Love you much,
Dad

May 20, 1995

Dear Anne,

About halfway through the mothballing of the *Mertz*, our skipper, Lieutenant Commander White, USNR, called me into his quarters and advised that he had enough points to gain separation from naval service and he was going to take steps to leave as soon as possible. Accordingly, he had recommended to his superiors that I succeed him, since I would be the senior officer aboard and I was well qualified to be the Commanding Officer until the ship was formally decommissioned. So without having an opportunity to decline or refute, I was made the C. O. of the USS *Mertz* DD691. Well, I could handle it, but I didn't relish the idea, because the situation was getting more exasperating with good men leaving everyday and overall morale not the best. Everyone, both officers and enlisted men, who were not regular navy just wanted to get out of there and go home. Only about 20 percent of the crew were USN and didn't wish to leave the Navy.

For a while I had serious thoughts of staying in the regular Navy, but after the nuclear bombing in Japan, the scuttlebutt was that most of the oceangoing vessels of the future would be nuclear powered and the prototypes would be naval warships. My experience had been in conventional steam powered ships and the idea of re-educating myself to run nuclear power plants wasn't appealing. Anyway, I elected to remain in the service until I had enough points to leave. Actually, this would occur just about the time the *Mertz* would be decommissioned. So for the next month or so, I was the commanding officer. The only time I took the conn underway was when we moved the ship from our mooring area to a drydock. Took a couple of hours, but I was in command and responsible for everything that happened. One nice thing about my being the skipper was that it went into my officer's record that Lieutenant AGG, USNR, was Commanding Officer of the USS *Mertz* DD691.

There were many personnel problems to handle as skipper. Haven't time to mention all of them but will give you one as an example. I was awakened from my bunk about 3:30 A.M. one night by the officer of the deck. Said I had an emergency phone call from ashore. So I got up and answered the phone. It was Crowley, my First Class Electricians Mate. He was in deep trouble. He had been out on the town in San Diego and brought a girl back to his room on the eighth floor of the Grant Hotel. He couldn't remember details because he had been somewhat intoxicated, but they were awakened about 3:00 A.M. by the hotel manager. Apparently he had taken a shower before falling into bed. The trouble was he left the shower on and the water hadn't drained. The shower stall overflowed, the bathroom overflowed, his room had a couple of inches of water and it was leaking into the hall and the floor below until someone discovered it. The manager called the cops and wanted him arrested. He also wanted to know who was going to pay for all the damages—and Crowley was broke. Somehow we got things straightened out and brought him back to the ship. I can't remember how this thing was resolved, but it was. The problems one had as the skipper.

Turning to the lighter side of our stay in San Diego, the remaining single officers aboard had their fun. I can remember having some great times at the beautiful Coronado Hotel. It was an elegant place and remains so after all these years. It had several stories of "circular" rooms similar to those at the Grand Hotel in Point Clear, Alabama. I bumped into several old friends from home who were there—Bill Ellis, his brother John, Ed Sanford and others. On one occasion shortly after we arrived in San Diego, we went over to the Coronado and I met an attractive girl, Helen Courtney Chircop, who turned out to be the private secretary of the admiral who was Commandant of the Ninth Naval District—the top naval post in this region. She lived only three blocks from the hotel and had lots of girlfriends, so she fixed up my fellow officers with dates and we had some great times going to San Diego nightclubs or going up to LaJolla to some fine restaurants or to the beaches in that direction.

One of our officers, Roger Bozzone, was a California native from Manhattan Beach. He introduced us to those marvelous California salads. They were huge, had everything, and were always a full meal.

Later we went to another one of those socials for officers given by the young and fair single girls of San Diego. This was an opportunity to meet some nice "uptown" girls. In the process I met another very attractive girl, Heil Vandervoort. Her parents owned the biggest florist shop in San Diego. Had a number of dates with Heil. She was attending San Diego State and always got dates for my friends with her sorority sisters. We would double- and triple-date to all kinds of places, mainly The Tops, a very fine club that catered to those who were twenty-something. We also went to the Pacific Square dance hall, where Harry James's band was playing. Heil was a marvelous dancer. I'll admit I was sweet on her all the way up to the time I left San Diego to go home. Several weeks later I received some mail from my shipmates who were still in San Diego. The only thing in the envelope was a picture of Heil in the local newspaper social section announcing her engagement to a Lt. Robert Ricketts who had returned to his home in San Diego just after I left. Turns out they were going steady before I met her, but she never said anything about it.

Some of the other officers on the *Mertz*, the *Monssen* or the *Remey* introduced me to the game of golf. Consequently, I played a few times on some beautiful courses in the San Diego area.

In mothballing the ship, we were to put everything in place—refill all spare parts boxes, containers, etc. All machinery was covered with a plastic and sprayed with gray paint—everything looked like a bunch of cocoons. All compartments were also to be sealed. Eventually the entire ship was to be sealed and installed with equipment to ventilate and keep the humidity low and the temperature reasonable. Lots of our gear was identified as Title B. This included our wardroom record player and cabinet where we kept all of our V-disc records. Bill Sanders and I were sealing up the record chest one day and we wondered why such items had to be kept aboard. Naval regulations insisted that they remain on the ship. We were tempted to steal a few of our favorites but didn't. They are collector's items today.

It came about that I finally had enough points to depart from naval service about three weeks before the ship was to be decommissioned and mothballed in the Nineteenth Reserve Fleet. I was conscientious, loyal, and patriotic up to a point—and that point was reached, so I turned the C.O. job over to Bob Harding, who reluctantly accepted, because he wanted to leave as well.

I packed my gear, bid all my buddies farewell and left for home in May of 1946. Since I hadn't taken much leave during my active duty, I rated almost three months' terminal leave with pay. I was officially separated from the Navy on July 14, 1946. This occurred out at the Naval Air Station on Lake Pontchartrain in New Orleans.

I had often wondered about the old *Mertz*. Thought it would be nice to return to San Diego someday and step aboard the vessel that was my home for close to three years. Some of these reserve fleet destroyers were recommissioned during the Korean War or the Vietnam conflict. Some were sold to a number of third-world countries that wanted to start or expand their navies. But not the *Mertz*. She stayed in San Diego for years. Finally, it was sold for scrap for the sum of $160,000 to—guess who—the Japanese.

I started to list all of the campaign ribbons that anyone earned if they were aboard the entire life of the USS *Mertz* (I was one) but that's all passé. If we wished, we could wear ribbons on our uniforms that reflected earning thirteen battle stars. To paraphrase General MacArthur, "Old Navy salts never die, they just slowly fade away."

The other day I finished reading an excellent account of the Battle of Leyte Gulf in the Philippines. I was reminded of how very lucky we were on the *Mertz*. We could have been blown out of the water in seconds by the Japanese Fleet coming down the east coast of Samar. We could have been severely damaged a dozen times in the Pacific by enemy aircraft, or mines, or torpedoes, or kamikazes. We somehow survived all the horrible carnage that many sailors experienced. The man upstairs spared us.

As you know, I started writing you about as much of my life as I could remember. Took you through grade school, high school, college and now my naval experience. If I were to write a book of my early years, I could appropriately title it *Growing Up in New Orleans,* but in adding my career in the Navy, perhaps I would have to revise the title to just *Growing Up* because I really didn't mature until I completed my tour of duty. The armed forces always said, "Send us the boy and we'll return you the man." They're probably right, but when I came home I was still only twenty-three years old.

Must go.

Love you so much,
Dad

Addendum. Graduation Lists

ALCEE' FORTIER HIGH SCHOOL GRADUATES-JUNE 1931

Robert M. Adams
Paul A. Arceneaux
William W. Ayres
Sam A. Barkoff
Purcell T. Baumgartner
Gladwyn H. Bell
Adolphe C. Billet
Henry S. Blake
Barnett Blitz
Adam Fritz Blumer
Frederick W. Boelte
Edward M. Bostick
Albert C. Boyd
Henry E. Bredow
Martin E. Burke
Augustus G. Cambias
Harry B. Caplan
Stephen L. Cefolia
Salvador Civilette
William L. Clauset
Joseph K. Clay
Harry J. Collins
Jesse C. Connelly
Myron A. Copland
Gustave H. Crais
James F. Crawford
John B. Daly
William J. Daly
Thomas A. Davenport
Phillip Del Corral
Albert F. Dugan
Frederick I. Dymond
Sidney Ellis, Jr.
Harry M. England
Frank Ernesto, Jr.
Cornelius J. Everett
Thomas C. Fischer
George R. Fisher

Francis T. Folse
William E. Frantz
Lucius J. Freiberger
Alton P. Frymire
Samuel P. Goldberg
Jack J. Griffin
Patrick D. Hale
Benjamin J. Haney, Jr.
Robert E. Harris
Atchie Heilman
Preston Van F. Henley
Ernest J. Holloway
James J. Howe
Davis C. Humphreys
William C. Jacobs
George Janvier
Lawrence J. Jaubert
Bruce P. Jillson
Woodrow M. Knobloch
Elmer E. Kramer
Max A. Kreh
Albert A. Levin
Melville L. Levy
Raoul Livaudais
Humberto M. Lopez
Julian H. Lorenzen
Lee H. Lorenzen
Stanley M. McDonald
William McHardy
William C. Maher
Newman D. Maier
Irwin Massman
Arthur E. Merchant
Jerome C. Mimeles
Anthony F.V. Miranti
Edward J. Muth
Herman Nebel, Jr.
Allen B. Nicholas

Albert M. Norwood
Daniel Nowak
James R. O'Leary
Michael Offner
Jackson M. Olivier
George Pelias
Nathan Pillawsky
Crawford J. Powell
Edward J. Preis
Roy M. Pullen
Thomas T. Quigley
William L. Ray
Robert Y. Rivera
Eugene G. Robichaux
Sam I. Rosenberg
Howard J. Sambola
Payton R. Sandoz
Saul Singer
Williard G. Smith
Carroll Stahl
Joseph D. Starr
Parks H. Stearns
Henry H. Stengel
Frank D. Stigler
Fred Stockton
Arnaud P. Texada
Clinton U. True
Richard S. Tuite
Frank D. Tuller
Lewis H. Twyman, Jr.
Charles P. Ward
Joseph Wainberg
Max Wexler
Charles G. Wright
James A. Wright
Alvin N. Zander
Philip J. Zellinger

ALCEE' FORTIER HIGH SCHOOL GRADUATES-JANUARY 1932

Wilbert A. Argus
Billy A. Barnes
Gilbert R. Barth
Rich L. Bazin
Albert Benard
Emile Birtel
Louis C. Bisso
Malcolm P. Boley

William M. Brewer
August J. Brodtmann, Jr.
Irving Burglass
Howell P. Cairns
Howard A. Despommier
Abram Diaz
Ernest H. Doerries, Jr.
Aaron Epstein

William C. Epstein
Oliver W. Evans
Philip R. Farnsworth
Edward J. Filleul
Ralph Fishman
Morris Gerber
Byron W. Glass
Jack F. Goran

Cleve A. Heath
Albert E. Hodapp
Gordon B. Hyde
John J. James
Bruce M. James
Robert L. Johnson
Edward J. Kane, Jr.
Peter E. Kissgen
Isaac Levy, Jr.
Tom S. Lobrano
Alex F. McCarthy
Donald W. McKay
William C. Mattern
Paul Novoselsky

Karl Oldstein
Junius H. Payne
Lionel M. Ricau
Frank J. Rosato
Herman S. Phillips
Hugo R. Phillips
Charles A. Prechter
Frank E. Rose
William H. Schlotterer
Lee Schroeder
Salon C. Scheppegrell
William L. Seaman
Harold P. Shalleross
Wilbur K. Shear

George Smill
Claude R. Smith
Joe H. Sperling
Solomon Teles
Norman E. Tharp
Gordon Veith
Fred J. Vogel
John A. Warner
Joseph G. Weddington
Ben F. Welborn
Felix Welsch
Edward L. Winstine

ALCEE' FORTIER HIGH SCHOOL GRADUATES-JUNE 1932

Edward A. Adey, III
Moise M. Alaynick
Biddle W. Allen
Robert H. Anderson
Charles W. Arby
Al S. Ballance
Roy P. Bartels
Clarence E. Bennett, Jr.
Edward B. Block
Duncan Blake
Hobart W. Blakeslee
Howard L. Boddan
Julius Bowsky
Charles W. Boyle
Bernard M. Bowman
L. Waymon Branch
Jonas R. Brooks
Robert C. Bradford
Charles A. Burton
Walter H. Bush
J. Taylor Caffery
Rich E. Callihan
Russell A. Casey
Harry E. Charlestrom, Jr.
N.J. Chetta
John B. Chotin
Walter H. Claiborne
Hector A. Carrillo
Roy K. Clifton
W. Sherwood Collins
William H. Coughlin
G.F. Counce, Jr.
Edwin P. Crozat
William J. Culver
John E. Davenport
Joseph E. Daum, Jr.
John S. Devlin
Jacob DeCorte
John J. Donovan

Walter P. Diaz
Farrar R. Dodge
George H. Douglas, Jr.
Billy V. Dunne
Charles Dusenburg
Leonard L. Drown
Michael A. Ensenat
Louis A. Ensenat
Jimmy Eustis
Joseph G. Edwards
Fred A. Eigenbrod
William F. Fagan
Harry Feinhartz
Wilfred Finkelstein
Albert T. Foley
Walter H. Fuchs
Abraham V. Fuchs
William E. Gilbert
Robert E. Gillaspie
John S. Guth
Rudolph Haisfield
Samuel J. Goldberg
Grant V. Hastings
Hayward H. Hillyer
Augustine L. Hogan, Jr.
Fred R. Hwigart
Robert L. Hullinghorst
William A. Hardaker
Charles W. Hoyle
John Jacobs
Theo P. Jamerson
Kermit B. Jaubert
Albert E. Johnson, Jr.
Herman G. Janssen, Jr.
William K. Janssen
Douglas Kelly, Jr.
Joe H. Kahn
Jacob Klegar
William R. Konrad

Sterling J. Knight
Thornton A. Kuntz
Frank C. Lanata
Charles A. Levy, Jr.
Thomas W. Lawson
Justin J. Lazarus
Louis E. Landry
Marcus E. Landau
Edward F. LeBreton
Joseph E. Loper, Jr.
Ernest H. Lockenberg
Bertel A. Luke
Thomas H. McGladdery
Joseph D. Martin, Jr.
James B. Massey
John E. Mahner
Justin L. McCarthy
William McElheney
Joseph S. Monaghan
Fred M. Mendez
John E. Morrill, Jr.
John E. Monroe, Jr.
Clyde F. Morrison
Theo E. Nesom
Waldemar S. Nelson
James B. Norris
Clifton R. Newlin
Maurice Pailet
Norman Pailet
John J. O'Neil
Burt R.O'Rourke
P.J. Perry
Edward Plant
Morris H. Portnoy
Richard F. Price
Jack E. Perkins
William R. Rebentisch
John S. Randall
Joseph W. Radebaugh

Fred A. Rhodes
James L. Rhoden
John R. Riley, Jr.
George M. Robinson
Julius Rowsky
Robert Russo
Theo A. Schlueter
George H. Schmidt, Jr.
Fred C. Schroeder
Karl W. Seeman, Jr.
Theo H. Shepard
Horace Simon, Jr.
Edgar M. Smith

Howard K. Smith, Jr.
Fred M. Sondes
Joseph Spadaford, Jr.
Edward R. Stassi
Joseph E. Steib
Bartholomew P. Sullivan
William B. Seaskind
Fred R. Swigert
Edward B. Taylor
B. Simeon Titus, Jr.
John B. Tabarlet
Gilbert J. Victor
Zeb Ward, Jr.

Warren Welmon, Jr.
Charles J. Wetta
Joseph M Woodward, Jr.
Charles D. Wright
Clifford G. Webb
J. Leche Youngs
Philip Zito
Louis J. Zollinger
(Possible)
Thomas H. Gladdary
Augustine L. Haydn, Jr.
Carlos A. Salazar

Ruldolph Halsfield
John K. Magruder

Carlos A. Polamar
Cummings A. Sanborn

Walter B. Moses, Jr.

ALCEE' FORTIER HIGH SCHOOL GRADUATES-JANUARY 1933

Dan J. Arroyo
Ray H. Bartels
Lionel G. Bernard
Alex B. Bloch
Robert B. Boyd
Winston V. Bradburry
Donald Brady
Russell J. Cantelli
Lawrence R. Collins
Charles J. Conner
William Culver
Bert Davis
James Eddy
Sam K. Eddy
Tom H. Elliott, Jr.
Edwin R. Ferguson
James L. Finnin
Owen Gahagan
Louis B. Gonzales
Paul P. Gonzales

Sidney S. Graff
Andreas Horcasitas
Achille Klotz
Robert J. Linton
George Lucas
David McCooo
Robert McGivney
John K. Magruder
Bradford J. Monroe
Walter B. Moses, Jr.
J. Von H. Muller, Jr.
James F. Oliver
Philip Oliver
Washburn Paul
George Plotkin
Enrique H. Reid
Edmond P. Rordam
Ragnvald B. Rordam
Horward Rowley
Cummings A. Sanborn, Jr.

Beryl Samuelson
Boysie Sanford
Charles Sanford
Joseph D. Sansoni
Malcolm E. Schmiego
George H. Schwing
Henry B. Shepard
W. Sidney Singleton
Alberto Smith
David Stuart
Edward B. Taylor
Gernon Z. Tolmas
William Porter Tull
George E. Valervich
Clifford C. Walker
Roswell J. Weil
William George Young
Henry L. Waskowski

ALCEE' FORTIER HIGH SCHOOL GRADUATES-JUNE 1933

Frank M. Aguirre
James C. Alleyn
Claiborne Andrews
Herman Antis
Justin J. Aron
John S. Arthur
Lawrence C. Atkinson
Milton T. Aufdemorte
Lloyd E. Barrios
Joseph G. Berdon
Coleman Bernstein
Walter M. Berry

Frank J. Bertucci
William H. Bohne
Richard E. Bond
Delwyn W. Bonds
John C. Bowman
John Brandt
Lazar Brener
Tom P. Brooks
Charles D. Broussard
Robert B. Burkes
Chester B. Brennan
James Brodie

Edwin M.........
Nicholas T. Campbell
Robert M. Causse
Eugene J. Cazenave
John Centanni
William D. Chapman
Godfrey T. Coate
Harry Cohen
Mayer Cohen
Charles E. Colombel
Rex Conn
Sam S. Corte

G. Eddie Cornwell
Charles Irwin Crais
Robert J. Crawley
Louis J. DeLassus
Godfrey D. Donovan
Menard Doswell
David M. Drown
Gus Dufilho
Ewell E. Eagan
Charles J. Eberts
Caswell P. Ellis
John W. Enos
Alvin J. Eppling
Henry C. Eustis
Harold G. Faust
Milo R. Fausterman
William B. Fisher
Jacob L. Fischman
Frank Flack
Albert S. Fossler
Farris R. Fox
Dobin Friedman
William J. Friichter
Charles L. Fultz
Tom E. Furlow
Cameron B. Gamble
Louis W. Geier
Vance A. Geier
William D. Grace
William A. Green
Sidney S. Grodsky
Melvin H. Grosz
Harry Guriesvsky
Ray A. Haar
Harris Harrigin
Monte Hart
John E. Heckert
Robert Henriques
Merlin R. Hoerner
Paul H. Hoerske

Henry Hoffman
Emile Holzenthal
William S. Huey
James D. Jackson
Samuel Jacob
J. Gordon Jardet
James J. Jaubert
Paul A. Jensen
Charles A. Johnson
E. Douglas Johnson
Elwood S. Jones
Pierre Jovovitch
Nathan Kaufman
Richard Keenan
Calvin Kennedy
Alf Klaveness
Paul W. Kluchin
John V. Koehl
Paul Keretzky
Lionel Landry
Sabin P. Landry
Alvin F. Latura
Edgar J. LeBlanc
Thomas J. Lee
Arthur F. Leibe
Hilbert A. Leibe
John S. Lemann
Frank P. Lewis
Wesley A. Lewis
Fenwick E. Lisso
James M. Lisso
Joseph K. McCollum
Horace A. McKey
Boyd R. McKirahan
Ernest W. McNeil
Charles J. Mange
Robert M. Martin
John S. Mayer
George Mayoral
Adolph E. Mazurette

Fred W. Miller
John F. Mitchell
Anthony J. Monjure
Marion S. Monk
John A. Montgomery
John E. Morrison
Joseph A. Murphy
Elisha B. Meyers
Nestor B. Newlin
William H. Newman
Treadwell J. Nobles
Paul E. Odendahl
Louis R. Otto, Jr.
Angelo J. Palmisano
Robert Vernon Payne
Lars N. Pedersen
Eugene S. Pennebaker
George J. Perez
Morris L. Perlman
Milton E. Pick
Horace Pitcher
Alfred M. Porth
Norman Pozinsky
George W. Prechter
Herman Robinowitz
Charles E. Reed
Ralph Reins
Henry R. Richmond
Perry R. Roehm
Charles Rohm, Jr.
Herbert E. Romagosa
George E. Roper
Ernesto L. Rosell
Leonard H. Rosenson
Kurt O. Rubisch
John F. Ryan
Bernard Samuel
Lawrence Sauer
Richard A. Sharpe
Merrill J. Scherer

Henry S. Schill
Roy L. Schmidt
Norbert G. Schopp
Jack A. Schupp
Frank J. Serio
Phillip M. Seymour
Saul E. Silverman
John W. Sims
Lerey Z. Slater
Federico Smith
Roby H. Spaar
James C. Spotts

William S. Stacy
Shelton S. Stanton
Wilfred J. Steib
Joseph H. Steiner
Ernest M. Sutter
William M. Swayne
Henry L. Thompson
William G. Troeseher
Sidney J. Varney
Richard G. Verlander
Wendell D. Vicknair
Irwin E. Volker

Frank C. Voss
John C. Wallace, Jr.
James M. Ward
Edward W. Welch
Clarence C. Weiser
Philip Werlein
Edward W. White, Jr.
Melville E. White
John W. Whitty
Paul L. Wiggin
Fred J. Wolfe, Jr.
Richard E. Wright

ALCEE' FORTIER HIGH SCHOOL GRADUATES-FEBRUARY 1934

Adolph E. Asher
Edward E. Badeaux, Jr.
Harry C. Baldwin
J. Reyna Barrios
Royal R. Bastian, Jr.
Calvin K. Benedict
Nester T. Beyer
Edward Bives
Morris G. Blockwell, Jr.
Ike Bloch, Jr.
Richard E. Bond
Irving Breen
Ben W. Brook, Jr.
Robert D. Burkes
Jules L. Cahn
David L. Cappel
George A. Carroll
George J. Casara
Frank Cerniglia
J. Scott Chotin
Nathan Cotlar
Oliver J. Counce
Louis R. Daray, Jr.
Henry Davies
William J. DeArmas
Alex Dimitry, Jr.
Richard E. Donegan

Lewis P. Eaves, Jr.
Williard A. Eastin
Morris M. Elliot
Gerson Finkelstein
Jacques L. Fortier
J. Lewis Fredrick
Lloyd Gahagan
Cameron B. Gamble
Charles W. Genelia
Floyd L. Getsinger
F. Wesley Gleason, Jr.
Sidney S. Grodsky
Graham J. Haddock, Jr.
John E. Hall, Jr.
Cornelius Hecker
Arthur C. Hollister, Jr.
Melvin O. Johnson
J. George Jones, Jr.
William P. Kaiser
Birger V. Kaurin
Karl M. Klein
Gustav A. Kuper
Charles McGinnis LaCour
Leo E. Lucia
Fred W. Marks
Francis Dodd Menge
Shelby Moore

William D. Morton
Amedee J. Nelson
Tom O'Leary
George J. Peterson, III
Herbert N. Pettigrew, Jr.
Louis C. Phillips
Charles G. Quinlan
Herman Rabinowitz
Jay Weller Rice
Lawrence E. Robins
Charles M. Samuel
Roy L. Schmidt
Norbert B. Shelby
Howard J. Smith
William F. Standke, Jr.
Joseph H. Steiner
John W. Starliper
Chaster C. Stetfelt
Chadbourne Steward
Richard T. Taylor
Marshall K. Vignes
Earnest G. Vocke
Donard O. Ward
Sidney A. Williams
George L. Wimberly
Welville H. Wolfson

ALCEE' FORTIER HIGH SCHOOL GRADUATES-JUNE 1934

Charles T. Althans
Thomas B. Anderson
David Antin
W.S. Atkinson
Hamilton K. Avery
Phillip J.J. Aviles, Jr.
John P. Ayres, Jr.
Louis L. Babin
Lawrence M. Barkley
Walter M. Bartlett
John T. Basile
Edward A. Becker, Jr.
Arnold J. Bennett
Eric A. Benson
Hector E. Bernadas, Jr.
Louis L. Bernard
Walter L. Beyer
Harold Blenn
Sidney H. Blessy
Ernest L. Bliss
Laurence H. Bohne
William P. Boizelle
Alvin G. Bothner
Carol S. Bowsky

Cyril T. Breaux
Edward S. Bres, II
William A. Briant
Edwin L. Brock
Fred Bronfin
B.W. Brooks, Jr.
Tom B. Brooks
H. Bowers
John Buchanan
Robert J. Caire
Frank T. Calongne
Joseph R. Capaci
Sidney D. Carp
Arthur C. Carter
Louis J. Champagne
Frank B. Chapman
Stephen A. Chavez
Joseph F. Cheleno
J. Ralston Chopin
Karl H. Clauset
Henry H. Collins
Pete J. Campagno
Richard H. Corales, Jr.
Michael A. Costa

Edward Elwell Counce
William T. Craig, Jr.
John B. Cressend
Harry G. Crossen
Jack Cruze
Marion F. Culver
Richard C. Davidson
Julius T. Davis
William J. DeArmas, Jr.
Baptiste J. DeJean
Joseph G. Delatte
William T. Dewhurst
Donald W. Doyle
Everett L. Drewes
Walden A. Drysdale
James A. Ducos
James Dupas, II
Owen S. Eckhardt
W. Byron Edgar
William C. Ellis
Herman J. Estrade, Jr.
George H. Evans
Walt H. Eversmeyer, Jr.
Peter J. Failla

Monte B. Farmer
Billy Ferguson
William W. Fellom
Nathan L. Fendig
Sidney E. Finkelstein
John B. Fitch
Nolvil F. Fortier
Edwin J. Fredrichs
Charles H. Frierson, Jr.
Charles F. Frisco
Lloyd Gahagan
Emmett W. Geary
Floyd L. Getsinger
Frank A. Giardina
Harry S. Gidiere
John E. Goebel
Michael N. Goldberg
Carl F. Goll, IV
Ben C. Gore
Joseph G. Greenwald
Harry Grosz
Rene A. Gaus
Malcolm G. Haas
Robert L. Haney
Ringgold Hardin
Tom F. Hardy
Guy C. Harris, Jr.
Weeks T. Harrison

Peter L. Hassinger
Murray F. Hawkins
George M.B. Helm
Abe L. Horshberg
Maunsel W. Hickey
Neil Himel, Jr.
Cerf Hirsch
Alvin L. Holzenthal
Wilber Hooper
William O. Hudson, II
Paul J. Jastram
E. Lee Jones
J. George Jones, Jr.
Fred C. Jung, Jr.
Sam Kancher
Henry E. Kane, Jr.
Label A. Katz
James E. Kelly
Maurice A. Kenny
Tom A. Kimbrough, Jr.
John C. Kirkpatrick
Val E. Kissgen
Odd Klaveness
Hanckes A. Klein
Arthur W. Koon, Jr.
Solomon Koretzky
Abe B. Kupperman
Arthur B. Lacour

Arthur N. Lambert, Jr.
Neil Lamont
James W. Larkin
Victor K. LaRocca
Shepard M. Latter
Robert E. LeCorgne
Gilbert E. Ledger
Fred E. LeLaurin, Jr.
Harold B. Levy
Salon M. Levy
Boyd H. Lewis
John Locantro
Idas Western Lohmann
Leonard Lozano
James H. McCaskill, Jr.
Charles E. McKinley, Jr.
Charles Ben Maginnis
Don A. Maginnis, Jr.
Sam S. Maggio, Jr.
Alcide St. Cyr Mann
Robert H. Manning
Fortunato Mannino
McMeen Hepburn Many
Ralph E. Mattes
Adolph E. Mazurette
Edward A. May, Jr.
Luis A. Mayoral
Alvin F. Mitchell

Robert E. Millelstaedt
Cornelious Modinger, Jr.
Frank V. Moise, Jr.
Hal E. Monroe
Greer O. Moore
W.C. Moseley
Warren G. Moses
Elisha B. Myers, Jr.
Floyd W. Newlin
J. Warren Newman
W. Raymond D. North
Calvin G. Norwood
Theo Offner
Norvin P. Oliver, Jr.
Tom P. Orr, Jr.
William F. O'Toole
Stanford J. Otto
Edward W. Owen, Jr.
Jo Robert Persons, Jr.
Arthur E. Phillips
Joseph R. Pistorius
Paul N. Pizzo
Robert W. Polchow
Arthur C. Porter

Henri Prudhomme
George Queyrouze, Jr.
Gus V. Rabito
Anthony A. Reese
Frazer L. Rice
Francis J. Richardson, Jr.
Ashton Ives Rivet
Charles O. Rogers
J. Robert Rombach
Marx Rosenzweig
John M. Ruch
Charles F. Sauter
John H. Schaeffer
Bernard J. Schmaltz
Gayle Schneidau, Jr.
William Sellers
Frank Sheel
Maurice J. Simon
Gilbert L. Simoneaux
James A. Sinclair
Harold Singer
Henry N. Smith, Jr.
Robert F. Spangenberg, Jr.
Malcoln A. Stephens

Carl F. Stockmeyer, Jr.
Robert E. Lee Stolzenthaler
Jack C. Stone
Edwin F. Stumpf
Jack A. Sutherlin
Richard T. Taylor
Horace A. Thompson, Jr.
Juan J. Trillo
Felix J. Troxclair
Leonard S. Ungar
Robinson Miller Upton
Bernard Volodarsky
Walt Van Hoven, Jr.
John F. Waguespack, Jr.
Donald O. Ward
J. Berwick Watkins
Felix H. Webster
Dan T. Wetta
George F. Williamson
George L. Wimberly
Charles H. Wirbel
Andrew Michael Wolert
Adolph M. Wolff

ALCEE' FORTIER HIGH SCHOOL GRADUATES-JANUARY 1935

Allen D. Acomb
John H. Ahrens
Paul B. Alker
Edward A. Anthony
Charles P. Alcklen
Bernard Aronson
Jacob Becker
Frank L. Beier
Ralph W. Bond
Sylvain C. Bouche
Eric P. Breidenbach
Tom E. Carty
Charles E. Chambers
Eugene C. Coolley
William J. Conrad
Jack P. Crumhorn
Claude H. Dannemann
Stanley F. Diefenthal
Josph M. Dicharry
Peter J. Fitzpatrick
John L. Gallegly

Emil Greenwald
Alvin B. Harrison
Harry A. Heinz
Winter A. Holbrook
Alden B. Johnson
Gerald E. Kahn
Philip M. Kenner
Beverly T. Kincaide
Edward L. King
John J. Lane
Ashton G. Lestrapes
Elmo LeBlanc
Oscar S. Lima
Edward McQueen
Paul Marsh
William Manning
Charles Melhado
Perry K. Moon
Harold L. Morris
Arcadius H. Norris
Ellis Pailet

G. Constantine Pelias
Joseph R. Pistorius
A. Erwin Ralston
Norbert M. Redmond
Marcel F. Romagosa
James F. Richmond
William B. Richter
Jean Pierre Roven
William G. Ryals
Jacob T. Schmidt
Ben F. Simms
Wardwell Smith
Calvin L. Stengel
Simon L. Streiffer
Floyd E. Terranova
Tom E. Thorpe
Harold J. Upton
George Will
Edward W. Wynne
Edwood Zatarain

ALCEE' FORTIER HIGH SCHOOL GRADUATES-JUNE 1935

Edward M. Aguirre
Fred H. Ahrens
Woods Allen
Harold S. Andry
William A. Atkinson
Clarence Barbier
David Hanlin Becker
Kenneth Q. Berger
Emile J. Bernard
Lawrence B. Berthaud
John L. Bertucci
William D. Billingsley
Clem B. Binnings
Jules F. Blass
Louis J. Bock
Phillip W. Bohne
Tom Boone
Shirley B. Braselman
Frank Brightson
Darrell M. Brisbin
Thomas G. Broussard
Bob W. Browning
Trufant J. Burguieres
Norman Burnstein
Gailon T. Bryan
Hubert N. Byrnes
John H. Cahn
Anthony J. Calagno
George S. Cambias
James C. Cammack

Joshua N. Caplan
Franco Carvajal
Henry J. Cearns
Henry W. Chapman
Wilfred H. Charbonnet
Marshall J. Charlton
Neil L. Chavigny
Bob Carson Chinn
Phlip B. Clerc
Fletcher Cochran
Demcey D. Colley
Louis J. Correjolles
James A. Cosgrove
Robert D. Cosgrove
Felix H. Cotton
Stewart M. Crais
Frederick H. Crane
Frank F. Cristina
James A. Cullerton
Leonard Culotta
Fernando J. Cuquet, Jr.
Rene L. Dechard
Marion Dailey
Allen J. Dancy
Vincent B. D'Antoni
William D. Davis
William N. Deimel
Stanley L. Diefenthal
Curry C. Dixon
Donald J. Duclaux

John D. Duffy
Celestin J. Dumestre
William H. Dunstan, Jr.
Conrad A. Duvic, Jr.
Norman E. Eaves
Joseph C. Ebling
William E. Eldridge, Jr.
James A. Ermon
George Falkenstein, Jr.
Oscar E. Fasquelle
Leon Feldman
Roger H. Fellom
Alex G. Finney
John C. Finney
George R. Foerster
Edmond J. Foret
Morris S. Forsyth
Owen H. Foss
William Foss, Jr.
Charles J. Freitag
Carl M. Fremaux
Julian P. Freret
Warren G. Furlow
Freddie Generes
Norton R. Girault
David S. Gissel
Andre D. Gomez
Miller Gordon
Frank R. Green
John T. Green

Charles W. Greenmayer
Tilden H. Greenbaum, Jr.
Frederick C. Grieshaber
Paul J. Guma
Boris C. Haase
Edmond C. Haase, Jr.
David Hackney
Arthur B. Hammond
Frank H. Hardenstein
Thomas S. Harllee
John Harper
Lew R. Harris
Maurice H. Hellman
Herbert B. Hendricks
Edward N. Herrmann
Julius U. Herzog
Milton E. Hills
Charles S. Hincks
Norwood N.J. Hingle
Julian F. Hirsch
George W. Hopkins
John O. Hoyt

Herman J. Janssen
James Johnson, Jr.
Ernest Jones, Jr.
Warren Joubert
Paul S. Julienne
Walter J. Jung, Jr.
Leo J. Kachel
Arthur J. Kahn
Thomas J. Kennedy
Edmond Kimble
Charles L. Knight
Nestor B. Knoepfler
David M. Korn
David G. Kostmayer
Paul Krail
John T. Kramer
David A. Kraus
Morris Krilov
Bill W. Kuhn
Vincent A. LaBarbera
Paul M. Lagarde
Arthur C. Lazarus

Joseph L. Leber
Robert E. Legendre
Louis Levy
Stanley S. Levy
Oswald B. Lodrigues
Russell B. Long
Arthur L. Lowe
Alfred Lozano
Richard J. Luck
Cosmo W. Manalle
John F. Manson
Peter F. Maroney
Edward J. Marquez
Rudolph J. Marshall
Cloyee Matheny
Harvey C. May, Jr.
George N. McAlister
Alden McLellan, Jr.
C. Fred Melcher
Julius J. Meyer
Jacob C. Minor
Edwin E. Moise

Harry B. Moore
Harold J. Morris
Charles D. Muller, Jr.
Louis P. Muller
Bryant A. Murray
Charles W. Nelson
Arcadius H. Norris
Arvin H. Northup
Clarence W. Nutting
Fred W. Oser
Lewis C. Parrish
Diego A. H. Patron
Frank Pattie, Jr.
Einar N. Pedersen
George H. Penn, Jr.
Armand B. Pepperman
Karl E. Pottharst
Everett S. Pratt
George H. Queyrouze
Arthur R. Ramirez
Spencer A. Rappold
Charles F. Read
James P. Reaser
W. Ford Reese
Ernest J. Reidenauer, Jr.
Jack R. Renfro
William S. Resor
Atwood L. Rice
Robert M. Richardson
Thomas F. Richardson

Nicholas P. Rivet
Albert J. Robinson
Robert G. Rogers
William B. Rose
James J. Rosenberg
Julius M. Rosenberg
Paul A. Ross, Jr.
Bernard M. Roth
Eugene Ruiz
Joseph Sanders
Roy B. Schaefer
Val Scheurich
Joseph V. Schlosser
Arthur T. Schreiber
Curtis F. Scott, Jr.
Richard C. Seither
Samuel Simkin
James L. Slaughter
Frederick W. Sinclair
Afred L. Solomon
Alwyn Smith
Emmitt L. Smith
Eugene F. Smith
Joseph C. Smith
Jack E. Sparling
Clarence J. Steeg
Ferdie B. Stern
Sal Sterbcow
Richard E. Swann, Jr.
Martin K. Thomen, Jr.

Thomas A. Tomeny
George J. Tregle, Jr.
George Triche
Raul A. Trillo
Audubon A. Truxillo
Ruffin G. Truxillo
Jules G. Tuyes
James M. Vail
Andrew L. Vasquez
George W. Vicknair
George A. Vivirito, Jr.
Adam H. Volk
William Wait
Leslie Lee Watson
Seth J. Weldon
Thomas H. Wells, Jr.
Andrew M. Wilkinson
George Will
Louis T. Williams
George E. Williams
Walter C. Williams
Allan E. Wilmot
Donald E. Wilson
James N. Wilson
Philip H. Witherspoon
Edward E. Wynne
Gails Young, Jr.
Arthur D. Zaldrondo
Allison O. Zansler

154

ALCEE' FORTIER HIGH SCHOOL GRADUATES-FEBRUARY 1936

Joseph P. Abele
Walter Antin
J.D. Babin
Floyd T. Bajon
Millard C. Baker
Lowe A. Barnett, Jr.
Eugene J. Barrett
Meyer Berger
Louis R. Bertucci
John F. Blancaneaux
Joseph M. Bistowish
Raymond V. Bouche
Frank Meyers Bray
John William Bray, Jr.
Stuart Brehm
Lewis Cahn Bryon, Jr.
Pierre F. Carriere
Robert R. Cazaubon
William E. Cazauhon
Marvin A. Clement
Louis N. Collins
Kent H. Courtney
Joseph O. Covert
Charles V. Delerno
Richard J. Dempsey, Jr.
Charles A. Desporte
Edward L. Dickinson
Albert T. Diermayer
Theo E. Ducos
Charles J. Eagan
Edward Ecuyer
Gus G. Eckart
Joseph Everhardt
August F. Fisher, Jr.

Ernest L. Fisher, Jr.
Charles L. Fisher
Leonard K. .....
John Burns Fitch
Milton L. Fletclinger
Frank P. Ganucheau, Jr.
Marcel G. Gelpi, Jr.
James L. Giangrosso
David Gore
Wilton Hagardorn
Ringgold B. Hardin
Emmett L. Harvey
Edward E. Hebert
Louis N. Hodges
Hector J. Horcasitas
Byron Q. Iverson
Phillip H. Jahncke
Woodrow W. Kelly
Thomas C. King
Ben Koretzky
George LaBorde
Harold Lagroue
Nelson Landry
Robert Lanier
Robert S. Leigh
Max B. Levin
Joseph Lockhart
George Lopez
Eduardo N. Lores
Arne Lorentzen
Richard T. McCurdy
E. Mann
Joseph A. Mann
James P. Marquar

Robert G. Moeller
John H. Morton
George A. Murphy
Elisha B. Myers
John D. Olson
Marshall F. Ordemann
Carlos Orfilla
William D. O'Regan
Edgar E. Otto
John S. Patterson
Roland T. Pertuit
Edgar U. Peyronnin
Jay Powers
Sam L. Prochaska
Russell S. Rheams
Alfred A. Rouillier
Nash Charles Roberts
Albert F. Sanchez
Ben L. Sandoz
Charles O. Shellany
Gus A. Schreiber
Walter G. Seaman
Edward G. Smith
Pete R. Sodergren
Allen Tichenor
Douglas P. Torre
Mottram P. Torre
Ernest J. Triche, Jr.
John R. Vallee
Harry M. Vitter
William B. Wait
Theo G. Walker
Eugene W. Wyman, Jr.

ALCEE' FORTIER HIGH SCHOOL GRADUATES-JUNE 1936

Herbert F. Adey, II
Arthur R. Amuedo
Joseph O. Anderson
John W. Anthony, Jr.
John E. Arnoult
Henry A. Babylon
Millard C. Baker, Jr.
Vernon N. Balovich
Pat F. Bass
Joseph V. Bell
Hilarius J. Bernard
John F. Blass, Jr.
Werner E. Blattman
Walter E. Blessey
Norman H. Blitch
Eustis R. Bordelon, Jr.
Michel E. Boudreaux

Arthur S. Bouyson
Julius L. Breaux
Joseph O. Braud
Francis Breaux
William W. Brierre
Irving Brown
Henry J. Bultman
Charles W. Burton
Harry B. Cable
George A. Canal
Joseph M. Cannizzaro
Jack M. Canovsky
M.A. Carso, Jr.
Andrew P. Carter
Franklin Chalmers
Walt B. Coleman, Jr.
Robert A. Collins

Louis A. Conner
Vern P. Connolly
Sidney H. Cook
Charles G. Corley
Justa P. Correa, Jr.
Alex W. Coulogne
Kent H. Courtney
John M. Couvillon
Joseph O. Covert
Roland C. Crenshaw
Roy B. Crews, Jr.
Dave F. Dabney
George B.C. Dangerfield, Jr.
Homer L. Davis
Henry L. DeColigney
Emannuel G. Defraites
Joseph P. Dermody, Jr.

Louis G. DeSonier
Henry F. Dognibene
Peter M. Dombourian
Walter E. Dorrah
Roger H. Doyle
Paul A. Drulihet, III
Joseph Ducote
Lionel Dufilho
Tom C. Dufilho
Elmer M. Dufrechou
James C. Dunphy
Henry T. Duvic
Robert H. Earhart
Henry S. Eason
Howard G. Elliot
James R. Eustis
James D. Fahs
Norman A. Falk
Enrique E. Fasquelle
Marice Feingerts
Maurice E. Felix
David Fichman, Jr.
William A. Fitzgerald, Jr.
Charles H. Flower
Edward J. Frank
William T. Fray, Jr.
Theo T. Freese, Jr.
George N. Frishie, Jr.
Charles J. Gadmer, Jr.
Joe Gernsbacher
Carl E. Geyer
Julian R. Gissel
Addley H. Gladden
Fulton Godat
Davis C. Gore

Ben A. Grasser
Henry B. Greenburg
Leon Greenberg
John D. Greenhorn
Gideon B. Griffin
Charles Guess
Louis D. Haeuser
Tom C. Hall
William A. Hamann
Edward J. Harmeyer
Ray J. Hart
James E. Harvey
John H. Heath
Howard J. Hebert
Wilfred J. Heintz
Royall Hellbach
Neil C. Herberger
George J. Holzer
Rosslyn P. Hotard
Charles T. Isaminger
Roger N. Jaubert
Calvin P. Jones
Sol C. Joseph
Bidwell W. Jumel
George B. Jurgens
Ray R. Kenny
Henry B. Kerr
Norman R. Kerth
Louis J. Kistner
Leon Klein
Leon J. Knecht
Garner J. Knoepfler
Marion B. Kotch, Jr.
Bryce W. Krogman
Hubert R. Kuehne

Nelson F. Kurz
Don A. Landry
George J. Landry, Jr.
H.J. Lane, Jr.
Charles D. Lanphier
Dabney H. Lea, Jr.
George M. Leake, Jr.
Maurice M. LeBreton
Hebert Lee
Robert E. Lee, Jr.
Alfred A. Leafe
Homer F. Leifeste
William Leon
Newell Levy
Herbert S. Livaudais
Pierre Livaudais
Herbert J. Lopez, Jr.
Diebold W. McCall
Ora X. McClellan
Joseph J. Marchese
Clark L. Marks
David L. Markstein
Albert C. Martin, Jr.
Edward B. Martin
Leo T. Marzoni, Jr.
Albert Mason
George B. Matthews
Mario V. Medina
Richard J. Melancon
Charles W. Menendez
Sidney S. Menshel
Ralph L. Monaghan
Malcoln W. Monroe
Anthony Montalbano
Milton K. Morrison

Harry H. Muller, Jr.
Reginald T. Muller
Robert A. Muller
Joseph E. Munn, Jr.
Charles P. Murphy, Jr.
George A. Murphy
John A. Murphy
John W. Myers
George J. O'Keefe, Jr.
Anthony Palmissano, III
Paul J. Panquerno
Harold N. Parker
Julius A. Payne
David A. Pecot
Gus M. Peterson, Jr.
William S. Pfaff
King Pipes
Randolph Pipes

David F. Porter
John E. Pottharst, Jr.
William K. Pratt
Robert R. Prechter
Peter G. Rappold, Jr.
Tom J. Rennie
Claude A. Richter
Russell S. Rheams
Everette C. Roberts
Horace R. Robinson
Rudolph B. Roessle, Jr.
Robert B. Rogers
Raoul M. Rome
Albert H. Rordam
David L. Roth
Emile C. Rufin
Hyman Samuelson
P.J. Sanchez

Alex D. Sapp
Eugene V. Schanerille, Jr.
Allen J. Shexnailder
Melville H. Schmidt
Leon L. Schwartz
Gus A. Seeber, Jr.
Henry D. Seeling
James C. Senter, Jr.
Walter M. Sessums
Sam G. Shepard
Ralph G. Sneed
Richard D. Sneed
Alex C. Solomon
Ernest Spence, Jr.
Juilius Spizer
John H. Stark, Jr.
Charles H. Steele
Roy A. Steger

Saul Steinman
Reinhard A. Steinmayer
John W. Stewart
Mike R. Tamberella
Emile J. Tercero
Lovik P. Thomas
William J. Thomas
George H. Thomen
Chester R. Thomson

Ray E. Trask
C.K. Tricou
Sam A. Trufant, III
Alvin J. Truxillo
Woodrow W. Truxillo
James F. Turnbull
Stanworth Verdier
Charles N. Vosburgh
Winston W. Walker

William H. Wallace
Kenneth W. Ward
George A. Wedemey
Carl L. Weiderten
Sam P. Wright
Hal R. Yockey
Bernard I. Zoller, Jr.
Harry Zoller

ALCEE' FORTIER HIGH SCHOOL GRADUATES-JANUARY 1937

James R. Adair
Edmund J. Anderson
Albert Aschaffenberg
Adam F. Authement
Merlin J. Barrios
Elroy E. Barth
Robert D. Barth
John R. Buttaloro
Charles A. Bertel
John H. Bird
Vincent A. Brennan
James E. Carberry
William M. Campbell
Edward J. Clark
Paul E. Coe
Thomas Collins
Joseph M. Cannizzero
Joseph C. Danner
Joseph P. DeCorte
Peter M. Dombourian
Donald F. Ellison
Henry C. Dosky
Alex N. Dussel
William H. Eggerton, Jr.
Henry B. Eason
James D. Fahs
Lawrence E. Fagen
Arthur T. Feaster
Riley B. Fell
Albert D. Flair
Octave J. Folse
Paul B. Fossier
Roy Funes

Maurice J. Gelpi
Joseph J. Gennusa
Richard M. Gira
Thomas M. Gooch
Charles A. Graver
Earl R. Haas
Virgil R. Harmon
Charles R. Harrison
William W. Hazel
Alvin D. Hellbach
Edwin J. Hiller
Max Hiller
Taylor A. Hopkins
Leonard C. Joseph
Julius R. Jung
Herbert W. Kaiser
Raymond M. Keese
Sam G. Kreeger
Charles A. Lanaux
Victor J. LaRocca
Nelson J. LeBlanc
Dan S. Lehon
Thomas Lewis
Fred G. Lotka
Fred C. Lincks
Dan L. Mayer
Henry L. Mayer
Jack P. Meyer
Edward L. Merrigan
Albert N. Miranda
Edward D. Moseley
Louis C. Mounicou
Albert J. Nugon

Eldred D. Oasterle
Bernard Oppenheim
Gustave Pailet
Maurice Pailet
Joseph A. Palermo
Henry F. Parker
Robert L. Parker
Harris P. Pierson
C. Dan Pique
William C. Reidy
Henry W. Reininger
Charles R. Robinson
Owen D. Ryan
Patrick H. Ryan
Edwin M. Schaffer
Cyril E. Schoen
Herman A. Singerman
Ambrose M. Smith
Ralph G. Sneed
Waldorf A. Steeg
Hermann W. Stumborg
Einar N. Svendsen
Howard M. Tull
Art W. Turner
Walter J. Verlander
Warren C. Vivirite
Irving Warahaver
Frank L. Werner
Frank W. Woodruff
James E. Wright
Lawrence A. Zibilich

ALCEE' FORTIER HIGH SCHOOL GRADUATES-JUNE 1937

Webster A. Acomb, Jr.
Robert W. Adamson
Michele Albans
Norman Anseman
William L. Aydelotte
Harold B. Ayres
Allen L. Babin
Charles C. Babylon

William D. Barcelo
Martin Belasco
Robert T. Bassnett
John L. Bell
Robert E. Bell, Jr.
Jack L. Berlin
Peter L. Bernard, Jr.
Warren Bernadas

Edward M. Bezou, Jr.
Walter J. Binnings
Rodney A. Black
Roy F. Blondeau
Stanford K. Blum, Jr.
Morris F. Borge
Alvin W. Bosch
Robert L. Boswell

Lloyd L. Boudreaux
James A. Bowers
George J. Bravo
Leopold Breen
Charles Brown
Engie R. Broderick
Norman E. Brownlee, Jr.
Harold A. Bruchie
John H. Bruno
Art A. Calix
Anthony J. Capozza
John M. Carstens
William H. Church
Oliver L. Clarke, Jr.
Thomas W. Collens, Jr.
Fred Hunter Collins
Robert M. Conn
Herrick Ames Conners
Thomas P. Cooke
Fred Corales
Paul D. Cordes
James Crain
Harry Crane
John C. Culbertson
Dewey F. Daigle
J. Palfrey Dameron
John V. Dorsam, Jr.
Harry R. Davies, Jr.
George L. Degan
Carlos DeLaVega
Manual J. DeLerno
Lee H. DesBordes
Victor Dognibene
Francis P. Dolese
Samuel Domilise
Robert E. Donegan
Thomas M. Drury
John M. Dunn, Jr.
Louis Durigneaud
James T. Dwyer, Jr.
Ray Arthur Dyke, Jr.
Emile P. Eckart, Jr.
J. Douglas Eustis
John L. Evans, Jr.

Lloyd P. Fadrigue
Julius Finkelstein
Edward D. Finley
Marley R. Fisk, Jr.
William Fitzmorris
Peter Favalore
Raymond Flemming
Alvin Flettrich
James H. Fortson
Fred Forstall
George R. Fowler, Jr.
Benjamin A. Foy
Ernest H. Francis
Irwin Frankel
Louis T. Frantz
Harry W. Fristoe
Christopher Gadsden
Charles R. Gage, Jr.
Robert B. Galt
Marino Garrido
John M. Gaunt
Alvin A. Gautreaux
Arthur W. Goodwin
William J. Goodwin, Jr.
Frank C. Gough, Jr.
Lewis B. Graham
Berkley Green
Stephen L. Guice
Juel G. Guillot
Douglas C. Haley
Seymore Harris
James E. Heard
Richard A. Harred, Jr.
William B. Hefhelms
George R. Hercher
Martin L. Huber
Marvin L. Hyland
Albert M. Jeager, Jr.
Rodney C. Jung
Hurman Junker
Jerome W. King
.........ier, Jr.
Frank L. Lambert, Jr.
Leicester Landon

Bart LaRocca
Erwin A. LaRose
Benigno Castallano Larrea
George W. Lauriat
James W. Leake
Paul R. LeBlanc
Edward Leclier
Andre L. Lesartre
Morris E. Lepow
Arnold J. Levy
A. Herbert Levy, Jr.
Henry Lindner, Jr.
John D. Lockwood
Harold Loeb
J.F. Auguste Lorber
Louis C. Lozes
William B. McCampbell
Herbert J. McCampbell, Jr.
Martin L. McCoy
Philip McHargus
George Macdonald
Kay G. Magas
John M. Mahlen
Alex C. Maillbo
Bernard Manning, Jr.
George D. Martin, Jr.
Leonard S. Marx
Richard L. Mayes
William E. Melkild
Walter Menendez
Earl L. Mertzweiller, Jr.
Lloyd E Meyer
Norman J. Mitchell
Thomas H. Milligan
Julius R. Moore
Lucien Moret, Jr.
William Murry
John P. Noble, Jr.
J. Denver Normand
Charles J. O'Neil
Tom F. P. O'Neil
Francis J. Ory
John Pappas
Peter M. Pelegrini

George E. Perira, Jr.
Ernest R. Perez
Austin G. Phillips
Benjamin M. Phillips
Louis S. Pick
Robert Powell
Tom H. Pretorius
Leonard C. Ramon, Jr.
Lamar A. Ramos, Jr.

Bruno D. Redmond
James S. Rees
Frank B. Reid
James E. Reid
Charles S. Reily, Jr.
James H. Rester, Jr.
Leon Rich, Jr.
Harold F. Richter
Philip G. Ricks

Theodore B. Robinson
William Ryan
Edward Scanlon, Jr.
David H. Schueremann
John W. Schlosser
George T. Schneider
Armond F. Schroeder
Tom G. Schwalm
Robert Segura

Walter Shepard
Allen N. Smith
Irvin S. Smith
John P. Smith
Paul M. Smith
Charles A. Snea
John R. Sonderegger
Joe W. Stamps
James W. Spencer, Jr.
Joseph W. Stanley
George F. Sterkin
Sol B. Stone, Jr.
Jefferson Stewart
Edward M. St. John, Jr.

Julius Stone
Arthur W. Stout, Jr.
Harold H. Stream
Sam J. St. Romain, Jr.
Roy J. Tarontino
Durwood J. Thibodaux
George S. Thimish, Jr.
Oscar J. Tolmas
Roy P. Tooley
Anthony Tramontana
Israel Trestman
Leon M. Trice, Jr.
Michel Uspeh
Robert R. Vignes

Jean L. Villere
William E. Wakefield, Jr.
John R. Warriner
John J. Watzka
Martin S. Watsky
Billy A. Weisfeld
Albert W. Weller
Vernon S. Welman
David J. Wolbrette
Henry Worner, III
Max P. Zander
Edward Zinkow

ALCEE' FORTIER HIGH SCHOOL GRADUATES-JANUARY 1938

Harry D. Arnold
Albert G. Aufdemorte, Jr.
Earnest M. Barber
John P. Barnes
Hiram W.K. Batson
John P. Baudois
Christopher H. Bellone
Rudolph S. Bils
Walter C. Blattmann
Louis L. Brothers
Andrew B. Booth
James B. Booth
Robert J. Bosworth
Gerald B. Bulot
Aubry F. Buras, Jr.
Henry C. Carby, Jr.
Russell G. Charles
Edward J. Clement, Jr.
Robert M. Cole
Edward J. Collins
William H. Costa
Joseph A. Cuccia
John C. Daller
John R. Dearing
Theo W. Dietze
James F. Domingues
Edward F. Downing, Jr.
William T. Dowty
Richard F. Dicharry
Joseph E. Draube, Jr.
William M. Duffy
Donald B. Ehrhart
Charles A. Emling, Jr.
Edmond L. Faust, Jr.
Maurice C. Felix
Herbert Thayer Fichman
Arthur E. Fielder
Oswald F. Fischer

Harry Fischer, Jr.
Theodore Frank
Stephen P. Gasperocz, Jr.
James W. Googan, Jr.
Louis S. Gurvich
Leicester Hannibal, Jr.
Ray F. Harmeyer
Richard C. Hebert
Jed S. Henderson
Jacob J. Hess
Charles C. Hoerske
George P. Guthrie
Clarence R. Holloway
Sidney A. Holt
Leon Jacobs, Jr.
Walter I. Kahn
Gustave B. Keller
Robert J. Kelly
John H. Kimsey
John A. King
Matthew D. Logan
Henry J. Lamousis
Frederick Larson
John Lathan
Guy L. Leefe
Oliver Legendre
Myron C. Leidinger
Ellis Levin
Edward J. McGlaughlin
Lloyd A. McGlaughlin, Jr.
Patrick J. Manning
David Melville
Theo F. Middleton
Bennet C. Miller
Valdemar C. Mogensen
John E. Moragas
James A. Morgan
Ralph Moskowitz

Lloyd E. Mulligan
Charles P. Murphy
Walter M. Negrotto
Wesley G. Nutting
Percy H. Moise
Francis Jeff Oser
Charles P. Pertheux
John W. Perkowski
H.F. Pique
Leo C. Possen
William H. Pusch
Corwin B. Reed
William H. Reinhardt
Lucien W. Rolland
George T. Rouse
Albert P. Spaar, Jr.
Clifford L. Schmidt
Albert G. Schwartz
Robert W. Schupp
William D. Shaffer, Jr.
John W. Shepard, Jr.
Elliot Silverman
Stanley T. Smith
David Spizer
William F. Titton
Edward J. Thurber
Daniel L. Schmucker
Hyman C. Tolmas
Herman J. Twilbeck
Arthur S. Tycer
William H. Urban, Jr.
Albert T. Wakefield
Ralph Weaver
John D. Wilson
Bernard P. Wolfe
Samuel L. Wolfson

ALCEE' FORTIER HIGH SCHOOL GRADUATES-JUNE 1938

Domenic Arthur Albano
Franklyn J. Albrecht, Jr.
Paul Edward Arbo
Charles Conrad Armbruster
Edwin Weaver Arny, Jr.
Douglas Carrick Augustine
Stanley Lee Aultman
Harrie Wilson Backes, Jr.
Martin S. Baer
Gus Charles Bahn
Bruce Baird, Jr.
George Mutzen Baker
Leonard Francis Banowetz
Alfred Mason Barnes, Jr.
Francis Rowen Barnard, Jr.
David Norman Barr, Jr.
Roy Robbins Bartlett, III
Wilbur R. Beckman
Floyd Joseph Becknel
Ernest Arno Beier
David Bernstein
Frederick Crockett Billingsley
Ralph Herman Blattmann
Rocco Frank Bonura
Alfred Joseph Boudreaux
Leo Ve. Bradley
Albert Joseph Breaux, Jr.
John Thomas Brennan
Clarence Pitman Browne
Saul Charles Bruchis
William Peter Buckley, Jr.
Robert Leonard Bulot
E. Derwood N. Buniff
Thomas James Byrnes
Myron Burnstein
Simon Dresner Caplan
Raymond H. Capriotti
Joseph John Carboni, Jr.
John Francis Caruso
Maurice Samuel Cazubon
Charles J. Christina
Robert F. Clothier
Lester Ferdinand Coleman
Stephen Dennis Collins, Jr.
Eugene C. Coman
Norman David Copland
William McCubbin Costley, Jr.
William Biggs Cox
Timothy Albert Crain
David Emile Crais
Benjamin Crump
Charles Vincent Cuccia

Joseph Wilkerson Dale, Jr.
Edward R. Dannemann
Benjamin Bynner Davenport
James DeVeney
Edward Carlton Dietrich
Lawrence Losch Dillon
Walter E. Douglas, Jr.
Charles Alexander Dorhauer, Jr.
John Thomas Eagan, Jr.
Holmes Earl
William Howard Edwards
Lawrence Bres Eustis
Jacob B. Fallo
Warren P. Feldner
Edward Robustiano Ferro
Stanley Fink
Charles Louis Fischer, Jr.
James Stanford Fisk
Richard Curtis Fitzgerald
Jack P. Fitzner
Francis Lawrence Fitzpatrick
Lloyd James Fremaux
Charles Friedel, III
Kermit Frymire
Raymond Joseph Flanagan
Raymond Gauche, Jr.
Harold Hubert Gauthe
George A. Geerken
Casper Philip Gelbke, Jr.
Matthew Edward Genovese
Anthony Roy Giardina
Norman S. Glueck
Irving Diez Goldstein
Jack Gordon
Bernard Albert Grehan
Joseph Neville Grenier
Samuel Gilroy Gremillion, Jr.
Joseph V. Guidry
Leon J. Gullo
Richard Guthrie
William Ringler Hall
Nathan Halpern, Jr.
Jesse H. Harrell, Jr.
Edmond Milton Haley
Elmore Bernard Hauch, Jr.
Manuel Anthony Head
John C. Heausler, Jr.
Hector Joseph Hebert, Jr.
Frederick Jacob Heebe
Herman Hellman
Wolf Karl Hellmers
Sol Joseph Hershberg

Donald Hugh Higgins, Jr.
Harry Hirsch, Jr.
George August Hoffman
Paul M. Holzenthal
Albert L. Hopkins
Walter George Hoppmeyer, Jr.
Floyd Howell, Jr.
Charles Stanley Huete
Wallace Hunter
Ted Pearson Hutslar
Louis Adolph Ittmann
James M. Jennings
Ernest P. Johnson, Jr.
Robert Thomas Johnson
James E. Jomes
George Alexander Jorns, Jr.
L.J. Joseph
Theodore Charles Jourdan, Jr.
Myron Kass
John Edward Keff
John Alfred King
Floyd E. Keen
George Chester Koffskey, Jr.
Theodore John Kruse, Jr.
Anthony Edward LaBarre, Jr.
Sanford Jarold Joseph LaBorde
Delwin Peter Leguens
William J. Langlois, Jr.
John St. Paul Lanius
Milton Hinrichs Lasker
Richard Donald Lay
Lawrence Joseph LeBon, Jr.
Rene LeGardeur, III
Alan Jerry Lenovsky
Sydney Daniel Levy, Jr.
Edward B. Leverich
Wilbur Noel Lincks
Bernard Irving Lipkis
Theo F. Middleton
Gordon E. Lipscomb
Robert Warren Little
Matthew Louis Longuefosse
William Wright Loyal
Charles Wilson McArthur
Alvin George McCormick, Jr.
Jesse Steed McGee
Paul McGill, Jr.
Howell McMahon
Laurence Joseph Macaluso
Ronald Leslie Macke
Paul Kenney Malone
Michele N. Manalle

Roy Henry Manning
Spalding Kenan Manson, Jr.
Gordon Clayton Markel
John Warren Marshall
Robert P. Marshall
James H. Martin, Jr.
Harold Marx, Jr.
Ivan J. Mattes
Hunter W. May
Ernest Howard Mayrux
Joseph Allen Mayne
Albert Louis Meliet
William C. Menge
John Martin Miazza
Anthony Joseph Milazzo
Charles Lockett Miller
William J. Mogabgab
Neville Sidney Moise
Samuel S. Moody, Jr.
Thomas J. Moran
Owen Burton Munro
Michael Joseph Musmeci
Charles V. Nugent, Jr.
Alvin John Mut, Jr.
Roy O'Keefe, Jr.
Lionel Henry Orpin
Louis W. Ottermann
Pedro Flores Palma
Reginald Joseph Panquerne
Guy Raymond Parker, Jr.
William Sterling Parkerson
Benjamin George Perkowski
Shepard Francis Perrin
Carson S. Pettepher
Newby H. Pope
Benjamin Aby Petty
Tilden Pick
John D. Pique', Jr.

Frederick Walker Pitts
Joseph Anthony Prima
Robert N. Payette, Jr.
Maurice Antonio Ravelo
Irwin A. Rabinovitz
Emmette H. Reeks
Leo Ott Rhea
Raymond H. Rhode
Carlton Hubert Richard, Jr.
Richard Groves Riley
Manuel John Rivette
Earl Sherwood Robinson, Jr.
Frederick Edwin Robinson
Nicholas Alphonse Rouse
Albert M. Rush
Harry Charles Sadler, Jr.
C.W. Sanders, Jr.
John W. Sanders
Norman Joseph Sarrat
Ludwig T. Scherer, Jr.
Peter Charles Schmidt
Philip Christopher Howard
Schmidt
Oscar Schneidau
Donald Peter Scott
Stephen Joseph Scully
Silvare Alwyn Seeling
John Senac, Jr.
Alfred Gilbert Serio
John Joseph Sheppard, Jr.
William Francis Sherwood
Ashley Jacob Shocket
Julius J. Simon
Maurice Singer
Louis Fred Sivori, Jr.
Lee Slaughter
Edward Langdon Smith
Maxime L. Smith

Albert Lee Soule', III
Peter Joseph Staffoard
Hansen Hall Steele
Clovis Steib, Jr.
Carl Robert Stauss, Jr.
Glenn Erwin Taylor, Jr.
Charles Henry Tefft, Jr.
Davidson H. Texada
Joseph Guy Thibodaux, Jr.
Jack Waddell Thomson
Richard L. Thorpe
Jose' E. Torres
Jean Joseph Towne
Warren Edmund Trask
Rene J. C. Tricou, Jr.
William B. Troendle
Walter Tynes Tull
James Hugh Tullos
Jno. A. Usner, Jr.
Richard Gonzales Vela
Jorge Maldonado Villegas
Alvin Henry Vogt
Eugene Anthony Wagner, Jr.
Jesse Lee Wimberly
William Richard Wakeland
David A. Warriner, Jr.
Edward H. Watermeier, Jr.
John Drayton Williams Watts
William Joseph West
Charles Perry Willis
Holman R. Wherritt
Benjamin Franklin White, Jr.
Harold A. Whitman, Jr.
Florville Francis Whittaker, Jr.
Thomas Francis Williams
Issac Yambra

ALCEE' FORTIER HIGH SCHOOL GRADUATES-JANUARY 1939

Franklyn Albrecht, Jr.
LeRoy Allain, Jr.
Nathaniel Angell
Laurence Baird, Jr.
George Bartlett
Christen Berg
Bayard Bingham
Kenneth Blackwell
Lionel Charles Brietze
Theodore Broderick
Edmund Brown, Jr.
John Carughi, Jr.
Ferdinand Cefolia

Wilton Clay
Thomas Colley
Albert Collins
Henry Cook
Gutman Cranow
Nicholas Cromwell
Richard Cromwell
Warren Carrier
John Dean, Jr.
Edward Desforges
Joseph Devenny, Jr.
Charles Donnaud
Charles Eakin

John Earley
Benjamin Edwards
Harry Englebrecht
Harold Farnsworth, Jr.
Charles Felker
Emile Fenasci, Jr.
Ralph Friedel
Earl Forstall
Harold Fuchs
Peter Garrilli, Jr.
Richard Geisenheimer
Chester Georger
Edward Gerstner

Irwin Gibbs
Alfred Lopez Gonzalez
William Goodrow
Lloyd Gordon, Jr.
John Grush
George Gumpert, Jr.
Alfred Hale
Hector Hebert
Stanford Herron
James Himel
Herbert Hirtb
Ernest Huete, Jr.
John Ibert
Ellis Joubert
George Kane
Henry Katz
John Keff, Jr.
Bernard LaHasky
Joseph LaPlace
Albert Lambert

Robert Landry
Edward LaRose
Elmo Levy
Alexander LoCascio
Thomas Lupo
John McCarthy
James McCrary
Louis McFaul, Jr.
Claude Markbart
Harold Mayeur
Douglas Miller
Aaron Mintz
George Montgomery
John Murat
Bryden Pease
Joseph Power
Earl Perry
Samuel Rabinowitz
Simon Reems, Jr.
Clarence Sanders

Eugene Schaffer, Jr.
F. Dixon Schweinfurth
Salvadore Segreto
Murray Spindell
Lyall Shiell, Jr.
Charles P. Smith
Abraham Stabinsky
Dale Stancliff
Ralph Taylor, Jr.
Stephen Thorwegen
Herman Ungar
Edmund Vales
William Valls
Elroy Wasmuth
William Watlington
Harrison Weber
Thomas Wood
Louis Young

ALCEE' FORTIER HIGH SCHOOL GRADUATES-JUNE 1939

Richard G. Andry
Donald R. Angers
Warren Arceneaux
Frank Argote
Malcolm R. Arnoult
Norman A. Aronson
Thomas Ashley
Michael H. Bagot
H. Kieth Barnett
Earl P. Bartlett, Jr.
Herbert Barton
Carl S. Bauman
Bennie H. Bell, Jr.
Charles S. Bell
Linden D. Bentley
Peter R. Bertucci
Rudolph L. Bittman
Mose F. Bloomensteil
Milton D. Blumenthal
Henry Porter Boardman
Arthur W. Bohmfalk
Chandler G. Boswell
Henry B. Bradford, II
Oliver Bradford
Ervin B. Breazeale
Edward Joseph Brou
Victor H. Bruno
Warren C. Cable
Robert R. Cahal, Jr.
L. Beryl Canovsky
Gilbert M. Carp
Joseph J. Casselberry
John F. Clemmer, Jr.

Henry R. Cocreham, Jr.
Marx Cohen, Jr.
Paul H. Collette
Peter A. Constanza
John M. Cooner
Louis S. Copponex
R. E. Lee Cornwell
Harold J. Counce
Robert E. Courtin, Jr.
David Covert
William B. Craft
Paul J. Cresap
Sidney J. Crochet, Jr.
Lear W. Dane
Edwin E. Danner, Jr.
Rosario J. DeCorte
Ira T. Dell
Samuel P. Denmark
Walter A. Doucet, Jr.
David F. Douglas
John F. Delany
Robson B. Dunwody
Frank C. Dutrey
Lloyd E. Eagan
James L. Earhart
William R. Eason
Randolph R. Edwards
John K. Elgin, Jr.
Fernando J. Estopinal
Even Evanoff
Charles R. Evans
Charles J. Falkenstein
Joseph P. Fasullo

Charles F. Fee
Joseph V. Fein
Paul A. Ferara
George B. Fiegle
Elmer H. Flair
Howard J. Fleck
David M. Fraiser
Charles W. Frank, Jr.
Charles N. Frisbie
Peter Fumusa
Gordon Gaille
Richard D. Gaille
Robert M. Gaines, Jr.
Peter Garrilli, Jr.
James C. Garrison
Edwin Henry Gebhardt
Walter F. Gemeinhardt
Green B. Gillespie
Alvin G. Gottschall
Osmond B. Green
Bernard J. Grieshaber
Darrell E. Griffin, Jr.
David Haas
Broos R. Hall
Leonard Halpern
Dan Handleman
Charles A. Hanson
Edward W. Hardin
Edward N. Hecker, Jr.
F. Jack Higgins
Edward C. Hingle, Jr.
Francis X. Hoeffner, Jr.
Julius W. Hohenstein

Kenneth M. Holloway
John A. Homes
Hamilton H. Howry, Jr.
Earl L. Ittmann, Jr.
Harold C. Jackson, Jr.
William J. Jacobi
Bernard L. Jacobs
Thomas A. James, Jr.
Edwin George Jane, Jr.
Ellis Jaubert
Neils W. Johnson
Arthur B. Johnson
Robert T. Johnson
Gordon L. Joseph
Ashton S. Junker
Joseph T.A. Katz, Jr.
Leon D. Katz
Raymond T. Kelly
Michael E. Kenny

Joseph F. Keppel, Jr.
Harry L. Kirkland
Victor F. Kirschman
David M. Kleck
Leon Klinger
George F. Klumpp
Edward H. Knight, Jr.
Wilkes A. Knolle
Ernest W. Koehler
Allen B. Koltun
Joseph Krail
Herbert G. Kurz
Roger J. Laderer
Joseph M. LaLande, Jr.
J. Marcel Lambert
Norman Lamont
August C. Lang
Anthony Joseph LaRocca
Rosario LaRocca

Stanley K. Lawrence
Earl F. Lea
Raymond J. Leicht
Leonard Leon
LeRoy J. Leonard
Julian M. Levy
Joseph E. Lewis, Jr.
Edward G. Luck
Edward G. Ludtke, Jr.
Burley B. Lufburrow
Roy M. Lusher, Jr.
Gehard E. Maale
Charles Maginnis
John D. Maginnis
William Maginnis, III
Hubert G. Manning, Jr.
George E. McCaskey, Jr.
William L. McLeod
Ernest E. McSpadden, Jr.

William K. McWilliams, Jr.
Lloyd C. Melancon
Walter C. Meyer
Allen L. Miller, Jr.
Aaron Mintz
Charles L. Modenbach
David Monroe
Bernard P. Mooney, Jr.
Jay Merrill Moter, Jr.
Alvin J. Muller
Henry J. Mumme
Charles T. Myers
David Neuhauser
Robert E. Newlin
George C. Nungesser, Jr.
Arthur E. O'Connor, Jr.
Ward F. J. Odenwald, Jr.
Herbert O'Donnell, Jr.
Frank B. O'Leary, Jr.
Charles J. Olson
Stanford Opotowsky
Joseph E. O'Sullivan, Jr.
Earl Paddock
Carlo J. Palermo
Edwin M. Palmer
John J. Palmer
Sam H. Parkerson
Tom B. Parkerson
John J. Pastorek
Jan N. Pedersen
Malcolm S. Peters
Earl Pizzo
Francis C. Poche, Jr.
Thomas W. Pope, Jr.

Frank Anthony Porretto
Anthony Ragas
William A. Rappold
Jacob L. Rasch
Rodney F. Redmond
John B. Regan
Huston C. Reynolds
Joseph V. Riccobono
John T. Roberts
Donald James Rodriguez
Gordon W. Rohrbacker
Louis J. Rosenbohm
Joseph H. Rosher
John B. Ross, I
Fred L. Ruckert, Jr.
Charles F. Russo
Paul J. E. Rydell
Anthony Sachitano
Bernard A. Salomon
David H. Scanlan
Herbert A. Schaffer, Jr.
Vernon L. Scharfenstein
Clifford H. Schlessinger, Jr.
Parker Schneidau
George C. Schroeder, Jr.
Fred J. Schuber, Jr.
Charles Schwartz, Jr.
Angell J. Segreto
Warren C. Shankle, Jr.
Ralph F. Shiver, Jr.
Foster Silva
Salvadore J. Simeone
Harry V. Sims, Jr.
Charles Singerman

Fred J. Smith
Otto R. Smith, Jr.
Homer D. Solanas
Clay Spencer
Leonard M. Spiegel
George H. Stanton, Jr.
William W. St. Clair
Maurice I. Stewart
Lester M. Stockard
Edwin W. Stockmeyer
Russell T. Surridge
Maurice A. Theriot
Clarence H. Thomas
Charles F. Thomason
Harold A. Timken, Jr.
Leo J. Trahan, Jr.
James R. Tranchina
Joseph J. Tricou
Ralph L. Trosclair
Creston R. Troxler, Jr.
Gordon E. Trunnel
Stanley Udin
Daniel Leon Verges
Daniel H. Vliet, Jr.
Michel C. Volz
Engle C. Walker
Robert B. Wallace
Louis T. Walsdorf, Jr.
John McCarthy Ward
Richey L. Waugh
Robert J. L. Waugh
Gerald N. Weiss
Morris G. West
Robert N. Wiegand

Robert L. Willard
William Wiss
Edgar J. Wolfe

Calvin J. Worrel
Stanley H. Yarborough
Edward J. Zatarain, Jr.

David N. Zoller

ALCEE' FORTIER HIGH SCHOOL GRADUATES-JANUARY 1940

James Robert Alexander
Paul Michael Andrieu
John Christopher Arnos, III
Edward James Arpin
George B. Barnett
Hubert C. Barrios
LaMar McCormick Barthet
James P. Basha
Merritt Charles Becker, Jr.
Daniel Thomas Becnel
Donald S. Biewer
Hilton Melvin Blalock
Leonard Joseph Bowers
John M. Breslin, Jr.
Frank V. Boylan
Henry Gerod Bulliard
Steve Carra
Paul Jung Cavanah
Francis I. Cervantes
Anthony J. Chimento
Hubert Clotworthy
Lyle A. Crews
Christian Crusta
Walter Daniel
Warren A. Delacroix, Jr.
Wallace B. Diboll, Jr.
Byron E. Dodd, Jr.
George Paul Dorsey
Noel T. Dressel, Jr.
Wayne Phillip Ducomb
Anton Ericksen
Pratt Farnsworth
Frederick Fiegel, Jr.
John C. Freese
Louis Raymond Frey
C. Walter Gray
Jack Gerald Gray
Nathan Greenbert
Gordon Gsell

Broos R. Hall
Nathan Hamilton
George Higgins
Roland Higgins
Richard L. Holman
Willliam M. Hughes
Edwin Isolani
Irving E. Johnson, Jr.
Jules Zang Johnson
Harry N. Jumonville
Carroll Ketteringham
Vernon R. Kistner
George Lagroue
William Lagroue
Clarence W. Lane
Benny L. Lampo
William K. Lewis
Kirby J. Lindsley, Jr.
Adrian L. McAuley
James Samuel McCormack
Duggan H. McCrary, Jr.
Thomas E. McLaffon, Jr.
Adolph J. Maier, Jr.
Jack Peter Mancuso
Richard McKinney Meyer
Earl Frederick Minning, Jr.
Fernand Mire
Eugene Meyers Moppert, Jr.
Joseph R. Oelkers, Jr.
Rodney Gipsy Olsen
Marechal N. O'Quinn, Jr.
Edmund N. O'Rourke
Gilbert Ory
Lawrence Ory
Gustave Pailet
Jack Stephen Pereira
Sam Salvadore Perino
Ray Carter Perry, Jr.
Anthony J. Pillittere

Nolan Pittman
Ellis Michael Pisciotta
William Alfred Poche
Warren Raymond Puneky
Frank H. Roark, Jr.
John Walter Rock
John P. Rooker
Milton I. Rosenson
Edwin Noon Rossiter
Frank J. Russell, Jr.
Edward H. Sanford
Harry E. Schafer, Jr.
Charles C. Schenuck, Jr.
Frank Schneider, Jr.
Jefferson Schneider
Hebert E. Schussler, Jr.
Frederic D. Schwarz
William H. Seither, Jr.
James K. Simpson
Milton B. Singleton
Clyde Richard Stanley
Samuel A. Steeg
David Weill Stern
Rees Daniel Stith
Tommy Stokes
William Thomas, Jr.
Roy A. Troendle
Harrison Troop
Robert L. Vaccaro
Jack West
Gerald J. Whitman
William L. Whitman
Sebastian S. Wilkinson
James A. Williams
Milton B. Wise
William B. Wise
Leonard Sol Wolf

ALCEE' FORTIER HIGH SCHOOL GRADUATES-JUNE 1940

Bernard Abadie, Jr.
John W. Adams, Jr.
Arthur M. Adolph
Henry R. Alker, Jr.
Henry L. Anderson
Fred George Anepohl
Sidney H. Antin
Lloyd J. Arbo

Ellis Aronson
Stanley V. Asbury
Richard C. Ashman
James S. Assunto
Daniel S. Babin
Joseph M. Barkoff
Richard A. Barnes, Jr.
Robert Hopkins Bartley

Reginald W. Barry
Quintin L. Bennett
Landry J. Bernard, Jr.
Joseph Bernstein, Jr.
Edmond P. Bertheaud
Russell R. Biaggne
Laurence F. Bienvenu
Roy J. Billet

Harold L. Block
Taylor B. Bodkin
Robert R. Bond
Charles E. Bordes
Herman H. Bothner, Jr.
Richard B. Bowes
Wallace W. Bradford
Ben B. Brill, Jr.
Wendell B. Brock
Clarence M. Buckles
Wilmer J. Buckley
Henry G. Buse
Elroy J. Cain
Donald G. Callaway
Joseph C. Cangelosi
Ewell C. Cantey, Jr.
Roy Glenn Cappel
Lyle F. Carriere
Leslie B. Case, Jr.
Henry G. Casserleigh, Jr.
George M. Chester
William W. Christy
Hays B. Clark, Jr.
Albert H. Cohen
Allen D. Colley
James D. Connell
Lucas S. Conner, Jr.
Charles Conrad
George E. Conroy, Jr.
Milton John Cook
Asahel W. Cooper, Jr.
Harris Copenhaver, Jr.
J. Edward Couper
Elgin C. Cowart, Jr.
John F. Crawford
James H. Crosby
Prentiss L. Daffan
Robert F. D'Aunoy
Clyde L. Davis, Jr.
Gem R. Davis, Jr.
Michael A. DeCorte
Joseph DeLerno, Jr.
Walter G. Doell, Jr.
Leonhard L. Dowty

Leonard L. Dreyfus
Lloyd S. Durmeyer
Alvin E. Duvernay
Hunter Lee Early
Peter Elorriaga, Jr.
Edward L. Emling
Eugene A. Esparros, Jr.
Hugh Edward Evans
Walter E. Evans, Jr.
Thomas J. Feehan
Irving Feltenstein
Harold Raymond Ferro
William B. Finney
Edward J. Fischer
John A. Fitzgerald
Phares Frantz
Alex S. Freedman
Narvin B. Frickman
Carl R. Froeba
Gaudern Gadmer
Warren J. Gadpaille
Robert B. Gage
Roger C. Gardner, Jr.
Maurice B. Gatlin, Jr.
Pierre Gelpi
Francis J. Gillane
Jefferson J. Gillane
Eugene J. Gomez, Jr.
Henry E. Graham, III
Russell J. Gray
Joseph A. Guerra
Frederick H. Guidry
David P. Guinle
Carl A. Gumpert
Alden E. Hagadorn
Edward J. Hannahan
Richard D. Harang
Francis M. Harris, Jr.
Henry J. Haydel
Edward E. Heausler
Joseph F. Hermann, Jr.
Henry J. Hermes
Louis M. Heuchert, Jr.
Henry J. Hildebrand, Jr.

John D. Hinckley
Alois M. Hirt, Jr.
Warren H. Hoppmeyer
James D. Horney
Richard F. Hughes
Melville J. Jacobson
William E. James, Jr.
William J. Jason
Roy C. Jensen, Jr.
Daniel W. Johnston
Charles B. Jones
Ernest N. Kahn
John B. Kane
Norman J. Kauffmann, Jr.
Francis J. Kelley
Lewis J. Krail
Louis H. Krieger
Charles D. LaBorde
Lloyd L. Lacher, Jr.
James D. Lambeth
Leopold M. LaPoutge
Donald A. Lassus
Raymond L. Lee
Theodore J. Leres
Allison M. Levy
David P. Levy
Gus D. Levy
Michel Levy
Harper G. Lewis, III
Charles A. Lopez
Turner S. Lux, Jr.
Robert H. McCabe
Malone D. McCain
Lee F. McCrocklin
Nicholas Macaluso
David H. Machauer
Victor P. Maisano
Ray R. Marino
John D. Marshall, Jr.
William L. Marshall
Jack J. Martin
George J. Mattingly
Conrad L. Mavor
Daniel A. Mayer

Val. M. Menendez
Edward C. Merrill, Jr.
John H. Michell
Boyd P. Milburn, Jr.
Charles Miller
Ellis Mintz
Joseph P. Mitanti
Ridgley Moise, Jr.
Robert Mc. Montgomery

John F. Moser, Jr.
Robert E. Murphy
Cornel W. Nett
Paul S. Nobel
Douglas T. O'Keefe
Robert P. O'Neill
Searcy M. Parker
Godfrey R. Parkerson
Carroll Passmore

Gerald C. Pelias
Harold C. Pelias
Brewer F. Pense
Theodore Perlman
Louis F. Perret
Vincent R. Perrin, Jr.
Howard J. Pertuit
Urban J. Pfefferle
John L. Poche

William F. Polchow, Jr.
Paul C. Potthorst
Joseph S. Pourciau, Jr.
Louis V. Provensal, III
Robert E. Ratelle
Calvin A. Rauch
Warren A. Rauch
J. Robert Reinhard, Jr.
Joseph F Reith, Jr.
Alexander E. Reitz
Adrian F. Reynolds
Stephen J. Richard
Adolph J. Rinck
Edward R. Robertson
Houston L. Roby, Jr.
Francis L. Rock
Robert M. Rohrbacker
Vincent Roy Rosche
John C. Rourke
Harold M. Schambach
Jack R. Schega, Jr.
Donald B. Schell
Alvin F. Schlosser

Karl Schneidau, Jr.
Andrew J. Schwabe, Jr.
Angelo J. Sciortino
George A. Seaver, III
Joseph S. Serio, Jr.
Joseph P. Sexton, Jr.
William D. Sheppard
Herbert R. Sieger, Jr.
Harold Simmons
Leon Sinawsky
Charles Boerner Skinner, Jr.
Roland C. Smith
Joseph R. Spillmann
Thomas Snow
Charles E. Steidtmann, Jr.
Edwin J. Stewart, Jr.
Walter S. Stone
A. C. Suhren, Jr.
Robert J. Swayne, Jr.
Malcolm J. Tailleur
Edwin J. Taylor, Jr.
Charles G. Timish
Wieck W. Timish

James W. Tucker
William Van der Haeghen
Manuel M. Vega, Jr.
David E. Verlander, Jr.
Joseph A. Vignes
Edward J. Vives, Jr.
Thomas O. Wakeman
William E. Walker, Jr.
Walter G. Wedig, Jr.
Fred August Wendt, Jr.
William H. West
William T. West, Jr.
Thomas C. Wicker, Jr.
Charles B. Williams, Jr.
Knighton Williams
John F. Williams
Malcolm J. Williams
William A. Williams
Robert C. Wolley
Ronald A. Worrel
Charles F. Wusthoff, Jr.
Harvey T. Zammit

ALCEE' FORTIER HIGH SCHOOL GRADUATES-JANUARY 1941

Conrad H. Appel
Horace J. Arceneaux
Forest S. Aucoin
Henry D. Bacon
Julius R. Barr
Edgar L. Belsom
Jack A. Biquenat
David S. Binnings
John W. Boebinger
Edward D. Bourdel
William F. Burchardt
Paul I. Burtuccini
Clifford H. Cadis
Anthony L. Cefalu
Frederick Chatry
Ralph B. Chevis, Jr.
Karl L. Cooper
Joseph B. Corry
Leo P. Creel
John B. Cruell
Richard L. Daigle
Remy D. Delacroix
Randolph G. Dodd
Lawrence J. Dowling
Lawrence C. Dugan
Roy J. Duthu
Nicholas K. Edrington
Doug J. Ehrensing
Martial C. Esparros
Harold M. E. Faller, Jr.

Sal J. Federico
James S. Flower
Joseph P. Felix
James A. Fitzgerald
Lawrence P. Forstall
Warren A. Forstall
Roy F. Frantz, Jr.
Otto Gelsenheimer, Jr.
Thomas J. Gillane
Gustave A. Gondran
Earl P. Gore
Frank J. Graff
Gilbert Groetsch
Alton S. Hall
Roderick G. Heausler
Elliot J. Hebert
Lewis J. Heroy
Keith C. Hotard
John R. Hillery
Wilmer G. Hindricks
Gerald P. Hirt
Julius S. Hoffman
Alva B. Howell
Warren R. Hugo
Harold Husser
Irwin Isaacson
Warren E. Johncke
Shepard G. Jane'
Edward T. Jennings
Clifford H. Jordon

William C. Kelton
Frederick N. Kemp
Fred E. Kleyle
Frank J. Knecht
Clayton E. Kruse
Paul F. Lacey
Victor B. Larocca
Leo C. Lob
Harold B. McCarthy
Jesse McNeil
C. Edward Madere
John F. Maxwell
Harold Melville
John J. Meyer
Rudolph Moise
Theodore Moise
Edgar T. Morris
Richard P. Newman
George R. Newport
Earl L. Parker
Felecian Perrin
Chester A. Peyronnin
Monroe L. Porter, Jr.
Roy A. Provenzano
Joseph Raspilair
Plez Reid
Henry J. Rosche
Clifford M. Roth
Roland P. Sackett
Dave J. Sall

Kenneth J. Schmidt
Howard A. Schrieffer
Lewis W. Schuler
George K. Shaw
John M. Shay
Sam H. Singer
George J. Stark

James R. Stiles
Roy M. Streckfus
John M. Stumborg
Thomas Tomeny
Charles D. Tuyes
Louis J. Uzee
Ludwig H. Von Gohren

William V. Walker
Bernard B. Waller
Edwin K. Wilkins
Esmar K. Williamson
Harold L. Zebal

ALCEE' FORTIER HIGH SCHOOL GRADUATES-JUNE 1941

Charles Adams
Louis Adam
Mario Aguilar
Karl Aijian
Philip Albrecht
Roy Amiss
Curtis Amuedo
Warner Anthony
Morgan Atwood
Butler Avery
George Baccich
Robert Bain
Clifton Baker
Raoul Barrios
Gordon Bangs
Michel A. Becnel
Bernard I. Bennett
Quintin Bennett
Denis Bergeron
Harold J. Bergeron
David Bierhorst
Harold Blaum
Benjamin Bourgeois
Louis Bourgeois
Walter Brauer
Samual Breen
Harold Bres
Edwin Brooks
August Brown
George Bucher
William Burbank
Arthur Burdon
Louis Burkes
James Byrne
Joseph Cali
Frank Calix
Gabriel Cassagne
Elroy Citron
John Clement
Philip Closmann
Max Constantine
Hansford Cowart
B. Rex Cross
Roy Deck
Joseph M. DeFraites
James Denny

Douglas Diboll
Robert Dillon
Edgar Dixey
Henry Doell
Ernest Drackett
Edwin Dressel
Harris Dulitz
Albert Dureau
Frederick Elliott, Jr.
Coleman Ezkovich
Norris Fant
Francis Favaloro
Calvin Fay
Wallis Feigler
Raymond Ferran
William F. Fink
Ashton Fischer
Charles Fisk
Brown Fortier
Louis Fortier
Arthur Foss
Jerry Frances
Alvin Frechter
Arthur Freeman
Lafayette Gaines
Louis J. Gallo
Richmond Galbreath
Peter Galiano
Glenn Gardner
Edward Gauthier
William Geagan
Louis Gernhauser
Peter Giuffria
Leon Goldblum
Herbert Goldstein
Kenneth M. Goll
James Gore
Oscar Gomez
Cyril Gray
Adolph Grishman
Frank Grunewald
Hoffman Guidry
James Gulotta
A.J. Gumina, Jr.
Charles Hadler
Henry Haffner

Lionel Hammock
Raymond Hammond
William Hawkins
Joseph Hebert
Douglas Henriques
Henry Herbert
William Herbst
Joseph Hero
Charles Herrick
Aubrey Heumann
Calvin Hoppmeyer
Merril Hughes
Elliot Hull
Robert Jacks
Arthur Janneck
A. Metz Kahn
Charles Kahn, Jr.
Eugene Katz
Morton Kaufman
Clarence Keller
William Kellner
Lloyd Kelly
Noell Kerr
Edward Keiler
Norman Kientz
Edward King
Paul Kohlmann
Stanley Kolton
Yngvar Krantz
Fred Kreger
Albert Lachin
Louis Gallo
Nevil Lambert
Frank Lamothe
William Lang
Edwin Lankston
Roy Lassus
Harold Lawrence
Raymond W. Lawton
Chester Leathers
William J. LeBlanc
Albert Ledner
Maurice Levin
Bernard Levy
Oscar Levy, Jr.
John Lozes

George Lucas
Sam McArthur
Thomas M. McBride
Thomas McCoy
Patrick McHugh
Armand Manning

Charles Martin
John Miller
Kenneth Miller
John Miner
Albert O. Mohr
George Montalbano

John Moore
Leonard B. Morais
Kenneth Muller
Richard Muller
Earl Nall
Warren Negrotto

Albert Nierzwicki
Allen Oden
Charles D. Oliver
Ray Olsen
Henry Oppenheim
Wilmer O'Rourke
John Parham
Charles Parra
Richard Pastorek
Lucius Patterson
Louis Perrilloux
Salvadore Perino
Steve Perino
Roy Perry, Jr.
Calvin Phelps
Richard Piske, Jr.
Arthur Pitcher
Ross Pizzitola
Williard Pounds
Alvin Prechter
Leo Radosta
Lucius Raffield
Robert J. Reinhardt
Leon Reiss
Joseph Ritter
Elmer Robeau
Alan J. Robinson
Vernon Robinson
Palmer Roessle
Harold Rosen

Robert C. Rourke
Edwin Roux
Armand Ruffo
George Ruhlman, II
Dan Scharff
Louis Sharfenstein
George Scherer
Albert Schipplein, Jr.
John Schluter
Howard Schmalz
Edward L. Schmidt, Jr.
Ricker Schmitt
Harold Schweitzer
Carl Schneider
Frank Sciacca
Philip Sciortino
Elroy Scott
Fulton W. Seale
Robert Senter
William Shepard
John Sherrouse
Warren Silva
Stephen Simoneaux
Jerry Sims
Irving Singer
G. W. "Jimmy" Small
Arnold Smason
Perry Spanier
William Stahl
Daniel Stark

Leo Stein
Lee Stentz
Eugene St. John
Roy Stoll
Sam Sulli
Richard Tarlton
James Thompson
Pat Tomeny
Herman Triche
William Trufant
Milton Tucker
Herman Wagner
Harold Walzer
Maurice Weinstein
Neol Weintraub
Clifford Welsh
Harmon West
Norman West
Alvin Wexler
George White
John Wiggin
James Williams
Louis Williams, Jr.
Robert Williams
David Winston
Harold Woods
Robert Woolfolk
Maurice Wynne
John Youngblood
Earl Zander

ALCEE' FORTIER HIGH SCHOOL GRADUATES-JANUARY 1942

Cyril Lloyd Acomb
Alfred Alder
Chester L. Alba
Charles Joseph Alfortish
Louis B. Ampolisk
Charles Jules Aronson
Lawrence Baird Ashman
Hubert J. Badeaux
Lucas R. Bagnetto
Saul H. Barber
Walter Sidney Barnes
William H. Bartlett, Jr.
Clifford L. Bennett
Joseph B. Bethancourt

Richard F. Blake
Thomas Edwin Bonner
August Steven Bono
Harry W. Bourgeois
Albert Henderson Bowes
Allden William Bowman
Charles Edward Bright
Delfin V. Brooks
Gerard T. Brotmeyer
Jordan Brown
Edwin L. Bruchis
Hoffman G. Brulet
Charles Joseph Buckley
Frank Joseph Canale

Lee Roy Cavin
Albert Maurin Charlton
Ignatius Paul Chairello
Ralph Edward Compagno
Albert Emerson Cook
Henry J. Crocheron
Norman A. Davis
Edwin William Doerries
Alonzo P. Emerson, Jr.
Lawrence A. Ferran, Jr.
Thomas Clifford Ficken
John O. Folse
Hollis Ganier
David Gansar

A. D. Geoghegan, Jr.
Henry P. Goodwin
Fred Maybin Gore
William Caruthers Graves
Scuddy Paul Gross
Angelo Gumina
Elbert J. Hodge, Jr.
Andrew C. Hoffmann
Ralph Raymond Hogan
Kamiah L. Johnson
William G. Johnson, Jr.
Allen Jumel
William Kimble
Irving Klein
David Paul Kloete
Herman Kobrock
Alden A. Krebs
Herbert J. Kuperman
Clancey A. Latham, Jr.
John Callan Leefe
Marvin L. Leonard
Walbert G. Levy
Sherman Lew

Horance Little
Carlos Joseph Lozano, Jr.
Pierre Lannaux
Waren J. McGovern
Albert Bruce McGraw
Norman W. McLeod
John L. Mahoney
Edward Makofsky, Jr.
Richard F. Maxwell, Jr.
Daniel L. Mendel, Jr.
David Scott Moodie
Lloyd Edwin Moppert
Patrick Joseph Nain
Julian Katz Opotowsky
Patrick H. O'Reilly, Jr.
Charles A. Perrenod, Jr.
F. Raymond Pfister, Jr.
Charles E. Polchow
Julian B. Rauch
Edward George Reppel, Jr.
Norman deLos Rice
Harold George Richard
Lynwood J. Rodriguez

William Firstbrook Rogers
Richard William Rooney, Jr.
Warren Payne Rosenthal
Norman Frank Sauls
Emile A. Schayot
John William Schill
Paul Elwood Seemann
Saul Silverman
S. Sharpe Stanfield
John E. Stephens, Jr.
Leo Arthur Stubbs
J. Arlon Thedy
Donald W. Urquhart
Leon J. Valley
Joseph Vanderbrook
Malcoln A. Vignes
Lester W. Wainer
Stephen B. Webb, Jr.
Dave Tobias Weinstein
Joseph Wilhelm
David Hoover Yockey
Andre H. Zilbermann
Marks Zion

ALCEE' FORTIER HIGH SCHOOL GRADUATES-JUNE 1942

Marshall Elliott Adams
James Franklin Albright, Jr.
Luis Guillermo Alvarez
Walter H. Amspoker
Albert Field Andre
Frederick Robert Andrews
Vincent Angelo Antara
Calvin Leo Astredo
Thomas Carl Babington
Joseph William Balmer
Herman J. Bankston
John Morgan Bass, Jr.
Thomas Loyal Bate
Ernest C. Belmont, Jr.
Raymond Wright Benfield
Ned William Berkermer
Richard George Black
James Buchanan Blitch
Harold Joseph Blum
Donald Forbes Blythe
Conrad Oscar Bostrom
Lloyd Raymond Bothner
Kenneth Francis Bowen
Robert Wells Breeden, Jr.
Stanley Marion Bressler
Charles Herbert Brewer
Robert Earl Bridges
Eldon Emmet Broders
Douglas Joseph Brown
Edward Samuel Brown

Percy Bernard Brugier
Ralph Edmond Burt
Matt Alphonse Buillung
William Denman Burch
Edward Henry Bultman, Jr.
Louis Joseph Burg, II
John Edward Burga
Frank H. Cain
Gerald Caldwell Cambias
Edmund Howard Campbell
Gerard Norbert Casso
Jack Henry Celestine
John Hitchcock Chamberlain
Robert Joseph Cheatham, Jr.
Leon W. Chelette
Jourdan Mark Clapp
Thomas Dean Clark
Louis Ray Clements
William James Cloud
John Stuart Coleman, Jr.
Forres McGraw Collins
William Dreaux Collins
Joseph Jenkins Cornish, III
Ralph Sidney Covert
John Lawrence Crosby
Sandy Grueling Davies
Richard G. Davis
Edwin Peter Delaney, Jr.
Dalton Ewell Delph, Jr.
Theodore Louis Demuth

Robert Edward Doell
John Joseph Dowie
Robert Culpepper Drouet
Charles Harry Dryfoos
Robert Frederick Dykhuizen
Louis Joseph Elliott
Raymond D. Ellison
Roy Charles Englebracht
Donald James Estopinal
George Louis Evans
Willard Stanyon Evans, Jr.
John Adrien Falcon, Jr.
Burk James Fanguy
Bartley Woodrow Farrell
Edward James Favaloro
Leon John Feugas, Jr.
Milton Henry Finger
Charles Harry Flair
Prescott Herrick Sandys Follett
John William Fornof
Horace Frank Foster
Gerland Joseph Foucha, Jr.
Roy Allan Frazier
Philip David Leon Frank
Ross H. Freer
Charles John Funk
Bill Grant Gaffney
Roy A. Geerken
Clarence L. Geier, Jr.
John William Giardina

William H. Gillane
Louis Arco Gily, Jr.
Harry John Glass, II
John Elwell Goetz
Jules Aloysius Grasser
Norman J. Gremillion
John I. Griffith
Frederick Miller Guice
Jack Gurry
Theester Ambroze Hamby, Jr.
Thomas Joseph Haney
Phillip Sand Hansel
Carl George Hartman
Hans Norbert Heinemann
Earl Joseph Henry
Michel Murrell Herbst
Richard Donald Herr
Harold Louis Herrmann
Paul John Herrmann
Durell A. Hiller
David Dexter Himel
Charles Louis Hock
David Rolland Hooks, Jr.
Nicholas Huber, Jr.
Robert Leon Humphreys
Richard Ingolia
William Andrew Ingraham
Robert Adams James
Robert Ollie James
Abner John Jeansonne
Paul Edward Tyson Jensen
Carroll Allen Johnson
Richard McElhiney Johnson
David Kancher
Edwin Marvin Katten, Jr.
Frederick William Keese, Jr.
Benjamin F. Kelley
H. Bradford Kelly
Elias Klein
Milton Albert Kuehne
Robert Edward Kunz
Charles Ray Landry
Stanley Harold Langer
Eugene Hinton Lawes
Guy J. LeBreton, Jr.
Rene Lehmann
Grenes John Lennox
David Charles Levin

Douglas Pokorny Levey
Richard Leslie Levy
James Iddo Lewis, Jr.
James Alphonse Lindsay
Maurice Little
Coleman Lubritz
Richard Henry McCrocklin
Emanuel Thomas McEvoy, Jr.
George Edward McLean
Clyde Austin McLeod
John Lloyd McLeod
Stephen Ludlow McMurray
Frank Salvadore Mannino
Donald Joseph Maillho
William Emile Martin, Jr.
Walter J. Martiny, Jr.
James Donald Matheny
Robert Markus May
Frederick Thomas Miller
Robert Madison Moore
Anees Mogabgab, Jr.
Harold Emanual Morais, Jr.
Charles Elbert Munden, III
George Alwyn Muths
George Daniel Neumann
John Stewart Neville
Joseph William Nicoll
Murray Ned Padwa
Milton Pailet
Paul Gideon Parra
Leonard Peatross Parrish
Sidney Kirby Pate
George Edmund Pearce
Hector Louis Perez
Alvin Paul Perry
John Cooper Petagna
Donald Burvant Pfefferle
John Joseph Pfister
Calvin Jerome Pflug
Alan Sidney Pincus
Alvin John Pittman
Valentine F. W. Polchow, Jr.
Berkeley Lake Poole
Bartholomew Fred Ponze
Anthony J. Porretto
Glauco Joseph Posseno
James Arnott Pratt
Raymond John Pujol

Anthony Dominick Ragusa
Irwin Matthew Rappold
Arthur Robert Reeb, Jr.
Wallace Albert Reed
Leo Reilly
Richard Burke Reynaud
Luis Arturo Rivera S.
Emile Leo Rivette
Robert Edwin Rosenbohm
Joe Rosenfield, III
Kenneth Bryan Rutland
Ralph Ronald Santos
Edward L. Schambach
Charles Christopher Scheu, Jr.
Robert John Schnyder, Jr.
Alfred John Schorling
Ray L. Scully
Maurice Simon
Ira Sheldon Slobodien
Melvin A. Solomon
Evan Ragland Soule
Douglas Perret Starr
Julian P. Stern
Roy Stewart
Charles Gregg Stokes, Jr.
Powell Burton Stokes
Sam Payne Stone
John Albert Tauzy, Jr.
Kenneth T. Teague
Stanley James Tefft
George Philip Terrebonne
William Edward Tucker
Frederick Henry Vanderbrook
Ralph Gerard Watermeier
Bryson Reid Watts
Charles Hartwell Weatherly, Jr.
Conway Oscar Welch
Lawrence Henry White
Andrew Peter Whitman, Jr.
Howard George Wiedemann
William Harold Wilkes
Harry John Williams, Jr.
Thomas Bryan Wilson, Jr.
Horace Milton Wolfe
Miles Frank Wortham
David Lester Zerlin

ALCEE' FORTIER HIGH SCHOOL GRADUATES-JANUARY 27, 1943

Daniel B. Alexander
William R. Averill
James R. Barnes
Robert F. Bermudez
Russell V. Bevelarque

Edwin P. Bultman, Jr.
Wilbert E. Butz
Carl D. Charbonnet
Morris F. Fakin
Leo Finegold

Albert F. Finnegan
Ewald F. Groetsch
Joseph C. Guillot
Fred R. Haeuser, Jr.
Louis W. Harris

Charles E. Harvey, Jr.
Clarence F. Holthaus
Joseph J. Ingolia, Jr.
Morton B. Kloete
Maubrey J. LeBlanc
Chester G. Lob
Tom F. McConnell
John D. McWilliams
Fred J. Masset
Colin J. Mayne
Jay I. Molony
Hugh I. Morrison
Wm. R. Moser
Maldenor M. Mott
Stanley F. Netherton

Farrell R.J. Nicholson
Sam L. Norwood, Jr.
Collier R. Parker
Harold N. Pedersen
Earl J. Perilloux
Charles S. Pique
Albert F. Pons
Stanley M. Pulitze
Jacob C. Randall
Irvin A. Reiner
Marion J. Robinson
Maurice F. Rooney
Louis F. Rosenbaum
Seymour S. Rosenberg
Richard R. Rotharmel

Joseph L. Scanlan
Carl J. Schumacher, Jr.
Charles T. Sheppard
Howard D. Sheppard
Henry G. Simon
Nathan F. Simoneaux
Ernest K. Strahan
Clayton H. Timken
James F. Tomeny
John S. Treen
Bernard P. Tuss
Richard J. Wakefield
Leonard M. Wolff
Ron D. Yarbrough

ADDITIONAL MEMEBERS IN THE ARMED FORCES

Alanson Chenault
Wilburn Ellis
John Gjertsen

Charles Gogreve
Theodore Hebert
Ralph Holsten

Everett Lochie
William Tarrant

ALCEE' FORTIER HIGH SCHOOL GRADUATES-MAY 26, 1943

Edward R. Abernathy
Robert E. Andersen
Robert J. Anderson
Sylvan Antin
William D. Arbogast
Leonard D. Aronson
Gordon C. Austin
Thomas Y. Awalt, Jr.
Ralph Ayala
Robert J. Bannon
Wallace K. Babington
Christopher J. Bellone
Herbert P. Benton, III
Eugene H. Berkowitz
Joseph M. Bertucci
John R. Bise, III
Johnnie T. Blackman
William A. Block
Aloysius L. Bonnette
Tom G. Borden
Milton R. Bossier
William A. Boudreau
Alan E. Brang
John F. Burris
Henry J. Costello
Leonard E. Claret
Herman R. Cohen
John G. Collins
Bernard J. Conroy
James W. Cook
Richard R. Cook
Roy F. Cook

Hyman H. Cooper
Elmer L. Crosby, Jr.
Nathaniel C. Dalton
Edward J. Darrow
Paul E. DeBlanc, Jr.
William J. Dermady, Jr.
Frank E. DeSilva
Arthur E. D'Hersis, Jr.
Albert A. Dingraudo
Matthew J. Doran
Marvin P. Duncan
Hubert B. Edwards
Arthur S. Ellis, Jr.
Leslie L. Ellis, Jr.
Raymond H. Eppling
Lloyd D. Estes, Jr.
Rene A. Eugene, Jr.
William F. Fant
Donald G. Farrar
Ernest J. Fazende, Jr.
William M. Feaster
Robert A. Ferrell
Elmo J. Fischer
Werner E. Forfer
Robert M. Franklin, Jr.
Rayfield S. Froeba, Jr.
Joseph B. Gillman
Louis K. Good, Jr.
Murray S. Gordon
William L. Gordon
Hugh F. Griffith
Albert C. Guillot

Jefferson O. Hamby
David L. Hancock
Alfred S. Hardenstein
John L. Heausler
Albert I. Hendler
Henry J. Hindricks
Donald K. Hoover
Richard W. Hughes
Lindsay L. Jackson
Bonnie E. Johnson, Jr.
Leonard A. Katz
Charles C. Keating
John W. Kirkpatrick
Almen G. Kickwood
Mervis C. Kleinfeldt
Harry A. Klundt, II
Merlyn E. Knecht
Stanley C. Kottemann
Coleman Kuhn
George L. Kuntz
Cyril A. Lagan
Leonce P. Lanoux
Jack W. Lark
Golden R. LaRose
Randon M. Larson
Henry F. LeMieux
Solomon Lepow
Raymond F. Lewis
Royal T. Liles, Jr.
Byran Lindsley
Charles Longo
Richard Lotapisch

Edward Lozano
David McArthur
Donald R. McCurley
Leo McQuernin
Jerold McIntoch
Thomas McIntosh
Donald McKay
John McNamara
Sproule McNeely
Andrew McWhorter
Charles Mahia
Seymour Malkin
Alfred Marks
Wade Martin
Nick Matrana
Burt Matthews
Anthony Mayoral
Julius Mercado
Daniel W. Milburn
George Millard, Jr.

Preston Mottram
Paul A. Newell
Stanley Netherton
George Nuslock, II
William Ogden
Edward Orftin
Robert O'Rourke
Kenneth Paisant
Arthur Pechon
Norvin Pellerin
Michael Pendergast
Robert Perry
Jaques Perrin
Charles Phillips, Jr.
John Plattner
George Price, Jr.
James Quintran, Jr.
Howard Raspilair
Irving Rau
Paul Raynaud

Maurice Rideau
Walter Rieger, Jr.
Martin Rivet, Jr.
Frank Roccaforte
Donald Rock
David Rooks
Lester Rosenzweig
Mansfield Roth, Jr.
James Ryan, Jr.
Ogden Salk
Ralph Schnacher
Malcoln Schroeder
Joseph Sciortino, Jr.
Warren Sciortino
Fenner Sedgebeer
Jesse Shelton
Chandler Sherwood
Joseph Shields
Louis Shiell
Harry Smith

James Snee
Leonard Spangenberg, Jr.
Otis Spillman
Frank Stainton
Wilbur Starr
John Stauss, Jr.
Bernard Steinau
Louis Startz
Jay Teasdel

Julian Tiblier
Walter Trahant, Jr.
William Travis, II
Adanelle Treigle
William Turner
Emile Vacasi, Jr.
Elbert Viz
William Vogt, Jr.
Burton G. Walker

Harman Ward
Robert Watkins
Harry Wells
Edward Whittaker
Harry Weigel
Melvin Woods
Louis Wyler, Jr.

ISIDORE NEWMAN SCHOOL-CLASS OF 1938

Margorie Jane Alshuler
Adeline Shirley Aronson
George Forbes Bastian
Dan Behre
John Frank Benham, II
Charles James Bloom, II
Curtis Webb Caines
Isidore Cohn, Jr.
Harold Cummins, Jr.
Charles Wogan Dureiux
Albert Fox
Fay Bettye Goldman
Gail Hausman
Dorothy Helen Hiller
Merwin Mercier Jamieson

John McShane Jordan
Hayden Eadras Lanois
Jefferson Davis Levine
Marie Louise Levy
Richard Bland Logan, Jr.
Fleurette Adoree Lurie
Helen Virginia Mattison
Edmund McIlheney
Bertha Rose Miller
Hilliard Eve Miller
Fannie Lee Nelken
Bertha Paglin
Annetta Lucille Pierce
Randolph Beauregard Robert
Douglas Scherer

Elaine Stevens Schwartz
William Mason Smith, III
Jeanet Irma Steckler
Peggy Rae Steinfirst
Sybil Wilkinson Stevens
Gerhard H.A. Thomas, Jr.
George Hamilton Tompkins
Harold David Victor
Jane Waldhorn
Raymond Bond Walker
John Beale Waterman, III
Hermoine Weill
Roy White, Jr.

ISIDORE NEWMAN SCHOOL-CLASS OF 1939

Samuel Arney
Helen Baldwin
Titine Clark

Robert Cummings
George Cunningham, Jr.
Lillian Durrand

Beverly Fink
Caroline Fletcher
Michel Fortier, Jr.

Ralph Ginsberg
Nina Glynn
William W. Goodell
Irwin Isaacs, Jr.
Louise Helen Jahncke
Nita Ethyl Kidd
Cora Alice Levine
Walter Levy, Jr.

Margeret Mayne
Schaumburg McGehee
Jane McNiven
Elizabeth Monrose
Saidee Montgomery
Malcolm O'Hara
William Rosenthal
Marvin Rosman

Margeret Saal
Glendower Salk
Clarke Salman, Jr.
Janet Seidenbach
Sylvia Weil
Lewis Wellford
McCrery Wheeler, Jr.
Rita Worms

ISIDORE NEWMAN SCHOOL-CLASS OF 1940

John Wesley Allee, II
Marilyn Barnett
James Michael Ber
Thomas Norton Bernard
Ted Bloch
Margorie Sybil Cahn
Norman Stephen Conroy
Sam Cornenswet, Jr.
Carol Dreyfous
Walter Raynold Ericsson
Clifford Freret Favrot, Jr.
Harvey Joseph Fitzpatrick
Hewitt Bates Fox

Margaret Freeman
Warren Leon Garfunkel
Richard Paige Garretson
Russell Mortimer Geer, Jr.
Lilyan Golden
William I. L. Haspel, Jr.
Himon Herbert Hirsch
L. Edward Lashman, Jr.
Ralph Pokorny Levey, Jr.
Douglas Colin MacDonald
Clare Joy Mayer
Bonnie Mae Miller
Margaret Nelson

Alice Batchelor Patton
Walter Flower Plauche
Ruth Provosty
Shirley Rosenberg
Albert Carl Schmidt
Ralph J. Schwartz, Jr.
Bernard Melville Solomon
Malcolm Renshaw Stouse
Delbert Pembroke Strong
Christopher Tompkins
Sidney Arthur Wales
Marion Wellford

ISIDORE NEWMAN SCHOOL-CLASS OF 1941

David W. Aiken
George E. Allen, Jr.
Ernest G. Asbury
Donald J. Balovich
Beverly Bisso (White)
F. Pearce Bradburn
Walter Carroll, Jr.
John A. Cochrane
Donald M. Coleman
George C. Cooksey, Jr.
Rupert Crebbin (Cheshire)
Betty Granberry (Moss)
Rufus C. Harris, Jr.
William A. Hilzim

Richard A. Hinckley
William H. Hodges
Edward LeMeilleur
Byron Lengsfield, Jr.
Lane N. Meltzer
Leo Miller, Jr.
Aubrey L. Moore
Lee F. Murphy, Jr.
Frank S. Normann, Jr.
Edward D. Parkhouse, Jr.
Jacqueline Provosty (Avegno)
Leonard M. Rosman
Richard W. Ross
Eugenie Sarre (Bolliver)

Benjamin Shanker
A.L. Shushan, Jr.
George C. Simmons
John B. Staples, Jr.
Joseph A. Sternberg
Joseph M. Supple
Elizabeth Tobin (Becker)
Joy Toney (Chilton)
Donald R. Wellford
Cornelius D. White, Jr.
Stewart M. Williams
William G. Zetzmann, Jr.

ISIDORE NEWMAN SCHOOL-CLASS OF 1942

William M. Barnett
Henry Batt, Jr.
Courtenay Bell (Winchester)
Doria M. Benton, Jr.
Emmy Lou Dicks (Cowand)
Brooke H. Duncan
Emile H. Ecuyer
Richard A. Farnsworth, Jr.
Adrienne Farrell (Kepper)
Jean Faust (Frymire)
Thomas B. Favrot
Charles Frank

Julius B. Fruchtgarten
Barbara Gardner (Payne)
Marjorie B. Garic
Julius B. Girard
Thomas P. Godchaux
Janis Goldman (Sabel)
Charles P. Gould, Jr.
Marcia Hathaway (Henderson)
W. Gordon Heffron, Jr.
Edward H. Hezlett, Jr.
Roy J. H. Hodges
Allen H. Johness, II

Harold L. Kearney, Jr.
Emile L. Kahn
Arnold C. Klein, Jr.
William Kohlman, II
Amelie L. LeBlanc
Louise Levine (Kombar)
Richard B. Levy
Tess Levy (Schornstein)
Marcel Livaudais, Jr.
G. Campbell Logan
Claude A. Lomax
Richard Lowenburg

James D. Maddox
Henry Magee, Jr.
Hugh Many
Bertha Marcus (Levy)
Mary Beaufort Matthews
John L. McCorkle
Malcolm M. Miller
Bella Mintz (Schlansky)
Sally Moss (Jellin)
William P. Parkhouse, III

Joseph K. Perloff
Cecile Pierce
Jack Rich, Sr.
Mathilde Ross (Holladay)
Charles Rosen, II
Alvin Pat Samuels
Marianne Sewell (Aiden)
Helen Skalka (Keen)
Joan Shwartz (Goldsmith)
Daniel N. Silverman, Jr.

Mercedes Sontheimer (Silverman)
Evan R. Soule
Harriet Stern (Rosenthal)
Joanne Stern (Gailar)
June Tremblay (Herold)
William Van Kirk
Roberta Volkert (Harrison)
Cecile Weil (Usdin)
Bertha Yaffe (Brohman)

ISIDORE NEWMAN SCHOOL-CLASS OF 1943

Lucie Abramson (Wing)
Walter James Amoss, Jr.
Adrian Benjamin, Jr.
John A. Bumstead, Jr.
Luther M. Byrd, Jr.
William J. Capo, Jr.
Signa Charbonnet (Cairon)
Lola Cochrane (Vale)
Milton H. Cohen
Paul M. Desbon, Jr.
E. Jane Dicks (Harris)
Ronald B. Dorning
Seymour J. Dreyfus
Dabney M. Ewin
C. Allen Favrot
Jerry Fitzpatrick
Julius W. Friend, Jr.
Jeanne Garretson (Lightman)
Louis A. Goldstein
Carol B. Hart
Evelyn Hodges (Gordon)
Paul E. Johnson, Jr.
Anne Kastler (Domec)

Helena Kelly (Elstrott)
Joanne King (Reckord)
Marian Louise Legendre
Ann Lejeune (Schneider)
Jack T. Lengsfield
Elaine Levy (Mintz)
Marian Leopold (Moskowitz)
Jacob Levine
Milton Jack Liberman
Katherine Burgess Long
Mildred Lubritz (Covert)
Berthe Marks (Amoss)
Berthia McCay (Brown)
Jean Nash (Abbott)
David R. Normann
Harold Patterson, Jr.
Marguerite Pierce (Rarick)
Michel O. Provosty
Sylvia Reiner (Shushan)
Walter Rooney, Jr.
Shirley Rosenthal (Rudolph)
Sue Rothrock (Menge)
Horace A. Sawyer, Jr.

Lois Seidenbach (Shepard)
John W. Sharp
Abe Silver, Jr.
John B. Smallpage, Sr.
James Charles Steidel
McDonald L. Stephens
Henry E. Stern
James H. Stewart
Marie Stouse (Van Kirk)
Henrietta Vallon (Bland)
J. Hubert Walker
William D. Weil
Phyllis Wellford (Fleming)
Margie West (Waller)
James C. Whattley
Louis Wingate
Marion Winstead
J. Barbee Winston
Eleanor Woodward (Westfeldt)
Miles P. Wynn
William Baker Wynn

NEW ORLEANS ACADEMY-CLASS OF 1931

Charles F. Gay
Jack C. Herman
Charles M. Klumpp

Edward B. Poitevent
Edward J. Putzell
John W. Stahler

Allen M. Steiner
S. Walter Stern, Jr.
Augustus Vreeland

NEW ORLEANS ACADEMY-CLASS OF 1932

Joseph Blythe, Jr.
Albert J. Flettrich
Carl Graffagnino
Edward Marks

Guy Malory
Gustaf McIlhenney
David Penn
Frank RePass

Raymond Samuel
Herman Schulze
Maurice Stern
Dolan Tipping

NEW ORLEANS ACADEMY-CLASS OF 1933

John W. Canone
Horatio S. Eustis
Herbert C. Flotte
Beverly V. Johnson

Robert L. Morris
J. Chaleron Penn
E. Earl Richards
Henry L. Trepagnier

Joseph L. Wymer
William Waller Young, Jr.

NEW ORLEANS ACADEMY-CLASS OF 1934

Clifford Atkinson, Jr.
Robert Blum
John Connelly
Frank deLatour

Laurence Fallon
Louis Graham
Charles Janvier
Norbert Markel

Longer Musson
John Walton

NEW ORLEANS ACADEMY-CLASS OF 1935

Woodruff George
Charles Healey
Henry Miles

Lee McMillan
Charles Miller
Peter Monrose

Devereaux O'Reilly
H.E. Pritchard, Jr.
Humbert Sandi

NEW ORLEANS ACADEMY-CLASS OF 1936

James Aldige'
N.C. Curtis, Jr.
Lloyd deLatour
W.J. Duease

Francis Gasquet
George Tabb
Marcel Gobert
John Guton

George Hopkins
Henry Laurens, Jr.
John Laurens, II
Alex Leonhardt, Jr.

NEW ORLEANS ACADEMY-CLASS OF 1937

Carroll Allen, Jr.
Ralston Cole, Jr.
Tom B. Denegre
Francis Gasque
Ellis Hinderman

Foster Johns, Jr.
William Leake, Jr.
Harborough Lill, Jr.
Curtis McKirahan, Jr.
Jack McMillan

Edward Means
John Muser
T. Robert Rudolf

NEW ORLEANS ACADEMY-CLASS OF 1938

William T. Coats, Jr.
John M. Collier
Clarence L. Dupre, Jr.
Robert E. Floweree
Robert S. Hart

Adolph H. Magruder
Stewart Maunsell, II
H.P. Moran, Jr.
Eads B. Poitevent
George B. Riviere

William B. Rudolf
R.F. Schneider, Jr.
Warren L. Stern
L.B. Stumph
Philip M. Walmsley

NEW ORLEANS ACADEMY-CLASS OF 1939

John U. Barr
Joseph A. Bisso
Pierre R. Dupont
Richard A. Faust
Robert L. Foster
Leonard M. King, Jr.

Franklin Laurens
Alfred LeBlanc
B.D.A. Lill
Leland S. Montgomery, Jr.
John R. Perez, Jr.
Raymond R. Perine

Robert H. Potts, Jr.
Samuel W. Ryniker, Jr.
Lester C. Smith, Jr.
Paul Tessier
Ellis M. Woodward
Edward Ziegler

NEW ORLEANS ACADEMY-CLASS OF 1940

Herbert J. Bremermann, Jr.
James Everett Eaves, Jr.
Gordon O. Ewin
Harry C. Ferrell, Jr.
Upton W. Giles, Jr.
Alvin S. Heumann

Stanhope Hopkins
Augustus F. Huge, Jr.
Charles H. Knost
James H. Kostmayer
John A. McLellan
Oscar J. McMillan

Merlin R. Markel
Robert E. Porter
Herbert P. Pursell, Jr.
Robert V. Whittaker, Jr.

NEW ORLEANS ACADEMY-CLASS OF 1941

Archie B. Bland, Jr.
John L. Blythe
Robert E. Catchings
Charles T. Curtis
Louis A. DeLatour
Frederick S. Ellis
Charles Stocker Fontelieu
Callender F. Hadden, Jr.

Alfred O. Hero, Jr.
Richard L. Hinderman
Melvin J. Jung, Jr.
Frank P. Krieger, Jr.
E. Howard McCaleb, III
Oliver B. Miles
Allen E. Querens
Louis V. Rand

Robert R. Richmond, Jr.
Harry Spiro, Jr.
W. Winston Weatherlow
Wallace O. Westfeldt, Jr.
Charles B. Williams
Harvey Windes

NEW ORLEANS ACADEMY-CLASS OF 1942

Richard P. Ellis
Charles L. Eshleman
Daniel B. LeGardeur
Leo A. Loubere

James L. McCall
William P. McCord
T.J. McMahon
Donald T. Myers

Blanc A. Parker
Charles W. Porter
A.P. Smith
William G. Zetzmann, Jr.

NEW ORLEANS ACADEMY-CLASS OF 1943

Ralp R. Alexis
Edward C. Alker
Edward S. Bagley
Albert Baldwin, Jr.
William P. Beatrous
Charles L. Cox, Jr.
T. J. Fontelieu, Jr.

Cyril P. Geary
Henry L. Hammett
George M. Helm
Thorn B. Himel
John A. Land, III
Richard J. Muniat
Henry F. Page, Jr.

Robert A. Pierpont, Jr.
Jules Rateau
James D. Rives, Jr.
John H. Williams
Charles W. Ziegler, III

NEW ORLEANS ACADEMY-CLASS OF 1944

Allen T. Bremermann
Joseph W. Buchanan, Jr.
George R. DeForest, Jr.
William L. Ferguson, Jr.
Paul Ned Graffagnino

Kenneth A. Langguth
Paul L. Loria
William R. Mattox, Jr.
Guy B. Mioton
Richard L. O'Connell

Charlton B. Ogden
Louis H. Rabouin, III
Arthur L. Robinson
Henry A. Soulie
Murdock M. Watkins, Jr.

NEW ORLEANS ACADEMY-CLASS OF 1945

Stanley R. Bremermann
Robert B. Bringhurst
James H. Cadzow, Jr.
John H. Counce
Ainsworth R. Cox
Prioleau Ellis, Jr.
Thomas Cargil Warner Ellis

John P. Hammond
Allan J. Harris, Jr.
John Ellett Jackson, Jr.
Frank A. Kruse, Jr.
Francis R. Lelong
Winston Carrington Lill
Philip R. Loria

Paul D. Mayer
Fernand J. Milhas
James K. Morris
Stanley S. Morris, Jr.
Dennis C. Rinerth
Mahlon A. Wetmore, Jr.

LOUISE S. MCGEHEE SCHOOL-CLASS OF 1937

Betty Bethea
Elsa Alyce Capo
Elinor Rosemary Crabbin
Amelia Honoure Craig
Roy Kaufman Beer
Margaret Fleming Dicks
Eleanor Elizabeth Dixon
Lucille Havard Ewin
Edith Fenno

Carolyn Thorn Himel
Sara Louise McLellan
Ida Luise Miller
Eleanor Nicholson
Margaret Paterson
Ruth Frances Pennebacher
Viola Josie Pottharst
Helen Louise Ritter
Marie Louise Ramelli

Aralee Marie Roy
Dorothy Alice Singreen
Harriet Sherman
Beatrice Elizabeth Shober
Mary Baldwin Smith
Muri Anna Umbach
Dorothy Rae Voss
Elinor Terry Welsh

LOUISE S. MCGEHEE SCHOOL-CLASS OF 1938

Mary Alpaugh
Grace Beatrous
Elliotte Beckner
Bruce Blakemore
Katherine Braselman
June Carpenter (Swearingen)
Corine Eshleman (Waldron)
Peggy Fenno
Patsy Geoghagen (White)
Mary Ann Hackett
Ruth Hackett
Gloria Hill

Elsa Hoehn (Terkuhle)
Alice Kinabrew
Virginia Kyle
Elaine Leverich
Bettie McCord
Hazeltine McCrocklin (West)
Edith McDonald
Nancy Miles (White)
Sally Mysing
Miller Owen
Cecille Parker (Westervelt)
Katherine Phillips

Eleanor Riess
Betty Schramm
Palmer Scott
Amelie Seaman
Margaret Terry (Tharp)
Olga Trepagnier
Sarah Villere
Corinne Waterman
Lee Wheatley (Woolfolk)
Harriet White

LOUISE S. MCGEHEE SCHOOL-CLASS OF 1939

Marilyn Baker
Wilma May Baker (Malhiot)
Jane Bruton
Gladys Buhler
Jean Bumstead (Williams)
Estelle Cable (Hathorn).
Saralee Creekmore (Peters)
Gloria Creighton (McGee)
Jane Dart (Maunsell)
Elaine Dicks (Floweree)
Yvonne Dureau (Dart)

Lydia Eaves (Trice)
Shirley Ernst
Carlotta Fowler (Pipes)
Gloria Garic (Anderson)
Mary Jim Goodwin
Betty Grant (Smith)
Barbara Hugg (Bowers)
Eleanor Logan
Barbara Martin (Parker)
Gladys Mayer
Aphra Morris (Perez)

Doris Morrison (Supple)
Jean Montgomery (Lewis, Jr.)
Patricia Page (Lambert)
Sally Gray Parker (Norman)
Barbara Perkins (Binnings)
Mary Rhodes (Hefter)
Evelyn Senter (Claiborne)
Elsa Schwartz (Parkerson)
Mary Jane Trevor (Eustis)

LOUISE S. MCGEHEE SCHOOL-CLASS OF 1940

Mary Aherns (Whittaker)
Jean Alpaugh (Stone)
Elizabeth Brown (Nettleton)
Doris Billingsley (Fletcher)
Aileen Cassegrain (Livaudais)
Nathalie Crump (Grehan)
Alice Dawson (Cox)
Mickey Dureau (Howell)
Betty Durland (Dupont)
Pat Farnsworth (Jones)

Katherine Gould (Hesslow)
Alma Hammett
Charlotte Hillyer (Dupuy)
Sally Holbrook (Boggs)
Lela Fournet (Vincent)
Anne Ivens (Robinson)
Janet Jones (Lorber)
Shirley Martin (Bassett)
Arthe Monroe (Duncan)
Rae Murphy (Wittenberg)

Memise Naef (Danielson)
Gertrude Munson (Hill)
Betty Pope (Christovich)
Libby Smart (Schneidau)
Althea Schulze (Martin)
Betty Stevens (Sherrill)
Kay Thompson (Vanderlin)
Barbara Vatter (Schupp)

LOUISE S. MCGEHEE SCHOOL-CLASS OF 1941

Patricia Ahrens (Carver)
Mona Aldige (Minge)
June Barkerding (Pigman)
Katherine Boulet (Favrot)
Bettie Brewster (Stockton)
Margeret "Peggie" Baker (Courtin)
Margaret Counce (Randolph)
Evalyn Dooley (Pitard)
Patricia Dickman (Barry)
Dottie Eaves (Kostmayer)
Ruth Fischofer (Martin)
Beth Glass (Caire)
Mary Grey (Macdonald)

Jane Hackett (Hardin)
Rosemary Janssen (Orphys)
Elizabeth Klipstein (Gautheir)
Minna "Polly" Lane
Katherine LaCour (Miller)
Lorraine Lyons (Carney)
Valerie Marchesseau (Trelles)
Jacqueline Mayhew (Ireland)
Margaret Martinez (Fortier)
Joy Nes (Richardson)
Harriott Phelps (Gay)
Mary Reynolds (Whitlock)
Jane Seeman (Crosby)

Adah Schneider
Virginia Smart (McIlhenny)
Ann Springer (Hopkins)
Nadyne Steinmayer (Manson)
Meg Stevenson (Henderson)
Anne Suthon (Laird)
Margaret Ann Trenchard
(Williamson)
Ann West (Caffery)
Audley Wheeler (Bethea)
Ellie Witherspoon (Caffery)

LOUISE S. MCGEHEE SCHOOL-CLASS OF 1942

Wilhemine Aragon (Salatich)
Dorothy Berea (Silver)
Harriet Blish (Robinson)
Catherine Burns (Tremaine)
Susan Caffery (Kirkpatrick)
Doris Carmer Clabaugh (Jadan)
Anne Clark (Gsell)
Mimi Clark (Cromwell)
Olive Eaves (Weigand)
Joan Durland (Benjamin)
Donna Demarest (Lydick)
Maudie Ellen Farrar (Farrar)
Connie Faust (Walk)

Patsy Gibbens (Caffery)
Alice Glenny (Shriver)
Grace Gould (Kayatta)
Beth Greenwald (Sweet)
Eleanor Hamilton
Bryne Havard (Warren)
Dottie Hecht (Cooper)
Mary Allen Jackson (Corder)
Kathryn Keyes (Guyer)
Martha McDonough (Matthews)
Jean McGivney (Boese)
Marie Odette Moran (Stahl)
Nancy Nunez (Carroll)

Patricia O'Hara (Knight)
Mary Pugh (Headley)
Baby Smith (Scoggin)
Kathleen Smith (Moore)
Jo Thomas (Collins)
Kathryn Verlander (Caire)
Marilyn Wellemeyer
Connie Wiener
Martha Witherspoon (Brannan)
Patricia Wogan (Warner)
Betty Woolf (Fowler)

LOUISE S. MCGEHEE SCHOOL-CLASS OF 1943

Robin Berckes (Richmond)
Charlotte Coats (Fanz)
Nancy Deane (Windes)
Elsie Gelpi (Rubin)
Beverly George (Rogers)
Roselle George (Brown)
Joan Guibet (Haase)
Betsy Hezlett (Chilelli)
Martha Helm (McCord)
Mary McNeil Hopkins (Gilly)

Olive Jewell (Randle)
Ann Johnston (Allison)
Delores Keyes (Schloss)
Barbara King (Amedee)
Jackie LeRoi (Bolton)
Gladys Malcolmson (Pevy)
Majorie Mauberret (Deano)
Marie O'Hara (Heintz)
Joel Oliver (Baldwin)
Elaine Querens (Helm)

Jeanette Renegar (Smith)
Ellen Schneider (Brooks)
Ellarose Sullivan (Carden)
Estelle Shirley (Nes)
Mary Margeret Todd (Monrose)
Eva Voelker
Jane Walker (Wallace)
Glendora Weigand (Brazy)

LOUISE S. MCGEHEE SCHOOL-CLASS OF 1944

Jane Alsobrook (Miller)
Francoise Billion (Richardson)
Betty Blancand (Flair)
Jean Boulet (McCarthy)
Betty Browne (Fouts)
Ann Burdette (Carroll)
Lou Cabral (Ford)
Lilyann Chadwick

Dale Dixon (Dewees)
Rosemary Gugert (Kennedy)
Dorothy Healey (Klundt)
Patricia Land (Stevens)
Claire Legai (Bishop)
Donnie MacDonald (Strayhorn)
Millicent May (Hamer)
Weezie Norton (Dillon)

Florence Edith Parker (Parker)
Elaine Prados (Musson)
Dorothy "Tee" Rand (Riviere)
Ernestine Saucier (Henkel)
Sue Saussy (Stewart)
Gayle Stocker (Denegre)
Mary M. Swords (Boehmer)
Jean Travis (Bousquet)

METAIRIE PARK COUNTRY DAY SCHOOL-CLASS OF 1938

James A. Anderson, III
Charles Bloom

Margaret Jean "Peggy"
Brodie"(Eckhardt)
Helen Anne Charbonnet

Barbara Cushing (Hoff)
John G. Pratt, Jr.

METAIRIE PARK COUNTRY DAY SCHOOL-CLASS OF 1939

Clifford Atkinson, Jr.
Theodore Boothby
Philip Duvic
Ruth Ellis (Layton)

Chesley Johnson (Dale-Arnurius)
S. Brucie Jones (Ballard)
Cynthia Landry (Clark)
Rene LeGardeur

Marion McCaleb (Marshall)
Margaret Muench
Mark Robinson
Frank B. Williams

METAIRIE PARK COUNTRY DAY SCHOOL-CLASS OF 1940

Edward B. Benjamin, Jr.

Titine Clark (Pottharst)

Mary Cutting

Manuel Duvic, Jr.
W. Brooke Fox
Frances Green
W. Lyall Howell

Katherine LeBlanc (Schoberle)
Mildred Lyons (Baldwin)
Carolyn Marshall
Calista Rault (Schneidau)

Newton Robinson
Edgar B. Stern, Jr.

METAIRIE PARK COUNTRY DAY SCHOOL-CLASS OF 1941

Alejandro Arguello
John Chambers, Jr.
Charlotte Clarke (Kirk)

Eugene Foster
Lorna Grayson
Lucy Herrera (Dyer)

Thomas R. Howell
Althea Leslie
Delord Mabry

METAIRIE PARK COUNTRY DAY SCHOOL-CLASS OF 1942

W. Mente Benjamin
Donald M. Bradburn
Evelyn Clark (Rogers)
Adair Chambers
Evelyn Clark (Rogers)
Deirdre Crager (Stanforth)

Baird Dentzler (Rice)
Kathleen Ellis (Sellers)
Towson Ellis, Jr.
Melvin F. Johnson
Stuart O. Landry, Jr.
Dorothy Middleton (Burguieres)

Loretto Richards (O'Reilly)
Louise Stoop
Barbara Strong (Harvey)
Jean Thompson (Daniel)
Mais Weston (Luikart)

METAIRIE PARK COUNTRY DAY SCHOOL-CLASS OF 1943

Jean Aschafenburg (Waterman)
Joan Benson
Ian Bradburn
John F. Clark, III
Irving Cummins
Patricia DeLancey (Kayser)
Suzanne Dennery (VanDijl)
Christine Farr
Kathleen Feibleman

Edith H. Field (Monsees)
Lois Foster (Robinson)
Gordon Frank
Louis A. Goldstein
Edward M. Heller
Laura Landry (McCall)
Thomas B. Lemann
Mary Menhinick (White)
Elizabeth Meriwether

Sydney E. Mix
George R. Montgomery
A. Miles Pratt, II
Avis Reynick (Ogilvy Moore)
Philip M. Stern
Watson Tebo
John H. Thomson, Jr.
Glendora L. Wiegand (Brazy)

ACADEMY OF THE SACRED HEART-CLASS OF 1938

Beth Jane Alexander
Jane Pauline Eastwood
Alleen Gutheridge
Ivel Jackson
Marian Legarde
Emily Locascio (Snellings)
Marie Alice Monrose

Isabel Morales
Carldad Quintero
Esperanza Quintero
Fe Quintero
Peggy Rickert
Mary Anna Rivet
Betty Roy

Elizabeth Russ
Jane Sandoz
Irma Valenzuela
Olga Valenzuela
Marguerite Waguespack
Joan Watters
Esther Wilson

ACADEMY OF THE SACRED HEART-CLASS OF 1939

Janet Bierhorst
Margeret Mary Byrne
Constance Claverie (Bohn)
Jacqueline Constantin
Marie Louise Dobelman
Jean Faust
Anne C. Friedricks

Margeret Joachim
Ruby Wilcox Lafferty
Betty E. Lemarie
Deborah Lyons
Marjorie Magee
Moonyeen Marion
Miriam Morales

Claire Reynaud
Yolanda Rodriguez
Dot M. Roy (Dane)
Betty Tinsley
Yolanda Volpe

ACADEMY OF THE SACRED HEART-CLASS OF 1940

Genevieve Bodet
Betty Bogron

Joel Bond
Olga Cantaro

Aileen Cassegrain (Livaudais)
Dixie Friedrichs

Jane Friedrichs
Elise Harris
Seville Jenny
Marianna Landrum
Zoe Leuer

Mary Ellen Mayronne
Mary Mikules
Marion Plauche
Ruth Claire Ryan
Marjorie Sigur

Marjorie Skelly
Lucille Smith
Imelda Volpe

ACADEMY OF THE SACRED HEART-CLASS OF 1941

Gilda Aragon
Dorothy Brock
Margaret Brownson
Geraldine Comeaux
Anita Louise Crozat
Anita Duncan
Jean Fisher
Amelie Generes

Patricia Grehan
Margaret Mary Guderian
Aileen "Lana" Hummel
Elaine Kernaghan (Coburn)
Eola Prowell (Lewis)
Lolita Martinez (Wegmann)
Barbara Rathe
Alice Remes

Emille Reynaud
Georgette Robert
Marion Sandoz
Marion Schexnaydre (Zinser)
Elizabeth Williams
Josephine Watters

ACADEMY OF THE SACRED HEART-CLASS OF 1942

Carol Bierhorst (Breeding)
Regina Daley (Boyle)
Betty Jenny (Magne)

Alice M. Marechal (O'Brien)
Felice Maurer (Lowe)
Elizabeth L. Quinn (Drury)

Erline R. Rutter (Peterson)
Patricia L. Streckfus (Clark)
Lois A. Weber (Bouchereau)

ACADEMY OF THE SACRED HEART-CLASS OF 1943

Yvonne Elder Brown (Collier)
Joan Burguieres (Brown)
Rosemary Carrere (Palfrey)
Shirley Hummel (Pratt)

Lillian Neguelona (Broderick)
Verinice E. O'Connor (Mayley)
Norma Rathe (Steele)
Patricia Saer (Brown)

Helen Stich (Plough)
Mary Adele Walton (Brown)
Nell Pape Williams (Waring)

RUGBY ACADEMY-CLASS OF 1935

George Atkins
Ted Atkinson
Edward Arceneau
Fayette Ewing
Richard Fitzgerald
Leo Frank
Roland Gerth

Vincent Haywood
Donald Jordan
Buckner Lawson
Ralph Lind
Sidney L. Menge, Jr.
Arthur Oldstein
Douglas Petitpain

Louis Rose
Jack Samuels
Raymond Salmen
Haywood Vincent
John Ward
Maxwell Wright

RUGBY ACADEMY-CLASS OF 1936

Edward Arceneau
Charles Drapekin
Elliott Clarke
P.K. Ewing
William Jackson

Virgil Jackson, Jr.
Frederick Leitz
Edwin Litolaf
George Mellinger
Francis O'Connor

Bernard Oppenheim
John Owens, Jr.
Ralph Rose, Jr.
John Ward, Jr.
William Waterman

RUGBY ACADEMY-CLASS OF 1937

William Louis Andry
Philip Adrian Bodet, III
John Drayton Clarke
Louis Grevemberg Davis
Jerry Harry Forst
Richard duJay Klorer

Charles Douglas Loog
William Anthony Massimini
Allen Jules Negrotto
Murray Edwards Petitpain
John Reising
James Reising

Alphonse Kenison Roy, Jr.
George Soule, IV
Byron Webre Stinson
Charles Julian Vaught

RUGBY ACADEMY-CLASS OF 1938

Edward R. Baldinger, Jr.
George W. Bohn, Jr.
Charles W. Bosch

Christos G. Kogas
Harold C. Lifsey
Folse Roy

Curtiss S. Schroeder
Jacob H. Simon
Harry R. Wakefield, Jr.

RUGBY ACADEMY-CLASS OF 1939

Carl Anderson
Maurice T. Benedict, Jr.
George A. Carpenter, Jr.
Harold F. Christadoro
Eddie Deckbar
Floyd a. Gruber
Edward P. Gurry
Thomas F. Jordan, Jr.

Harold C. Lifsey
Anthony M. Marhay, Jr.
Dominic J. Mumphrey, Jr.
Charles D. Patrick, Jr.
Fred Perkins
James R. Perkins
Earl Peyroux
Rudolph Ramelli

John Ross
Julian Rolfs
Anthony Russo, Jr.
Arthur J. Smith, Jr.
Miles Gordon Stevens, Jr.
Lester Stockard
Arthur Wood
J.L. Zemmer

RUGBY ACADEMY-CLASS OF 1940

Lester W. Bergeron
Herbert J. Chattenberg, Jr.
Walter F. Faust
Joseph Greco

Salvador J. Green
Samual H. McAfee, Jr.
Charles C. McGuire
Sydney L. Russell, Jr.

J. Schaffenberg
Frank A. Uddo
Charles S. White

RUGBY ACADEMY-CLASS OF 1941

C. A. Coulon
L. S. Hall
R. F. Kerner
I. A. Lindberg, Jr.
W. P. McLaney

W. P. Mollenkoph, Jr.
A. B. Murphy, Jr.
J. A. Ross
W. C. Russo
R. B. Sneed

H. J. Soland, III
K. L. Thrash
T. M. Wakefield

RUGBY ACADEMY-CLASS OF 1942

Frank J. Beyer, Jr.
Richard D. Carlton
Howard J. Cohen
Glenn Dietrich
Frank T. Doyle, Jr.

Frank N. Fradella, II
Charles B. Freeman
Noel C. Genevay, Jr.
Fred A. LeBlanc
Edwin M. Maye

Earl J. Peyroux
Edward T. Randolph, III
John L. Sarre

JESUIT HIGH SCHOOL-CLASS OF 1938

Joseph A. Achary, Jr.
Raymond P. Augustin, Sr.
Louis R. Ayala, Jr.
Victor E. Babin, Jr.
Edward W. Backer, Jr.
Nicholas M. Balovich
Gerald T. Barrett
George G. Baudean
Julian G. Baudier, Sr.
Thomas G. Beck, Jr.
Joseph G. Bernard
Adrian L. Block
Harry F. Blust, Jr.
Louis A. Bono

Allen I. Boudreaux
Louis C. Bougere
Floyd F. Bourgeois
William J. Bowen
Theodore J. Brown
George E. Burgess, Jr.
John E. Burke
John P. Byrnes
John L. Cahill, Jr.
James P. Caire
Wilfred F. Calongne, Jr.
Fred L. Caro
John F. Carrigan
Cyrus J. Caruso

Mahlon L. Cassidy
Clayton J. Charbonnet
Francis D. Charbonnet
Carroll A. Chauvin
Alvin R. Christovich, Jr.
John F. Ciolino
Vincent Colletti
William T. Coogan
Alfred F. Correnti
Edward J. Cousins
Stephen A. Cowan, Jr.
George A. Cox, Jr.
George E. Crane, Jr.
Edward A. Daspit

Joseph A. Diaz
Joseph S. DiFatta
Francis X. Donahue
Thomas F. Donelon
Thomas Donnelly
Robert J. Doskey
Lambert G. Durol
Edward J. Early
Clarence M. East, Jr.
Clarence A. Ehrhardt, Jr.
Russel J. Esser
James E. Fagan, Jr.
Albert G. Favot
Robert F. Fagot
Joseph A. Fahnert, Jr.
Robert E. Faubion
Gorden W. Faust
Hubert Fielder, Jr.
Peter E. Fineran
T. Stephen Fitzpatrick, Jr.
Harold L. Flettrich, Sr.
James L. Flood
St. Marc J. Flotte
Gerard L. Foley
Frank Fortier, Jr.
Falvey J. Fox
Aloysius M. Frechou
Frank C. Fromherz
Joseph F. Fromherz
Frank R. Gatti, Jr.
John J. Giarrantano
James J. Gilly
P. Edwin Golden, Jr.
Harry C. Graham, Jr.
Walter L. Gros, Jr.
William F. Grosch
Robert J. Grush
John B. Guarisco
William J. Guste, Jr.

Edward J. Harrigan
Warren Hauth
James J. Hecker
U. Joseph Hecker, Jr.
John L. Hein
Milton F. Hilbert, Jr.
Eugene J. Hoffman, Jr.
Carol J. Hooper
Harold J. Hooper, Sr.
Victor R. Imbornone
Charles K. Jennewine, Jr.
Alvin P. Jurisich
Paul R. Kalman, Jr.
James J. Kenny, Sr.
T. Hartley Kingsmill, Jr.
William A. Klein, Jr.
Joseph L. Kreller
Emile J. Laiche
Delery H. Lancaster
Ellwood J. Lawson
William H. Lawton
Milton L. LeBlanc, Jr.
Louis J. LeCarpentier
Paul A. Lemarie, Jr.
T. Ben Lockett
Louis M. Maduell
Charles L. Mancuso, Jr.
Herbert J. Mang
Dominic J. Martello
Anthony J. Matranga
Laurence W. Mazzeno, Jr.
Leonard J. McCaffery, Sr.
Albert McCoard, Jr.
Gerard F. McGinn, Jr.
Albert A. McVille
Joseph M. Meraux
Frank J. Meyer
James A. Meyer
August J. Mills, Jr.

Joseph G. Miorana
Edmund G. Miranne, Sr.
Anthony J. Monjure, III
Frank M. Montalbano
Raymond F. Montgomery
Peter E. Mouledous, Jr.
Neill F. Murphy
John J. Naccari
Robert E. O'Connor
John G. O'Hern
Moris A. O'Hern
Frank S. Oser, Jr.
Daniel W. Partridge
Joseph M. Perrett
Eugene J. Perrier, Jr.
James M. Perrier
Wallace C. Pfister
Edgar L. Plaeger
Ignatius N. Plescia
Roland F. Poche, Jr.
Frederick A. Pou
Jules J. Prats, Jr.
John A. Prejean, Jr.
Edwin P. Quilter, Jr.
Gus H. Rathe, Jr.
John F. Rau, Jr.
Louis L. Robein, Sr.
J. Mofield Roberts, Jr.
Warren J. Rogers, Jr.
Julian L. Roy
Henry C. Russell
Emmett W. Russo
Cornelius J. Ryan, III
James E. Ryder, Sr.
Albert C. Saer
Ernest L. Salatich
Edgar V. Schafer, Jr.
Earl J. Schneller
J. Garic Schoen

Mike W. Sciortino
Aubrey R. Seiler
Edwin F. Serpas, Jr.
Thomas W. Sheperd, Jr.
Raymond Sherrard, Jr.
Louis V. Sierra, Jr.
James J. Smith, Jr.
Morris L. St. Amant

Robert R. Taggart
Sidney L. Tiblier, Jr.
Anthony L. Tortorich
Stephen J. Von Norman, Jr.
Walt N. Veale, Jr.
Andre L. Villere
Bertney J. Weber
Francis X. Wegmann

William T. Welsh, Jr.
John E. Wheelahan
John A. Wilday, Jr.
Amador G. Windmeyer
Frank A. Zaeringer, Jr.
Harold L. Zeringer, Jr.

JESUIT HIGH SCHOOL-CLASS OF 1939

John J. Albrecht
Arthur C. Apffel
Dario F. Ballina, Jr.

Landry J. Bernard, Jr.
Alvin C. Bertucci
Nute A. Blue, Jr.

Leon T. Bomar, Jr.
Edwin C. Boudreaux, Jr.
Lawrence F. Brand

Philip A. Bruno
Gregory M. Burguieres
Robert E. Byrne
Joseph P. Cashen
Hubert W. Clements
Gerard F. Coogan
Edwin R. Cousins, Jr.
Richard A. Cousins
M. Judson Crane, Jr.
Thomas C. Creagan
Edwin A. Crise, Jr.
Marshall J. David
Frederick G. Deiler
Alfonso del Marmol
Edward L. Delery
Max J. Derbes, Jr.
James P. Dillon
T. Kenneth Dillon
Cleary J. Doussan
Richard J. Ducote
George L. Eastman, Jr.
John H. Elmer
Fred Erichson
M. Condry Farrell
James E. Fitzmorris, Jr.
Walter J. Flanagan, Jr.
Paul J. Fontana, Jr.
George F. Gaudin, Jr.
John J. Gaudry
Thomas L. Gaudry
Walter D. Gernon, Sr.
Thomas M. Gillin
Donald E. Graham
Harold J. Granen
Louis M. Grunewald
Louis L. Gueydan
Roy F. Guste
John F. Halligan
Thomas J. Hatrel

Norbert R. Hinckley
George A. Hoffman
W. Stanley Howell, Jr.
John G. Hyland, Jr.
Raymond J. Hymel
George F. Lagroue
John M. Lalanne, Jr.
Marian L. Larmann
John T. Leckert
Carroll P. Lincoln
Diego Andres
Bates J. Macgowan, Jr.
Evander Macgowan
Sal J. Maggiore
John L. Martinez
Claude B. Mauberret, Jr.
Bernard J. McCullum, Jr.
Charles A. Miller
Charles T. Miller
James H. Miller, Jr.
Rudolph G. Miller, Jr.
George F. Minor
L. John Monguillot
Wiley L. Mossy, Jr.
Warren E. Mouledoux
Ray B Myers
Walter F. Norton, Jr.
James T. O'Brien
Thomas J. O'Hare, Jr.
Maurice B. O'Neil, Jr.
John H. O'Neill, Jr.
Robert C. Oglesby, Jr.
William J. Oldenburg, Jr.
Edward B. Ortega, Jr.
Vincent A. Paciera
Allan N. Peirce, III
Henry C. Perret
Earl B. Philips
Paul O. H. Pigman

Michael S. Power, Jr.
Louis G. Reis, Jr.
Peter J. Ricca
Cedric F. Riche
Charles L. Rivet
Hilton L. Rivet
Labasse J. Robin Jr.
Winus J. Roeten
Leonard J. Rolfes
Robert J. Rooney
Frank J. Russell, Jr.
Howard J. Russell
Daniel B. Ryan
Philip F. Salles
Roy A. Sax
Russell J. Schonekas
Lionel A. Scott, Jr.
Walter M. Seidel, Jr.
Milton W. Seiler
Roger F. Shaw, Jr.
Emile S. Sherrard
Paul S. Stuart
John L. Taaffe
Pascal Taormina
George J. Taquino, Jr.
Joseph A. Tortorich
Malcolm J. Tuohy
Julius G. Villars
Trudeau J. Villars, Jr.
William J. Virgets, Jr.
J. Patrick Walsh
Daniel O. Weilbaecher
Maurice O. Weilbaecher
George V. Werner
John J. West, Jr.
George S. Wetzel
Robert E. Wheelahan
Andrew H. Wiebelt
Earl B. Wilken, Jr.

JESUIT HIGH SCHOOL-CLASS OF 1940

George H. Arbour
Joseph Armstrong
Frederick E. Barocco
Joseph F. Basset
Raymond P. Bassich, Jr.
Alton E. Bayard, Jr.
David P. Bernhardt, Jr.
Numa V. Bertel, Jr.
Richard J. Bohn
Edward T. Bomar
Joseph C. Bostick
Edward F. Bowman, III
Charles R. Brennan, Jr.
Ernest P. Brewton, Jr.

Henry J. Briggs, Jr.
Lester M. Brooks, Jr.
Wilbur C. Brummet
Henry J. Bryer, Jr.
John B. Burguieres
John B. Caire
Richard J. Carrere
Vincent D. Carruth
Clarence R. Caster, Jr.
John J. Cazenavette
James E. Champagne
Edward E. Chase
Samuel J. Ciolino
Thomas J. Conners

Blaise S. D'Antoni, Jr.
Lawrence F. D'Antoni
James R. Dalgarn, Jr.
John Dane, Jr.
Harold S. Dey, Jr.
Denis J. Downey
Ralph D. Dwyer, Jr.
J. William W. Earle, Jr.
Gerson R. Eberhardt
Thomas Edwards
James K. Faget
John W. Fanz, Jr.
John J. Farrell
Peter M. Ferguson

Louis J. Fricke
Ernest S. Gaiennie, Jr.
Charles A. Galiotto
William E. Garity
Charles G. Glueck
E. Carlton Guillot, Jr.
George F. Gurtner
Milton J. Hargis, Jr.
William A. Heausler, Jr.
Duval Hilbert
Willian P. Hindeland, Jr.
Joseph C. Howard, Jr.
George A. Issac, Jr.
Charles G. Jacques, Jr.
William H. Johnston
Michael C. Keller, Jr.
Thomas J. Kennair
Donald W. Kent
John M. Krebs
Albert J. Kuehn
Harold R. Lambert
P. J. Lauman
Bryce J. LeBlanc, Sr.
Owen V. LeBlanc, Sr.
Robert E. LeBlanc, III
Charles A. Leininger
Joseph B. Leininger
Robert F. Leon
Albert A. Levy, Jr.
Herman Lind, Jr.
Elliot J. Locascio
Fernand D. Lorio

Vernon C. Manint
Robert J. McHardy
Richard E. McNeely
W. Warren McPhillips
Emile F. Meyer, Jr.
Hirsch C. Meyer, Jr.
Ernest P. Miller, Jr.
Fred H. Mix, Jr.
Allyn M. Munger
Cyril J. Murphy, Jr.
Daniel J. Murphy, Jr.
Charles G. Nelson, Jr.
William C. Nelson, Jr.
Joseph A. Neyrey
Warren J. Nolan
Francis H. O'Donnell, Jr.
Ashton R. O'Dwyer
Carl J. Oldenburg
Blaine P. Olivier
Chalin Perez
Joseph L. Pittari
Francis A. Plough
Irwin F. Poche
Ewell C. Potts, Jr.
George Prassinos
James J. Puneky, Jr.
Joseph J. Quartana
George M. Quartano
James H. Quinn
Louis E. Ramos
August J. Rantz, Jr.
Paul J. Rau

Staigg G. Ray
Morris B. Redmann
Clarence G. Reuther, Jr.
Roy K. Rhodes, Jr.
Albert E. Richard, Jr.
Horace B. Rickey, Jr.
Erwin J. Robichaux
Robert P. Roth
Elmo C. Rousseau
Bernard L. Salvaggio
Frank L. Schneider
Paul W. Schott
Jack J. Scofield
Gerald R. Seely
Joseph D. Signorelli
Gustave C. Stubbs, Jr.
James A. Talbot, Jr.
Howard J. Taylor
Frank R. Thomas, Jr.
Fernand J. Tiblier
George A. Tormey, Jr.
Charles J. Vigo, Jr.
Peter W. Viscardi
John S. Watters
Theodore J. Weher, Jr.
William J. Wegmann
Garry S. Wilkin, Jr.
Joseph E. Windmeyer
Warren W. Wingerter
Emmett O. Woods
Lawrence L. Zeringer
Kent J. Zimmerman

JESUIT HIGH SCHOOL-CLASS OF 1941

Edward M. Alba
Harold V. Alfred, Jr.
Carl T. Avrard
Albert F. Backer, Jr.
James W. Barnes
Herbert L. Baylis
James D. Beck, III
Byron J. Berteau
C. Robert Bohn
Joseph A. Breaux
David C. Brennan
John P. Briant, Jr.
Alexander C. Brodtmann, Jr.
William Perry Brown
Stephen F. Browne, Jr.
Malcolm J. Brunet
Lucas F. Bruno, Jr.
Joseph S. Bruns, Sr.
Leon D. Bultman
Clendon J. Butera
J. Kenneth Butler, Jr.

John P. Byrne
Harry G. Caire
Jules A. Cambre
James Castrogiovanni
Edward S. Crist
Harold M. Clement
F. Fred Clerc
Walter T. Colbert
Brian J. Collins
Anthony J. Constanza
John M. Coogan, Sr.
George Coumes
J. Frederick Crane
Cedric A. Curran
John S. Dabdoub
Hartman C. Daniel
Anthony J. Delucca
Albert L. Diano, Jr.
J. Noel Digby
Leon P. Duplantier
Warren J. Dwyer

McMillan H. Elder
J. Philip Faust
Salvador Fazzio
Edward L. Fernandez
Leonard M. Finley
Charles F. Flack, Jr.
Michael J. Fleming
Joseph L. Fontcuberta, Jr.
Louis E. Ford
John G. Frick, Jr.
Thomas H. Fromhertz
William H. Gallmann, Jr.
Robert A. Generes
Eugene J. Gibert, Jr.
Edward G. Gillin
Edward J. Gilly
Bicford C. Graf
James H. Groetsch, Jr.
James E. Gros
James E. Hassinger, Jr.
Thomas M. Healy, Jr.

Donald J. Hebert
John G. Hill, Jr.
Charles A. Hoffman, Jr.
Paul F. Hoots
James L. Jansson
Francis L. Jaubert, Jr.
Ernest L. Joubert, III
Jack R. Kearney
Meade P. Kelly
Cyril F. Kirsch
Henry A. Kevlin, Jr.
O. J. Key, Jr.
Hebert A. Koster
Edward C. Kurtz, Sr.
Richard J. Lampton
Henry D. Lancaster
J. Browne Larose, Jr.
J. Charles LeBourgeois, Jr.
Albert L. LeBreton, Jr.
G. Wallace Leftwich
Daniel L. Levy, Jr.
Francis X. Levy
J. Paul Limont
Nickolas J. Liuzza
Stephen J. Loup, Jr.
Edward J. Ludman, Jr.
James Macauley
Edmund B. Martin, Jr.

Emile L. McMillan
Gerard T. McNamara
Warren J. Merrihew
Louise C. Meyer
Benjamin H. Miller
George Moisant, Jr.
Louis L. Moise
Roy J. Mossy
Glendy J. Munson, Jr.
Louis B. O'Neil, Jr.
Ramon A. Oriol, III
Russell P. Pennino
George Peter, III
Michael W. Pfister
George W. Pigman, Jr.
Louis A. Pilie
John L. Prendergast
Wesley A. Randall, Sr.
Joseph J. Ranna
Milton L. Raphael
Benjamin C. Raymond, Jr.
William G. Raymond, Jr.
Charles B. Richard
Louis E. Richard
Edward J. Romagosa
Ernest A. Roth, Jr.
Lawrence D. Roubion, Jr.
John J. Santos, Jr.

Gordon F. Schafer
Ernest Schluter, Jr.
George F. Schminke, III
Edward M. Socola
John R. Stample
Maurice J. Stouse, Jr.
William J. Tallant, Jr.
Anthony M. Tamburo
John B. Tamburo
Albert O. Tangue, Jr.
W. John Tessier
John W. Thomas
Robert M. Thomas
Stanley A. Thouran
Thomas J. Tiblier
Stanley L. Turegano
Raymond E. Vairin, Jr.
Jack L. Vigo
Thomas L. Villars
Francis X. Vinet
Vincent P. Vitrano
Gerard P. Walsh
John L. Walsh
Frederick Weaver
Thorton E. White, Jr.
Andrew A. Yuratich, Jr.
Jerome J. Zaeringer

JESUIT HIGH SCHOOL-CLASS OF 1942

John M. Adams
Frank J. Andel, Jr.
Robert B. Anderson, Jr.
John J. Archer, Jr.
Charles J. Babington
Lionel Barraza, Jr.
Bernard J. Barrett
Frank J. Basile, Jr.
George C. Battalora, Jr.
John E. Baudean
Raymond C. Baudier
Victor J. Baudier, Jr.
Harry T. Begg, Jr.
Gerard W. Bernard, Jr.
Robert M. Billet
Michael T. Blouin, Jr.
C. Adrian Bodet, Jr.
Donald B. Bohn
Lawrence G. Bole
Angelo A. Boudousquie, Jr.
Robert J. Brennan
Louis J. Brown, Jr.
Michael J. Butler
Raymond L. Caballero
Roy G. Caballero

Thomas L. Cahill
Etienne D. Cambon, Jr.
R. Lee Carmedelle
Lucien J. Caruso
Joseph A. Casamento, Jr.
John J. Casteix
James G. Coleman, Jr.
Kenneth J. Cox
John G. Cronan
John R. Curry, Jr.
Frank A. Cusimano, Sr.
John T. Daly, Jr.
Hilton G. Demare
Berchman H. DeHart, Jr.
Charles M. del Corral, Jr.
John R. DeSilva
John J. Devlin, Jr.
Anthony J. Debartolo
Malcolm S. Disimone
Patrick P. Donahue
Lloyd L. Drury
L. Joseph N. duTreil, Jr.
Joseph D. Early
William H. Ehrhardt
Richard P. Erichson

Robert B. Exnicios
Marvyn J. Fauria
John G. Finney, Jr.
John M. Flynn, Jr.
Roy G. Folse
Gerard W. Ford
Henry E. Fransen
Edward D. Gelzner, Jr.
Edward M. Gilligan, Jr.
Kennedy J. Gilly
William X. Graham
Charles D. Grenier
Arthur A. Grimsal
Joseph K. Hardie
Charles J. Heck, Jr.
Sidney F. Hecker
Gerard H. Hilbert
Mark Y. Hite
James A. Hooper, Jr.
Julian E. Hotard
Hugh E. Humphrey, Jr.
James I. Hymel, Jr.
Maurice G. Indest
Charles L. Jarreau
Charles C. Jaubert

George L. Johnston
Joseph A. Judge
Harry J. Keenan, II
Edgar J. Kehlor, Jr.
Charles J. Keller
William J. Keller, Jr.
Lawrence J. Kelley
Thomas J. Kelly, Jr.
Karl F. Klein
Joseph O. Kuebel, Jr.
Robert E. Lammond
Anatole T. Landry
John A. Dela Vallee
Joseph E. LeBlanc
John L. Lenfant, III
Ronald E. Lenfant
Vincent J. Liberto
James L. Lynch, Jr.
Joseph F. Maes, Jr.
Albert F. Majeau
Edward J. Maloney, Jr.
David B. Martin
Jose D. Martinez
Owen J. Martinez
Hugh J. McAuliffe
William T. McDonnell, Jr.
James D. McGovern, Jr.
Joseph G. Meiman
A. Albert Mercier, Jr.
Rene P. Meric, Jr.

Roy H. Miller
Patrick A. Mitchell, Jr.
R. A. Mix
Jack J. Moisant
George P. Montagnet, Jr.
Billy R. Moore, Sr.
Francis C. Moran, Jr.
Alvin B. Morgan
William D. Morgan, II
John E. Morrison
Joseph T. Murphy
Lawrence A. Murray, Jr.
Joseph N. Naccari
Arthur J. O'Keefe, III
Robert L. Ory
Louis G. Pascal, Jr.
Newton S. Perkins
James T. Perret
Roland J. Pilie
John W. Pitkin, Jr.
Bernard M. Plaia
Louis A. Poche
George J. Quartano
William J. Quilter
George E. Rapier
Philip H. Roach, Jr.
Angelo J. Rodi, Jr.
Joseph T. Ruli
William G. Scheppegrell, Jr.
Wallace B. Schmitz

Charles E. Schroll
F. Foerste Schully, Jr.
James T. Schulte
Jacob F. Schwab
Robert C. Seely, III
Charles J. Seifert, Jr.
Ronald A. Simone
William T. Smith, Jr.
George S. Stewart
George F. Sumner, III
Charles R. Swain
Maurice A. Taquino
James L. Tharpe, Jr.
Charles W. Tschirn
Lawrence Usner
Lachlan M. Vass, Jr.
Robert J. Villars
Allard C. Villere
James R. Von Meysenbug
Benjamin F. Walsh, Jr.
William H. Walsh
John W. Waters, Sr.
Robert J. Weicker
Thomas D. Wetzel
John C. Wheeler, Jr.
Edwin J. Williams, Jr.
George A. Williams
William D. Willig, Jr.
Paul J. Zerangue, Jr.

JESUIT HIGH SCHOOL-CLASS OF 1943

Charles A. Achee, Jr.
Leo J. Adde, III
Edward F. Arbour, Jr.
Edward H. Arnold, Jr.
Albert Baril, Jr.
Donald F. Barraza
Joseph A. Barreca
Courtney K. Bergeron
Warren A. Bernard
James A. Bertel, Jr.
Sylvester C. Blaize
Edward B. Bohner, Jr.
Charles Bordes, III
Robert N. Bose
P. C. Boudousquie, Jr.
Warren R. Brady
Harold C. Breeding, Jr.
Edwin T. Brown, III
Robert M. Brown
J. William Brownson
J. Robert Burvant
Thomas J. Byrne
Gerard F. Cali

Andrew P. Caneza, Jr.
Anthony B. Carimi
Chester W. Carr, Jr.
Lester E. Charbonnet
William J. Childress, Jr.
John D. Cieutat, Jr.
Felix J. Ciolino
Thomas E. Clapp
Albert L. Coman, Jr.
James A. Comiskey
Philip Cooper, Jr.
Calvin F. Christina
Ray A. Cureau
Lionel F. Currier
Mortimer F. Currier
Donald J. D'Antoni
George W. Davila, Jr.
John H. Denis
Edward D. DeRussy
George B. Dittmann
Harold J. Dittmann
Noel C.Duvic, Jr.
Albert R. Early

Lee W. Ecuyer
Thomas C. Erwin
Ronald L. Faia
Alvin J. Fazzio
William M. Feaheny
David B. Ferry, Jr.
Isidore J. Fisher
William P. Flanagan
Cornelius L. Ford
A. J. Fortier, Jr.
William J. Fraering
Harold C. Frederick, Jr.
Albert C. Frey, Jr.
Louis A. Gallo
Stanley B. Garlepied, Jr.
Leonard E. Gately, Jr.
Angelo J. Giolando
Carroll K. Gordon
Joseph C. Gorrondona
Peter J. Graffagnino, Jr.
Tom A. Greve
Herbert P. Grossimon
Maurice F. Hatrel, Jr.

Rudolph L. Heiny, Jr.
John A. Helmer, Jr.
Frank A. Herbert
J. Mansfie Hoerner
Joseph de T. Hogan, Jr.
Irby J. Hurst, Jr.
Adolphe W. Indest, Jr.
Niel J. Jarreau
Thomas Jenniskens.
James J. Kenney
John M. Koffskey, Jr.
Paul G. Lacroix, Jr.
Lloyd A. Langhoff, Jr.
Rene J. Lazare, Jr.
Raymond F. Leon
Ernest J. Leruth
Albert J. Lousteaux, Jr.
Donald V. Malarcher
Rene L. Mareshal
Joseph C. Morgavio
Raymond H. Martinez
Ernest L. Masson, Jr.
Louis D. Mathern, Jr.
E. Davis McCutcheon, Jr.
Joseph A. Melancon, Jr.
Thomas J. Meunier
Louis E. Meyers
John H. Miller
Vernon H. Moret
Donald G. Mullen

Robert D. Murphy, Jr.
Marcelin J. Nick, Jr.
Harold T. Nolan
Thomas H. Nolan
Patrick G. O'Keefe
Charles J. O'Shell
J. Nelson Oglesby
John H. Palmer, Jr.
John H. Pearson
Robert A. Philibert
Wilson J. Pollet
George T. Pourciau, Jr.
Ray L. Price
F. Pat Quinn, Sr.
Joseph M. Raspanti
Joseph M. Rault, Jr.
John W. Read
William V. Redmann
John F. Reilley
John B. Rew
Louis G. Riecke, Jr.
Cyril J. Robert
Kenneth B. Robert
John V. Robichaux
Armand J. Rodehorst, Jr.
David R. Rodrique
Vincent C. Rodriguez
Eugene T. Salatich
John S. Salatich
O. J. Schmidt, Jr.

Alphonse J. Schmitt, Jr.
Matthew P. Schneider, Jr.
John J. Schoenhardt
C. William Schroll
William G. Seiler
Francis V. Sherman
Jules E. Simoneaux, Jr.
Richard B. Spangenberg
Henry H. St. Paul, Jr.
Thomas B. Steen
S. Gideon Steiner, III
Pierre J. Stouse, Jr.
Hewitte A. Thian
Edgar J. Tiblier
Harry T. Tracey
Harry S. H. Verlander, Jr.
Joseph M. Vernaci
Anthony J. Vesich, Jr.
Louis Viau
Donald J. Walsh
Francis J. Warren, Jr.
William A. Watson, Jr.
George E. White, Sr.
Albert E. Widmer, Sr.
William J. Wild, Sr.
Joseph B. Williams
Stanley E. Wilson, Jr.
William V.Wolfe
Joseph E. Young
Charles C. Zatarain, Jr.

RIVERSIDE MILITARY ACADEMY, GAINESVILLE, GEORGIA-GRADUATES FROM LOUISIANA

IN CLASS OF 1938

Wilber Blackman, Alexandria
John Allen Brown, Denham
Springs

William S. Chadwick, Bayou Goula
Marvin Bell Farmer, New Orleans
August J. Mills, Jr., New Orleans

Leander H. Perez, Jr., New Orleans

IN CLASS OF 1939

Zachery Taylor Baker, Alexandria
Audio T. H. Bradford, New Orleans

Joseph Meraux, New Orleans
Charles S. Pitcher, Baton Rouge

IN CLASS OF 1940

Allen Thomas Ambrose, Baton
Rouge

IN CLASS OF 1941

Jack William Barnes, New Orleans
Herbert A. Durham, Shreveport
Herman E. Hall, New Orleans

Arthur Charles Mills, New Orleans
Nathaniel L. Whisenhant, New
Orleans

Michael H. Piper, Jr. , New Orleans
Charles R. Holloway, Baton Rouge

ST. STANISLAUS SCHOOL, BAY SAINT LOUIS, MISSISSIPPI

IN CLASS OF 1936

Edward D. Hogg

IN CLASS OF 1938

Jay Weil, Jr.

IN CLASS OF 1939

Milton J. Bienvenu   Carroll A. Giraud

IN CLASS OF 1940

Nigel E. Rafferty

IN CLASS OF 1941

James L. McConnell   Anthony J. Vizard

IN CLASS OF 1942

Felix A. "Doc" Blanchard   Julius H. Rolfs

WOODWARD ACADEMY (FORMERLY GEORGIA MILITARY ACADEMY) COLLEGE PARK, GEORGIA-

GRADUATES FROM LOUISIANA

IN CLASS OF 1938

Crane P. Fitzwilson, New Orleans   Arthur C. Herbert, New Orleans   Warner Mornhinvey, New Orleans

IN CLASS OF 1939

Charles G. Anzalone, Jr., Independence
Edward B. Baldinger, Jr., New Orleans

Benjamin W. Dart, Jr., New Orleans
David F. Dixon, New Orleans
John M. Parker, IV, New Orleans

Edmond Glenny Parker, New Orleans
Lawrence W. Stone, Jr., New Orleans

IN CLASS OF 1940

Carl B. Anderson, New Orleans
J. J. LeBourgeois, New Orleans
Troy H. Middleton, Baton Rouge

Don Maurice O'Donnell, Shreveport
Arthur J. "Moose" Porter, Jr., New Orleans

C. B. Shackleford, Shreveport
Chevis Webb Sherrouse, New Orleans

IN CLASS OF 1941

Harris D. Copenhaver, Jr., New Orleans
William M. Ellis, New Orleans
Edward D. Fischer, Jr., New Orleans

Walter A. George, Shreveport
Jerry I. Harless, Lake Charles
Joseph F. Heard, Shreveport
Thomas N. Lennox, New Orleans
Langdon Stone, New Orleans

Bob B. Slack, Shreveport
William J. Tessier, New Orleans

CHRIST SCHOOL, ARDEN (ASHVILLE) NORTH CAROLINA, GRADUATES FROM LOUISIANA

IN CLASS OF 1937

Douglas McIlheney, Avery Island

IN CLASS OF 1938

John Tilghman Robinson, New
Orleans

IN CLASS OF 1939

Arthur Carroll Waters, New
Orleans

IN CLASS OF 1940

Harry Clark, New Orleans   Samuel Logan, New Orleans

IN CLASS OF 1941

Grady Clark, New Orleans   Charles Wesley Robinson, New
Thomas C. Nicholls, III, New   Orleans
Orleans   Edgar H. Simmons, New Orleans

IN CLASS OF 1942

James Amoss, New Orleans   Thomas Favrot, New Orleans   George Logan, New Orleans

CLASS OF 1943

H. Harcourt Waters, New Orleans   George C. Durant, Jr., New Orleans   Edward Turner, New Orleans
John Clark, New Orleans   Dabney Ewin, New Orleans   Alonzo West, New Orleans

IN CLASS OF 1944

Charles Hancock, New Orleans   David P. Harris, Jr., Baton Rouge

GULF COAST MILITARY ACADEMY, GULFPORT, MISSISSIPPI

IN CLASS OF 1938

Robert J. Fabacher, New Orleans   Maurice K. Handelman, New
                                    Orleans

IN CLASS OF 1939

Neil P. Jeffrey, Jr., New Orleans

IN CLASS OF 1941

Boyce Nunnally, Jr., New Orleans

WARREN EASTON HIGH SCHOOL, NEW ORLEANS, LA

IN MID-TERM CLASS OF 1938

Benjamin H. Flake

Virgil M. Wheeler, Jr.

IN JUNE CLASS OF 1938

John J. Altobello
Hal C. Becker

Thomas S. Bloodworth, Jr.
Elliot H. Donnels

Edwin A. Lafaye, Jr.
Lloyd J. Reuter

IN JUNE CLASS OF 1939

Thomas G. Baffes
Wilton Duckworth

Julian J. Miester
Ward C. Purdum

Donald A. Ringe
Louis E. Thomas

IN JUNE CLASS OF 1940

John F. Caraway
Warren E. Ibele

Joseph J. Kyame
Michael J. Malony, Jr.

Lester J. Reed
Lloyd J. Roux

IN JUNE CLASS OF 1941

W. Wilber Ackermann
Benjamin S. Brupbacker

Kenneth M. Decossas
Herman E. Goodwin

HOLY CROSS HIGH SCHOOL, NEW ORLEANS

IN CLASS OF 1938

John Brennan

Thomas Salvant

IN CLASS OF 1940

John Fagan, Jr.
Henry Helm

Allen J. Schwark
Joseph White

ST. ALOYSIUS HIGH (NOW BROTHER MARTIN HIGH SCHOOL), NEW ORLEANS, LOUISIANA

IN CLASS OF 1938

Clyde J. Cucullu

Carroll W. Glynn

Albert H. St. Raymond

IN CLASS OF 1939

James R. Lamantia

Louis H. Schopfer

John M. Zibilich

IN CLASS OF 1940

Ben E. Abadie, Jr.

John Bonee'

James Zibilich

IN CLASS OF 1941

Albert E. Alba
Robert Schultis

Bernard Ward
William M. Zibilich

ELEANOR MCMAIN HIGH SCHOOL-MID-TERM CLASS OF 1937

Lillian Alexander
Mary Catherine Ayres
Marian Basile
Anne Beard
Bertha Bernstein
Dorothea Bordes
Marjorie Bruce
Dorothy G. Campbell
Virginia Clemmitt
Beth Cordes
Mary Crane
Billy Cummings
Margaret Dalferes
Laura L. Ernest
Leonora Fernandez
Jeanne Finke
Esther Fischer
Lois Ford
Helen Gerard
Katherine Godat
Elizabeth Gordon
Patricia Grant
Gloria Grimes
Maurine Griswold
Jean Hawkins

Jeannette Hecker
Merle Herbert
Carol Herfarth
Helen Kaften
Hilda Kenny
Lillian Kivetta
Gerd Klaveneks
Rosalie Lamouranna
Adele Levy
Henda Lewellan
Ruth Lewis
Annette Lisitzky
Marian Lloyd
Evelyn Luc
Mary McIntosh
Anna Lee Madere
Marjorie Maltry
Ardath M. Markel
Elsie Mattern
Elaine Melancon
Elizabeth Meyers
Jessie Mesmer
Mildred Minderman
Lisette Muller
Lee Paciera

Anna Palmisano
Eleano Pearce
Frances Pizzzalato
Lucy Platz
Floria Pollock
Ethelyn Railey
Audrey Reagan
Betty Ridnour
Nadine Robbert
Mildred Roch
Ardys Roussarie
Florence Scharfenstein
Joyce Shera
Margaret Smith
Constance Stina
Margaret Stucka
Bernice Swain
Jean Weil
Marilyn Whittaker
Gloria Wimberly
Marianne Yancy
Mary Ann Young
Stephanie Zigert

ELEANOR MCMAIN HIGH SCHOOL-JUNE CLASS OF 1937

Dorothy Adia
Virginia Avegno
Wanda Bailey
Dorothy Baltazor
Rita Benedict
Rose Mary Bertrand
Marian Billings
Lorraine Bordes
Elizabeth Brannan
Jeanne Brown
Helen Brugier
Rosemary Brupbacher
Virginia Buckner
Betty Bruns
Dorothy Bye
Barbara Campbell
Dorothy Cary
Beverly Case
Agnes Cassens
Ruth Chevis
Peggy Childress
Ethyl Christie
Myrtis Clarke
Julia Coltraro
Dorothy Constantin
Mildred Corkern

Rhea Cornman
Rita Couneil
Ethelyn Cryer
Bertha Mae Daigre
June Dailey
Beth Daniel
Helen Day
Carmen dela Ossa
Marie di Betta
Marie Doucet
Marie Douglass
Leila Dupree
Julie Duvis
Doris Engelhardt
Mary Jane Fargason
Helen Farrendou
Carolyn Fischer
Lorraine Fitzpatreick
Rosemary Folse
Lorina Fort
Shirley Fraiser
Elka Freeman
Marie Gamard
Doris Gardner
Carolina Garofalo
Delores Gehbauer

Marie Giardina
Anna Mae Goldstein
Irene Gomilla
Rita Gonzales
Hollie Gordon
Rosemary Grenier
Marion Griffin
Anna Mae Gueydan
Carmelita Gulotta
Dorothy Hass
Milledge Hass
Anna Mae Hagen
Lillie Hawkins
Mary Ellen Hayes
Millicent Hechler
Fanny Heim
Marie Hemenway
Audrey Hereford
Mildred Hiller
Kate Hodge
Lillian Holdsworth
Mary Hollis
Elsie Holzenthal
Jean Horsburgh
Gladys Howell
Norma Hummel

Georgia Hunter
Lorraine Hutchinson
Mary Jane Hutson
Anvel Jackson
Margaret John
Elsie Johnson
Helen J. Johnson
Shirley Jones
Alice Kancher
Flora Kearney
June Keating
Ruth Keff
Gertrude Klinger
Dorothy Lambert
Kathleen Lancaster
Anna Landry
Mary Leake
Lydia M. LeBlanc
Alma Leckert
Randie Ledbetter
Rosemary Legendre
Fanny Mae Levy
Marion Lhoste
Beulah Lieberman
Marie Louise Livaudais
Jean Lob
Sue Longupee
Enid Lopez
Melba Loubat

Patricia Love
Thelma Lynch
Naomi Lyons
Catherine Mackenroth
Nancy Magee
Eunice Mahl
Marion Marino
Doris Martinez
Beverly Mayeux
Shirley Mazzeno
Catherine McCrary
Catherine McDuff
Katherine McGill
Cornelia Meehan
Marion Merritt
Marguerite Mikulik
Irene Milan
Melva Mills
Jean Mitchell
Elise Moise
June Moise
Virginia Moreland
Clare Murphy
Margaret Murray
Theresa Myers
Ruth Nelson
Aline Nobile
Frances Occhipinti
Betty Odenwald

Mary O'Donnell
Emily Ohlsen
Carolyn O'Keefe
Nathalie Owings
Muriel Pasquier
Lucile Patterson
Jane Pearson
Irene Pfaff
Rose Phillips
Fern Pic
Isabella Pizzolato
Harriette Porter
Catherine Powers
Jacqueline Pugh
Lydia Ramirez
Audrey Ratigan
Elizabeth Raulins
Mary Ann Rizzo
Dorothea Rolland
Ernestine Rotureau
Beryl Roy
Anita Ruiz
Alma Salaun
Rita May Schaeffer
Yvonne Schaeffer
Yvonne Schwing
Belle Shubert
Margaret Sieger
Betty Smith

Edith Smith
Gloria Soule
Cecile Starr
Margaret Stathem
Gloria Stevens
Mary Agnes Sullivan
Rita Tangue
Gelpha Thompson
Betsy Tillotson
Emelda Tymon

Mary Uhlich
Marion Uthoff
Shirley Veazey
Dorothy A. Walker
Jessie Webb
Thais Weber
Margaret Wendt
Ruth Westerman
Audry Wetzel
Harrier Whilden

Doris White
Martha White
Irene Whitinger
Lucille Wiesand
Orient Wild
Ethyl Williams
Audry Wolz
Nettie Zahn
Lucille Zeman
Leona Zilberman

ELEANOR MCMAIN HIGH SCHOOL-MID-TERM CLASS OF 1938

Helen M. Abele
Doris C. Adam
Gloria A. Aicklen
Oralee M. Aiple
Josephine M. Aitken
Esther H. Alfred
Mary M. Archer
Ethel M. A. Aucoin
Anna L. Auger
Laura E. Aurner
Frances E. Ayres

Margaret M. Ball
Sue Barrett
Blanche H. Bentin
Betty B. Beyer
Ruth V. Biewer
Georgette Bottine
Ruby M. Boudreaux
Margie E. Boyd
Helen L. Brooks
Gwendolyn R. Buhler
Helen M. Burling

Lucy A. Byrne
Helen Cathalonge
Juanita M. Cecil
Naomi E. Chachere
Katherine D. Cockerham
Doris A. Coffey
Mildred B. Crews
Anna May Dalier
Frede DePolitte
Gloria R. Deuchert
Henrietta P. Diebold

Rhea E. Dinghaus
Dorothy Dowling
Dorothy C. Dubourg
Jane Eckford
Dorothy L. Eirmann
Mary C. Ellis
Audrey F. Eppling
Rosa M. Ferro Pascual
Gloria H. Gaunt
Georgiana Geisenheimer
Jean A. Greeen
Nellie M. Gunn
Rosemary C. Gutierrez
Dorothy Hartley
Leah R. Hellbach
Betty I. Hill
Gertrude R. Hopkins
Helen J. Hunt
Helen I. Huyghe
Margaret E. Judlin
Westley R. Kaiser
Mary L. Keefe
Lois R. Kelly
Anna Mae Keneker

Beverly E. Leopold
Dorothea H. Levy
Eloise E. Lochte
Maxine I. Martin
Viola D. McGregor
Marie E. McGuigin
Emily R. McGuigin
Emily R. Mehrtens
Elois A. Mentz
Helen A. Meyer
Verna Mae Meyer
Dawn Murray
Maria M. O'Connor
Frances E. Oestarly
Iris M. Ohlsen
Gloria L. Oliphant
Lydia M. Olivier
Dorothy M. Orr
Eleanora H. Paisant
Miriam Patrick
Marian Periman
Lillian Pitkin
Elsie F. Ritter
Barbara E. Roark

Carolyn E. Robert
Joanne Robinson
Margaret M. Rohr
Antonine A. Roppolo
Bella Rosenberg Sacks
Beth E. Salathe
Eunice A. Schmitt
Shirley V. Schoendorf
Lois Y. Schroeder
Marion M. Schule
Una Singer
Mary Jane Skinner
Stella M. Smith
Cecilia Carletrom Stewart
Marie L. Stewart
Leona E. Strawbridge
Mary Frances Strawbridge
Mary E. Sulli
Elizabeth M. Thompson
Ethel E. Treleaven
Yudas Vener
Emilie H. Villere
Irma L. Welch
Rita Mae Williams

ELEANOR MCMAIN HIGH SCHOOL-JUNE CLASS OF 1938

Carolyn Albrecht
Ruth Albrecht
Ruth Allen
Yvonne Anderson
Shirley Appollonia
Leah Backer
Mildred Bayer
Beatrice Behrens
Marie L. Blanchard
Rosemary Blum
Anna Bollins
Claire Brewster
Nancy Jane Brieger
Fay Brockman
Muriel Brown
Cordie Buckley
Mary Bulliard
Joyce Burnham
Rose Carr
Yvonne Carrouche
Beverly Carter
Gloria Castaing
Leah Costillion
Carol Conner
Eama Cook
Camille Costella
Eloise Costley
Rosejoy Danna
Yvonne de Latour

Edna Mae Dickey
Winniefred Drackett
Bessie Dulitz
Miriam Dulitz
Beverly Dumastre
Marguerite Duplantier
Evelyn Eck
Lorraine Edwards
Margaret Eicke
Virginia Ellison
Frances Ernst
Nathalie Feitel
Ruth Feldman
Elsie Field
Mary E. Fisk
Audrey Flautt
Hilde Forschler
Betty Foster
June Gahrs
Katherine Gallo
Shirley Garrett
Ruth Garard
LaRaine Gladden
Henrietta Gleason
Yvonne Goldenberg
Rose Marie Gruniz
Rosa Guaz
Annie Lov Guess
Elvia Hamilton

Alice Healy
Shirley Hebert
Sara Helm
Athea Hernard
Tatlana Hofstra
Beverly Hogan
Sara Hogan
Norma Hood
Edna Hurst
Nellie Ivey
Margary Jaubert
Helen Johnson
Margaret Johnston
Donal Jones
Miriam Jubas
Esther Kancher
Irene Keller
Mary C. Kelly
Gloria Kennedy
Patricia Kennedy
Margorie Kibbs
Ardath Klein
Mary Lachin
Nadine Landry
Ruby Lassen
Elaine Lear
Ursula Lee
Jacklyn Levy
Rita Licciardi

Lilian Lockhart
Muriel Lockhart
Jeanne Maddox
Marilyn Marks
Ethyl Mattes
Jenee Mayer
Willie McAllister
Mildred McConnell
Theresa McWhorter
Rebecca McWilliams
Mary Meighan
Nomi Meichert
Jenn Mertzwellier
Mary Lou Meyer
Vivian Meyer
Theresa Michel
Dorothy Midlo
Sabine Millet
France Misuraca
Gloria Monninger
Nancy Moody
Elvia Morales
Marion Muller
Helen Nazrytto
Louise Nelson
Helen Nicaud

Catherine Nixon
Margaret Nubar
Doris Oster
Helen Ourso
Fanny Pazarais
Shirley Penny
Ann Petagna
Marian Paytral
Gloria Pohlman
Miriam Pierce
Shirley Pitard
Patricia Prejean
Norma Porbes
Dorothy M. Reiner
Jewel Reis
Ella Richay
Lucille Rogan
Bobbie Sadilek
Louise Scaccia
Thyra Schaff
Marjorie Schneidau
Janet Schneider
Juliette Schonekas
Dorothy Schreiber
Elma Schroeder
Marjorie Seemann

Lydia Shamer
Dorothy Simkin
Margie Simpson
Gloria Skinner
Shirley Sneed
Yvonne Soniat
Gloria Sperier
Geraldine Sterling
Mildred Stewart
Elaine Stoll
Mary Sue Strahan
Matilda Sundmaker
Luana Thiel
Rosalie Vaccara
Connie Valentine
Barbera Vallas
Dorothy Van Lue
Mary Verlander
Dorothy Viosca
Marie L. Wakeman
Ruth Walker
Mary E. Warren
Eddieth Weathersby
Mathilde Weil
Pearl Wells
Ruth Westerfield

Geraldine Wetzel
Helen Williams
Anna Wilkinson
Marjorie Wimberley

Margaret Winter
Gene Wilkes
Ada Wynne
Marjorie Wymer

Kathleene Young
Marjorie Zengel

ELEANOR MCMAIN HIGH SCHOOL-MID-TERM CLASS OF 1939

Marie Accardo
Doris Alexander
Ruth Antin
Ellen Archer
Dorothy Artigues
Ruth Aufdemorte
Dorothy Azzona
Shirley Mae Babylon
Marie Balo
Katherine Mae Balmer
Marcella Barnes
Marguerite Barrett
Leslie Bartels
Evelyn Baust
Ruby Bourg
Kathleen Boyle
June Breitenbach
Doris Bryan
Marilyn Bryner
Marjorie Buesing

Elise Cambon
Gilda Casaxna
Gloria Daniel
Rosemary DeBray
Marie DeLerno
Martha Dennis
Dorothy Desforges
Mary Laura Dick
Jane Dinsmore
Elaine Dolze
Dorothy Dumestre
Barbara Duncan
Louise Eckart
Gloria Edwards
Marlelle Emling
Doris Evans
Elizabeth Fagan
Mabon Fleming
Margaret Gadsden
Margaret Gaines

Phyllis Griffin
Corinne Hannon
Jane Harlles
Hilda Hartman
Kathryn Healy
Hilda Heinemann
Madge Hemenway
Margarita Hofstra
Katherine Holmes
Ethyl Holzenthal
Bernice Hopner
Ruby Nelle Hoppmeyer
Thelma Jordy
Marjorie Karstendiek
Nellie Kaufman
Barbara Kessler
Vivian Kreider
Victoria LaNasa
Annabel Legen
Ethelise Lemarie

Kathryn Lewis
Margot Liepmann
Helen Malsano
Elizabeth McCoard
Mary Ellen McNamee
LaVerne Morris
Gloria Napolitano
Beulah Nelson
Carolyn Nelson
Betty Jane Nolan
Mary Nerney

Amelia Niedermann
Ruth Nungesser
Maud O'Rourke
June Powers
Marjorie Ragas
Malzie Reinhardt
Lucille Rickert
Lucille Ringel
Patricia Salvant
Marjorie Scharfenstein
Elizabeth Schmidt

Molita Seippel
Mary Louise Sheldon
Clarisse Steeg
Katherine Stewart
Thelma Touche
Lethia Veillon
Mary Lucy Wands
Doris Ware
Edith Wichterich
Ruth Yung
Catherine Zansler

ELEANOR MCMAIN HIGH SCHOOL-JUNE CLASS OF 1939

Beverly Abbott
Audrey Adams
Isabelle Adams
Marjorie Adams
Theodora Ahrens
Virginia Atello
Elaine Ames
Marjorie Babbitt
Adele Babin
Shirley Backes
Alice Baird
Mildred Banville
Carolyn Barbier
Nettie Barlow
Rosina Barraca
Graceh Bach
Julienne Benjamin
Frances Benson
Dorothy Benton
Beulah Bertel
Sadina Bertucci
Rita Mae Betz
Carol Bourgeois
Martha Bradford
Mary Jean Bringhurst
Joan Brooks
Margaret Brou
Mary Bua
Carol Byrne
Carolyn Campbell
Dorothy Campbell
Rita Cantrell
Joy Clay
Martha Cook
Laurin Cooper
Ellen Curie
Elolee Danahay
Helen d'Aquin
Melva Dinkel
Doris Dodd
Azema Ducamus
Mavis Duclos

Jean Duncan
Dorothy Dyke
Phyllis Eckert
Dorothy Ecuyer
Janet Edwards
Dorothory Eignus
Sarah Eldredge
Dorothy Epsting
Margaret Erskine
Dorothy Eversmeyer
Dorothy Fabacher
Marie Farrell
Leah Feldman
Anna Louise Figallo
Isabel Fisher
Lea Claire Fitzsimmons
Marie Louise Fitzsimmons
Helen Flettrich
Catherine Foerester
Dorothy Follett
Mary Ann Follett
Rosita Fossier
Marian Frankel
Paula Frankel
Marian Fraychinzud
Doris Frederick
Claire Fristos
Blanche Fuchs
Clementine Gibson
Hilda Giraud
Gloria Gluffria
Dorothy Glinky
Nathalie Goldman
Joyce Gordon
Marguerite Grady
Rosemary Gratia
Sylvia Guerchoux
Dorothy Gutierrez
Elizabeth Hall
Margaret Hanson
Mildred Hecker
Elaine Herbst

Marjorie Herman
Anna Herrmann
Alvia Heumann
Mabel Hoehn
Mildred Jane
Doris Johnson
Dorothy Jones
Dorothy Ann Jones
Betty Judd
Geraldine Jung
Constance Kahl
Billie Ketteringham
Jeanne Klepinger
Mary Louise Klumpp
Gloria Knecht
Edna Kuhn
Yvonne Landry
Bertha Langhoff
Ivy Nell LaRose
Jewell Latour
Dorothy LeBreton
Vida Ruth LeCron
Rosemary Legett
Dorothy Lammon
Esther Levin
Rhetta Loper
Lucille Loubat
Beth Lynch
Yvonne Lynch
Delores Mahony
Helen Marino
Marie Marquez
Rose Mary Mayes
Rose Marie McCaffery
Betty Jean McCall
Edna McCoy
Marie McCoy
Colinda McKenzie
Helener Markel
Nathalie Miester
Alma Lee Miller
Lettie Miranne

Evelyn Michel
Mary Allen Monroe
Carol Moore
June Moore
Darrel Morel
Mary Morrison
Lois Murat
Anna Mae Murphy
Lillian Nathaus
Dorothy Naquin
Marjorie Nettles
Jane Newton
June Parsons

Alice Patorno
Elise Pixberg
Constance Platt
Katherine Price
Bettie Prosser
Ellen Prowell
Angelina Randazzo
Virginia Ratenburg
Winfred Reeb
Rita Reider
Dorothy Reiner
Dorothy Jane Reiner
Audry Reinhard

Gloria Ribbey
Dorothy Rice
Dama Lou Riddick
Anne Riley
Joy Rogers
Claudia Rordam
Dixie Rosenthal
Antoinette Salzer
Edith Maxine Schanbien
Jane Scharfenstein
Marjorie Schexnaydre
Ethylyn Schmidt
Gertrude Schmidt

Irma Schwab
Noel Schwab
Margery Scott
June Sehrt
Claire Shannon
Elizabeth Shelton
Janet Shively
Freida Anna Shoaf
Olga Sickinger
Muriel Silverman
Mary Elizabeth Singletary
Alfena Smith
Ruth Stall
Ruth Staves

Beverly Stackler
Evalyn Stolaroff
Shirley Strabifo
Anne Strom
Carmelite Sullivan
Doris Tonet
Dorothy Turnbull
Ardith Van Gundry
Ann Virgin
Catherine Waddill
Dorothy Walker
Phyllis Watson
Mary Louise Weber
Shirley Weil

Rosemary Wenger
Janice White
Ruth White
Helen Whitman
Shirley Wichterich
Gloria Will
Dorothy Willem
Grace Witsell
Helen Wood
Elaine Worner
Crystal Wright
Amanda Zahn

ELEANOR MCMAIN HIGH SCHOOL-MID-TERM CLASS OF 1940

Elizabeth Abercrombie
Freddie Adams
Bess Anderson
Rose Anzelmo
Mildred Avegno
Theone Barry
Mary Belsom
Cidette Betz
Lynne Bodet
Maude Bordes
Gloria Boudreaux
Miriam Breecher
Wilda Bridger
Camille Buras
Shirley Burg
Marjory Burnham
Betty Clerc
Eileen Collins
Elizabeth Crowl
Alice Daly
Dorothy deRoode
Elaine De Silva
Rosalind Dismukes

June Duclos
Shirley Dumphy
Norma East
Wanda Elliott
Eleanor Ellison
Eleanor Ernst
Rose Finkelstein
Elaine Forschler
Martha Fraley
Jeanne Free
Isobelle Freebairn
Grace Gallagher
Althea Gebhardt
Conchetta Gendusa
Betty Gerhardt
Ethyl Gerth
Frances Goetz
Dora Harrison
Theone Heric
Lodonia Hess
Miriam Higgins
Alma Holz
Laura Hunter

Helen Jane
Yvonne Kempff
Gloria Knight
Grace Laguens
Oneida Landry
Gertrude Legett
Thoia Leopold
Elaine Levy
Jerry Liddell
Shirley Lupo
Angelina Macheca
Arsina McCay
Cornelia McChesney
Sophia Metzler
Perlin Meyers
Emelda Miller
Elizabeth Mitchell
Gloria Montero
Betty Moody
Sarah Morris
Phyllis Murdock
Catherine O'Hara
Laura Olsen

Lillian O'Reardon
Bessie Pailet
Mary Palmisano
Elleonora Perrilliat
Margery Peter
Helen Pfeffer
Rose Rabinovitz
Lois Redmond
Virgie Richard
Carmen Rivet
Shirley Roch
Norma Rosenson
Pauline Ross
Marjory Rotharmel

Lynette Rottmann
Leontine Rufin
Marie Sarrat
Gloria Savarese
Beatrice Scaruffi
Norma Schmidt
Dorothy Schneider
Myrtle Sievers
Audamese Simmons
Rhoda Simmons
Lois Skinner
Elfrieda Soland
Dorothy Soule
Guyitano Spano

Tingle Stevenson
Mary Stuart
Dorothy Tolmas
Myrtle Twickler
Louise Valdejo
Marjorie Valls
Mary Voila
Esther Webber
Georgette Wetzel
Shirley Wiederecht
Margaret Wiedorn
Gilda Wild
Gloria Yent

ELEANOR MCMAIN HIGH SCHOOL-JUNE CLASS OF 1940

Nina Adams
Odella Ahten
Dorothy Alcklen
Martha Albright
Helen Alexander
Leatrice Alonzo
Clara Lee Antin
Carmel Arceneaux
Shirley Babin
Gwendolyn Barlow
Gloria Barnett
Glynn Barnett
Helen Bartlett
Ruth Bell
June Beyer
Althea Bouchon
Betty Botie
Katherine Bougeois
Miriam Breen
Doris Brennan
Florence Brockhoven
Beverley Brown
Rita Brown
Daley Brupbacher
Velma Buran
Mary Belle Cahill
Joe Cameron
Marie Candela
Patricia Carey
Florence Cazayoux
Ethyl Chachere
Juliet Charlton
Alice Mae Chateau
Hope Cheney
Beverly Commander
Norma Conrad
Betty Cook
Sarah Courtin
Virginia Cullota

Ann Dandridge
Marjorie Darden
Helen Daspit
Vivian Dearing
Virginia Deck
Margaret Deegan
Yvonne de la Oses
Antoinette Dingraudo
Marion Doran
Jean Dresner
Shirley Dunlap
Elizabeth Dunn
Helen Eble
Camille Edwards
Louise Ellison
Jeannette Epperson
Elsa Federico
Betty Finnegan
Louise Foretich
Dorothy Frank
Carol Fraser
Mathilde Freedman
Carol Freret
Dorothy Fryer
Mary Gaillon
Mary Gatey
Pauline Gaudet
Hiuma Goldstein
Carroll Green
Helen Grethe
Doria Gros
Anita Guillory
Ruby Hall
Esther Hartmann
Eve Heinemann
Geneva Henderson
Mary Henley
Lucinda Hill
Jean Hirsch

Dianne Horowitz
Charleen Hutson
Dorothy Hyatt
Mildred Jumonville
Sybil Koeniger
Elaine LaBarge
Elaine Lambert
Muriel Lambert
Merle Landry
Gloria Lanoux
Gloria Lehman
Frances Levy
Vera Levy
Edna Mae Lewis
Leona Lewis
Shirley Liddell
Sania Liuzza
Joyce Loda
Thelma Mackenroth
Dorothy Magee
Dorothy Magruder
Joyce Mailhes
Lorraine Marchal
Janet Martin
Louise Mason
Genevieve Maurin
Vivian Maxwell
Rita Mayer
Gloria McCarthy
Stella McChesney
Gloria McEniry
Mildred Melancon
Lydia Melville
Lois Meyer
Marjorie Miller
Rosaria Munjure
Norma Mumme
Grace Murphy
Marjorie Murphy

Mary Alice Nelson
Janet Neuhauser
Laverne Newhouse
Lanier Neibling
Kathleen O'Conner
Frances Oden
Vivian Orr
Laura Oster
Doris Otto
Leah Park
Evelyn Perot
Lorraine Perilloux
Betty Pfirman
Ellen Pierre
Shirley Polders
Sylvia Portnoy

Dorothy Posceal
Elizabeth Prestes
Kathaleen Ralney
Alice Ramirez
Marie Ranlett
Theodora Ranlett
Haydee Ratigan
Jenny Ruth Reed
Gertrude Richard
Mary Katherine Rogan
Marjorie Rogers
June Rolfe
Claire Rouceau
Mildred Salzer
Kathleen Sandifer
Mary Scaccia

Rosemary Scanlan
Bettie Schaltenberg
Ethyl Schenck
Hedrica Schill
Betty Schneider
Dorothy Schneider
Eleanor Scott
Muriel Scully
Maryilyn Sehrt
Audrey Shubert
Shirley Shuster
Audry Simon
Gloria Simon
Eleanor Sinebeth
Jane Skelly
June Smith

Muriel Smith
Ottie Mae Smith
Cecilia Soldano
Florence Sonntag
Mae Jane Stern
Mary Stevens
Shirley Suffrin
Claire Suth
Cynthia Sutton
Olga Tolecto
Elsie Tillotson

Hazel Toledano
Rosalie Toussaint
Ruth Turgeau
Bertha Turnage
Margaret Vega
Leona Verges
Kay Viosca
Helen Warren
Margaret Watkins
Delores Watts
Margorie Wehl

Helda Westbrook
Marion White
Dorothy Williams
Leslie Williams
Margaret Wilson
Theresa Wolf
May Wong
Janet Worrell
Margaret Youngblood
Dorothy Zansler

ELEANOR MCMAIN HIGH SCHOOL-MID-TERM CLASS OF 1941

Betty Alexander
Emily Aldridge
Vera Baio
Camille Barnes
Betty Becker
Mary Beiger
Shirley Bellinger
Joyce Bickman
Lois Bock
Evelyn Bradon
Melba Braud
Catherine Brennan
May Brien
Ruth Bringhurst
Barbara Broderick
Beverly Burcks
Thelma Byrd
Frances Calamari
Hazel Cheney
Coral Daniel
Veda Davies
Marjorie Davis
Donna Dengler

Doris Dirhy
Carolyn Dietz
Jane Drackett
Rita Ducamus
Emily Dunn
Shirley Eberle
Catherine Eckart
June Eckart
Beverly Eckhardt
Yvonne Eiserloh
France Fort
Aimee Fortson
Camille Governali
Frances Governali
Athea Green
Patsy Grevenig
Eleanor Griffin
Dorothy Gotch
Shirley Hawkins
Betty Helwick
Dorothy Jensen
Clara Johnston
Jo Marie Jones

Lorraine Karstendick
Dorothy Kampen
Rosalie Katten
Louise Kelly
Catherine Kenney
Virginia Kerr
Mary Kline
Rae Kliner
Colleen Lawler
Lillian Lindsley
Clara Louper
Mary Lowe
Katherine Mascari
Rae Mattes
Elaine McFaul
Agnes Metzler
Dorothy Mesmer
Irene Meyers
Muriel Messenger
Bettie Moodie
Rose Muller
June Penard
Dorothy Peters

Grace Pizzuto
Jean Puderer
Shirley Reach
Lorraine Rehm
Leona Reilly
Lois Ribe
Dorothy Richard
Simone Richerand
Marjorie Ross

Myrtle Schumann
Shirley Spadafora
Mary Louise Stern
Imelda Sullivan
Lois Talbot
Betty Taylor
Mildred Taylor
Yvonne Thebault
Marion Thibodeaux

Melba Tricou
Lenore Ullrich
Ruth Waddill
Helen Waters
Dora Weisler
Beverly Wetzel
Joy Wild

ELEANOR MCMAIN HIGH SCHOOL-JUNE CLASS OF 1941

Jacqueline Ackers
Robin Ahrens
Florence Athena
Barbara Allen
Clare Allen
Marjorie Arbogast
Jane Atwood
Joanne Baker
Katherine Barnes
Rosemary Barr
Joy Barrett
Esther Barton
Vera Barton
Ellie Battalore
Shirley Besten
Shirley Mae Bergeron
Doris Berry
Margie Berry
Doris Berthelot
Barbara Boed
Muriel Bock
Veronica Bordenara
Joyce Boseh
Ella Bourgeois
Gloria Gourgeois
Jane Brehm
Jayne Brenna
May Bridger
Ruth Bringburst
Jane Buchanan
Mary Elizabeth Buerkle
Doris Burnham
Betty Cvadzow
Athea Campbell
Virginia Calalano
Nancy Chapman
Agnes Charbonnet
Audry Chevis
Sylvia Chinji Bing
Athea Clement
Rita Coales
Rita Comarda
Barbara Conroy
Shirley Coase
Jane Crane

Dorothy Croft
Claire Daley
Afton Denmark
Yvonne Doll
Olyva Drell
Mary Dubourg
Marjorie Duemling
Lorraine Eagan
Kasle Edwards
Doris Fiolayparia
Valerie Fitzgerald
Connie Fleming
Mary Jane Fourchard
Gloria Galle
Sybil George
Jennie Ben Germann
Coralie Giefery
Shirley Gitz
Madeline Green
Quinta Guillory
Rosemary Haas
Eleanor Handlin
Perry Harold
Gloria Hemenway
Leatrice Henderson
Margaret Henley
Henrietta Hennessey
Barbara Heron
Thora Hickerson
Agnes Higgins
Maxine Hilliard
Beverly Hingle
Ruth Hogue
Gloria Hunter
June Hutchinson
Dorothy Hutton
Edith Jacob
Gloriana Jahn
Ethelereida Johnson
Johnette Johnson
Sylvia Joyner
Blanche Katten
Margaret Kenny
Ada Kilb
Lola Kimbrough

Mary Knight
Carol Koller
Kathryn Laborde
Gloria Lachin
Norma LaGarde
Dorothy LaPoutge
Yvonne Laterriere
Mary Lawrence
Jean LeBlanc
Kathlyn Leger
Vivian Levy
Yvonne Llovergn
Betty Loch
Sadie Lomm
Clara Louper
Mary Ann Lyle
Balya Mallet
Julia Maloney
June Malter
Dorothy Mancini
Toby McCarty
Helena McClelland
Rita McGinnis
Barbara McNiff
Ophelia Melendez
Othella Menard
Aline Merlin
Doris Monnin
Joy Moore
Clare O'Donnell
Bernadine Owens
Etta Mae Palmisano
Alice Mae Pearce
Wilhelmina Pecot
Louise Perrin
Faye Petty
Marjorie Pflgter
Patricia Phillips
Helen Pitkin
Katherine Planchard
Ellen Ponder
Betty Porretto
Betty Prator
Shirley Pregeant
Patricia Price

Eola Prowell
Rebecca Pukof
June Ragas
Hazel Renaudin
Iris Riley
Dorothy Robinson
Doris Rock
Gloria Sall
Rosemary Santopadre
Gloria Schmitt

Miriam Schoen
Joycelyn Schully
Thelma Seiler
Inez Serpas
Katherine Serra
Eloise Sherrard
Mae Simmons
Maurine Simoneaux
Dorothy Staehle
Athea Steckler

Virginia Stone
Vivian Sundmaker
Anna Swartzfagar
Phyllis Terry
Gloria Thompson
Rita Trahan
Jane Trost
Cynthia Twigg
Bernadine Ulmer
Amalie "Tiny" Umbach

Shirley Vaeth
Lorraine Venza
Elaine Von Behren
Betty Vorbusch
Virginia Walker
Nell Walling
Frances Walther

Bettye Walsh
Margaret Ward
Claire Weathersby
Kathleen Wells
Jane Whiteside
Juanita Wild
Jane Willem

Emily Wood
Adele Yost
Shirley Zahn
Claire Zander
June Zatarain
Ivy Mae Ziegler
Geraldine Zoller

ELEANOR MCMAIN HIGH SCHOOL-MID-TERM CLASS OF 1942

Ruth Adler
Lille Allain
Rosemary Amedeo
Evelyn Anderson
Adele Aron
Carol Bayer
Naomi Benten
Betty Booth
Mercedes Bordelon
Doris Boudreaux
Gloria Buesing
Eleanor Byles
Maria Caserta
June Chandler
Lois Christoffer
Joyce Churchill
Dorothy Ciufi
Rosalle Cacchiara
Inez Coffey
Mercedes Coffey
Betty Cohn
Rita Mae Copenhaver
Arthur Merle Dabbs
Kathryn Dennis
Elaine Duclos
Rosemary Eckart
Charlsie Elliott
Esther Exsterstain
Constance Fell

Marjorie France
Vivian Grigg
Louise Hall
Elaine Hawley
Gerhard Heffron
Marie Hess
Constance Hinkel
Joyce Hymel
Rosalie Impastato
Catherine Jaubert
Mary Jeansonne
Estelle Kaylan
Rose Kass
Ella Katz
Marjorie Jeany
Dorothy Klimm
Louella Labiche
Floraine Leaman
Dorothy Lee
Amelia Levy
Rosemary Lombardino
Doris Mandella
Elma Mansicalco
Helen Mayeux
Audry Mead
Mary Elizabeth Menendez
Roselyn Mitchell
Bettie Moyer
Emilia Munch

Virginia Noxon
Hilda Olivier
Ann Osborn
Barbara Parker
Helen Price
Dorothy Dabalain
Mertie Reach
Elaine Redrock
Grace Schmidt
Catherine Schneider
Georgette Schwab
Gloria Shearin
Harriet Sherlock
Shirley Smith
Andrea Soyland
Elaine St. Julian
Muriel Stumph
Inez Sundmaker
Dorothy Sutter
Ruth Taylor
Betty Terroy
Verlie Thompson
Rosemary Vezich
Maxine Welks
Rosalie Willians
Mildred Williamson
Lucine Zahn

ELEANOR MCMAIN HIGH SCHOOL-JUNE CLASS OF 1942

Evelyn Adair
Elvie Adams

Kathryne Adds
Lora Mae Ard

Joy Atkins
Ruby Jane Badon

Kiki Baffes
Doris-Ruth Bagley
Rogna Jane Baker
Gayle Baldinger
Mary Camille Barefot
Barbara Barnes
Carol Barnett
Shirley Barth
Elderweiss Baxter
Miriam Becker
Marrelle Bellegarde
Doris Bennett
Marie Louise Bourdeu
Gwendolyn Breaux
Marjorie Breslin
Leila Bridger
Mollye Bronik
Sybil Broussard
Dorothy Brunet
Catherine Buchert
Marian Burvant
Lucille Calkins
Patricia Callahan
Coral Calongne
Kathryne Carson
Lois Chalona
Claire Chapman
Yvonne Chenoweth
Betty Clague
Dorcas Clotworthy
Peggy Cole
Lorraine Comiskey
Margaret Cooper
Patricia Cordes
Kathryn Cowser
Jamie Craig
Evelyn Crais
Carlotta Cruse
Helen Davis
Ida Fay Davis
Glendora deRouchel
Frances Desforges
Corinne DiLeo
Lura Clare Dixon
Marjorie Dixon
Helen Dowling
Mathilda Ducos
Dorothy Duett
Monitor Duvigneaud
Carolyn Earl
Evelyn Eble
Lois Elmer
Yvonne Franz

Vivian Fiegenschue
Doris Finnegan
Alice Fischer
Shirley Fischer
Shirley Floyd
Eugenie Forstall
Rachel Fortna
Jacqueline Frasier
Ida Mae Gagnet
Gloria Garon
Vera Gemeinhardt
Agnes Gesslier
Betty Goeddertz
Helen Gore
June Graves
Jane Gros
Frances Guidry
Helen Hay
Doris Hebert
Edna May Held
Marcel Heilbach
Lucille Hemard
Gloria Hoffman
Ruth Howerton
Carolyn Hubele
Gayle Hughs
Nita Jacobi
Bette John
Susan Johnson
Alma Jones
Ann Jones
Betty Jones
Loris Jones
Shirley Jung
Sybil Jung
Rosemary Kane
Emily Kaufmann
Miriam Kasting
Edlea Kelly
Mary Lee Kamp
Dorothy Keneker
Shirley Klein
Elsie Klinger
Wilma Knight
Mary Frances Kruse
Marjorie Kuntz
Muriel Latour
Ida Lavigne
Libby Levitan
Katherine Levy
Frances Liddell
Margie Little
Edith Lusch

Frances Macaluso
Margaret Maggio
Dorothy Magoni
Adele Maier
Marion Maler
Jeanne Marcoux
Betty Mason
Madeline Mason
Ruth Mason
Julie Mattes
Virginia Mazza
Beverly McClure
Mary McGowan
Louise McMahon
Marilyn McMaster
Chalita Menendez
Audry Merritt
Dorothy Meyer
Dorothy Miller
Jacqueline Miller
Beverly Malony
Jeanne Munaghan
Clair Gail Moress
Grace Muller
Mildred Muller
Rosemary Muller
Jeannette Mumme
Joseph Naquin
Kathryn Nelson
Jane Neutz
Betty Neuwirth
Anna Mae Nungesser
Eileen O'Brien
Meryl Ortis
Audrey Pailet
Marian Pailet
Marie Patrun
Lucy Perez
Audrey Pfeffer
Rita Pflueger
Marjorie Phillips
Gertrude Pierre
Margaret Poncet
Peggy Pozinsky
June Prejean
Lydia Prest
Janice Price
Marilyn Probst
Providence Pusatert
Frances Ragusa
Dorothy Reagan
Catherine Rebentisch
Gladys Reilly

Patricia Reilly
Ray Reynoir
Rita Riehlmann
Edwinna Ritter
Sybil Robelot
Marilyn Robert
Dorothy Roe
Virginia Rottman
Daphne Roy
Harriette Salzer
Patricia Sanchez
Ellen Sandifer
Norma Schaeffer
Shirley Schanbien
Adelaide Schmidt
Alberta Schonacher
Doris Schroeder
Jeanne Schroeder
Audrey Schwark

Lulubell Scott
Ami Sear
Gloria Seeman
Ruby Sharp
Marion Shaw
Sue Sibley
Doris Simms
Beverly Skelly
Jacquelyn Bouderes
Rosemary Spies
Audrey Spremich
Patsy Taggart
Carol Taylor
June Thaller
Lois Townley
Gloria Trelles
Catherine Trenchard
Sherril Tucker
Dorothy Tugel

Juliette Tureaud
Shirley Uhalt
Eva Villere
Audrey Virgets
Marilyn Wagner
Janet Wall
Eileen Waltzer
Jane Warren
Rosemary Weiss
Vera Wells
Sue Wild
Rose Mary Willingham
Gloria Winn
Gloria Winnige
Marion Woods
Christeene Young
Shirley Zinser

SOPHIE WRIGHT HIGH SCHOOL-MID-TERM CLASS OF 1937

Melba Alice Alexander
Doris Irene Ashley
Mabel Barnes
Geraldine Brenda Bartle
June Mary Barry
Ruth Edna Bertels
Mary Patricia Barth
Ruth Audrey Becker
Elma Florence Block
Edith Ann Brooks
Leona Esther Burg
Blanche Mildred Campbell
Norma Mabel Coates
Virginia Catherine Corte
Azilda Elenor Cuccia
May Jane Derby
Catherine Steele Duncan
Juanita Ernesto
Christins E. Esparros
Lant Van Dyne Farham
Shirley F. Farrell
Miriam M. Gould
Rita Ellen Graziani
Eunice Blanche Guess

Genevieve M. Hamann
Ruth Clare Harris
Rosemary M. Hazlauer
Jane Gibbs Haynes
Dorothy A. Herbert
Margaret E. Holcombe
Shirley A. Huxen
Edna Lee Jardet
Borghild I. Johannesen
Rita Shirley Johnston
Margaret Elizabeth Kampen
Mary Frances Keel
Pearl Annette Kerrigan
Mildred E. Kerth
Ida Koretzky
M. Marjorie Kramer
Doris Arlette Lankston
Marie Verna LoCicero
Dorothy Agnes Lopez
Katherine Marsalis
Rose Marie Mattes
Margaret Lee McCormick
Mary Clare McMahon
Mary Ann McWilliams

Anna Mae Melito
Ethyl Claire Miller
Marie Louise deMontluzin
Elsa Adele Muller
Joan Evelyn O'Toole
Bertha Emma Palazzo
Mary Josephine Piaciotta
Patricia Edith Pittman
Elizabeth Reynard
Freda Esther Robbins
Shirley St. Martin
Mary Nina Sandoz
Rosemary Sandoz
Rita Agnes San Salvador
Eva Albertine Seelhorst
Kathryn E. Sherman
Estelle Claire Simon
Emilie Virginia Smith
Sydney Stoney
Doris Odelle Thiac
Josephine Mary Tusa
Ethyl Bernice Weinstein
Rose Elizabeth Wiltz
Helen Marie Winchester

SOPHIE WRIGHT HIGH SCHOOL-JUNE CLASS OF 1937

Rosita Anguis
Corrie Ellen Babington
Shirley Kathryn Bachemin
Yvette Blanche Bagur
Josefina Banos

Kathryn Louise Barth
Edwina Giles Barthe
Norma Margaret Becker
Catherine Bellerino
Lorelei Rose Bennett

Thelma Marie Bourque
Louise Augusta Burg
Pauline Canatella
Anna Mae Canizaro
Geraldine Victoria Chaise

Grace Chavanne
Leila Elizabeth Chester
Miriam Mary Coates
Carol Caldwell Coe
Helene Marie Colomb
Annabelle Marie Colton
Angelina Columbo
Hazelle Elizabeth Cook
Betty Cooner
Abigail Blanche Cottrell
Yvonne Estelle Crumborn
Beverley Corrine Cuecia
Vera Mae Daniels
Doris Minge Dixey
Marie Dorea
Edna Marie Douglas
Helen Mae Draube
Anna Cecile Dremer
Leverne Dressel
Dorothy Clare Dupuy
Helen Demetria Evanoff
Clency Marie Falson
Myrtle Julia Fiegal
Rachel Leah Finegold
Margaret Marie Fortier
Thais Elizabeth Foss
Carolyn Lucie Fraenkel
Ines Frederick
Rosalou Jeanne Freeland
Carmelite Mary Fullmer
Ruth Rita Galliot
Marjorie Ganier
Amelia Geiger
Ruby Lorena Gibbs
Lucille Vivian Goeddertz
Frances Gertrude Good
Rosemary Goodspeed
Betty Lee Gough
Anna Mae Gros
Katherine Elizabeth Guess
Mary Mabel Guillot
Helen Rita Haney
Virginia Alberta Hardenstein
Martha Virginia Hawkins
Ruth Elizabeth Hawkins
Ruth Hayward
Gloria Marguerite Heebe
Anna Bertha Hoft
Dorothy Rose Hyland
Marjorie Jackson

Dorothy Mae Johnson
Marjorie Katherine Johnston
Rita Yvonne Jones
Margaret Louise Joyner
Norma R. Jung
Henriette Janice Kahn
Lois Florence Kampen
Naomi Marie Kane
Patricia Marie M. Keenan
Evelyn Louise Kelleher
Marie Frances Kern
Aline E. Hochet deKernion
Ethelda Louise Keyes
Lenore Genevieve Kihnel
Mary Emma Klotz
Audrey Mae Knecht
Rosemary Patricia Knecht
Mary Margaret Kotch
Mildred Davis Kramer
Mildred Mary Kurz
Helen Louise LaGarde
Doris Mae Lala
Marguerite Marie Lanaux
Gertrude N. LaRose
Lorena Sarah Leigh
Shirley Elise Lemley
Letechia Jane Livesey
Evelyn Thompson Lowe
Doris Mae Malone
Angelina Mancuso
Elizabeth Martin
Adele Margaret McAdam
Ethyl R. McDonnell
Iris Rita McGinley
Anna McGuire
Dorothy Kathryn McGuirk
Helen Grace McMurry
Rebecca Belle McMurry
Ethyl Louise McQueen
Marie P. Menendez
Renee David Miester
Adelia Camille Moore
Nelwyn Theresa Morvant
Edith Kingsley Motsch
Rita Mae Negrotto
Muriel Gwendolyn Murrell
Florence Katherine Nelson
Ida M. O'Donnell
Consuella Cameron Orlepp
Patricia Page

Gladys Mae Perdue
Augusta Stewart Pipes
June Ann Pittman
Rita A. Plique
Elizabeth R. Plotkin
Lorena S. Ponder
Edith Orion Pope
Ellen Lee Rasmussen
Jane Audry Reed
Edna Violet Rihner
Elizabeth Anne Roberts
Cynthia Robertson
Patricia Robertson
Earlene Robicheaux
Rita Jean Rose
Ruth Isabel Rothschild
Maxine Salem
Dorothy Beverly Samuel
Vendia Winifre Schelin
Stella Marie Schulze
Marie Cecilia Schwartz
Leatrice Joy Serpas
Dorothy Mortimer Shepard
Ruth Marie Shaver
Amelia Emily Shiell
Mary C. Sinclair
Margaret Elizabeth Skakel
Madaleine Mary Slaughter
Yvonne Dorothy Snakenberg
Delores Hilda Sonderegger
Helen Steinman
Mary Josephine Stone
Anna Virginia Strandvik
Marie Charlotte Sullivan
Myrtle Gladys Swayne
Rae Olive Tell
Louise Rita Thomas
Zubie Louise Thomas
Marjorie Paula Thorwegen
Sarah Jean McC. Tooley
Inda Carolyn Trout
Lillian Maya Tucker
Rosemary Tuna
Adele Catherine Voelkel
Shirley Mary Veeloh
Sarah Wainer
Olyve Ward
Janice Deane Weber
Edith Ruth West
Helen Robert West

Adeline Mary Whitfield
Marjorie Whitley
Hilda Claire Wolf

Ruthe Vivienne Wood
Evelyn Miriam Woods
Helen Murlel Woods

Clara Conde Yancey

SOPHIE WRIGHT HIGH SCHOOL-MID-TERM CLASS OF 1938

Florian Rita Barilleau
Emelda Marie Louise Barrios
Grace Margaret Barthelm
Walburga Rita Beaugez
Gloria Louise Bendzus
Margie Louise Bertin
Fanny Jeannette Bollag
Jennie Mary Bonewitz
Eleanor Clare Breen
Angela Ann Bucaro
Ann Byrne
Alice Bonnie Carruth
Lorraine Mavis Clement
Linda Jane Drisdale
Eileen Elson
Inga Rita Eyer

Louise Feitel
Mae Corrine Gerchow
Evelyn M. Gottesman
Willie Emma Groh
Elizabeth Helm
Audrey Saraking
Inez Ruth Koeneke
Maxine Rose Ledner
Dell Louise Lennox
Doris Anna Levin
Marie Louise Lipscomb
Catherine Rita LoCasio
Lucille Maloney
Elizabeth Daspit Myers
Martha Whitestine Orchard
Marguerite Lucille Phelps

Elaine Rita Pierce
Betty Riley
Bettye L. Rinkle
Elizabeth Rogers
Agatha Ann Roushar
Elizabeth Seaver
Cherrie Smith
Helen Elise Spyker
Marion Carolyn Startz
Beulah Sterbcow
Norma Ilma Stortz
Dorothy Rita Toole
Rita E. Traphagan
Florence Trellue
Sylvia Yonkelowitz

SOPHIE WRIGHT HIGH SCHOOL-JUNE CLASS OF 1938

Audrey Aicklen
Barbara Adele Allison
Lena Marguerite Amaden
Irene Elizabeth Arnoult
Catherine Atkinson
Clare Louise Auderer
Shirley Bertha Bartchy
Yvonne Elizabeth Benedict
Ethyl Evelyn Bergeron
Mildred Joyce Bermudez
Rita Rosalie Bermudez
Irene Louise Bernstein
Luna Bersadaky
Iris Norma Betz
Hazel Ruth Beuchot
Mary Louise Billiu
Audry Theresa Bistowish
Norma Angela Bourgeois
Mary Elizabeth Baylan
Jessie Brannon
Carolien Marifrances Brasher
Rose Marie Braud
Dorothea Thelma Brunner
Dorothea Lucille Burkart
Andrieu Catherine Burns
Martha Dale Butler
Anna May Cantelli
Joycelyn Rose Chapman
Henriette Claire Christensen
Catherine Steele Clark
Mar ty Louise Coe
Elsa Cohen
Helen Louise Collins
Mary Mae Collins
Marjorie Elaine Cooley

Constance Marguerite Cowart
Dixie Stuart Danese
Charlotte Elmira Danner
Paula Elizabeth Dauphin
Alice Filleul Dayries
Delores M. DeLatte
Angelina di Giovanni
Mary Catherine Doran
Josephine Celeste Douglas
Bryrelaine Dressel
Zoe Driscoll
Rose Mary Drullhet
Helen Frances Dreyfoos
Floria Mae duCote
Josephine Margaret Duhe
Marietta B. Ellison
Marie Louise Elmore
Vivian Louise Estopinal
Marie Jeanne Farrell
Nola May Felix
Margaret Lillian Fenerty
Nita Mary Fortier
Christine Louise Foy
Denise Isabel Freeman
Ruth M. Galatan
Helen Katherine Gallagher
Lucia Iniguez Garcia
Constance Gloria George
Juliette Graff
Frances Hodges Grayson
Lea Marie Graziani
Violeto May Gramar
Catherine Halpin
Florence Yvonne Hamakar
Valora Harris

Dorothy Emily Heim
Mary Spencina Hernandez
Jonnie Mae Herring
Estelle Margaret Hocke
Mary Elizabeth Hodge
Janice Hodges
Bettye Jean Huffmaster
Verna Mae Hoover
Marie Yvonne de la Houssaye
Sybil Rita de la Houssaye
Barbera Park Howell
Lois Magdelen Huber
Dorothy Bertha Hummel
Geneva Ruth Hybarger
Helen Grace Jackson
Ruth Marguerite Jennewine
Josephine Christine Jourdan
Rita Sultana Julian
Muriel Mary Juzan
Shirley Mary Juzan
Pauline Katz
Ruth Margaret Kelly
Mary Elizabeth Kernaw
Yves A. Kihnet
June Edith King
Dorothea Clara Kistner
Elizabeth Josephine Knight
Esther Jane Kron
Mary Ellen Lala
Elizabeth Jane Landstreet
Ethel Lois Laurent
Bernadette Rita L. Lawhon
Jeanne Althea LeBlanc
Lucille Louise LeBlanc
Ruby Elizabeth LeBlanc

Ruby Ruth LeBlanc
Irma Bertha Lecler
Frances Marie Leigh
Marcelle Yvonne Loetiger
Patricia Ellen Lillian Lusher
Muriel Mary Ann Lyons
Helen Mae Glashan
Hazel Alberyta Mancuso
Catherine Maroney
Florence Margaret Mayer
Nelva Laura Mayeux
Frances Pardue McCutchon
Martha Creighton McCutchon
Dolla Rita Melancon
Elizabeth Abnigail Moore
Estelle Rita Mullen
Rolly Agnes Osterberger
marcia June Owen
Katherine Marie Palazzo
Hazel Marie Patterson

Regina Constance Pelias
Genevieve Marguerite Petalta
Virginia Claire Perret
Thelma Mary Pertuit
Leah Pressner
James Holstnan Prochaska
Jeannette Marie Purves
Freida Marcelene Quarles
Josephine Louise Quartana
Consuelo Ann Redmann
Anna Elizabeth Reid
Agnes Genevieve Roberts
Aida Esther Rodriguez
Gertrude Rita Rome
Gloria Mary Ross
Doris June Roth
Claire Marie Rotis
Helen Marguerite Rotis
Kathleen Ruckert
Letitia Rosalie Schaefer

Ruth Mae Schaefer
Fannie Blanche Schmidt
Fabian Ann Schmitz
Alein Wilhelmina Schneller
Irma May Schwalb
Elsa Audrey Schwartz
Irma Mary Schwartz
Joycelyn Faith Stemann
Gaynell Mildred Serpas
Stella Mae Shepard
Alice Silverman
Adele Rita Stentz
Edith Rose Stentz
Marjorie Elinor Stephens
Bettye Maude Stulb
Gertrude Henrietta Sullivan
Rita Mae Tranchina
Mary Elizabeth Vezien
Lillian Mary Vogt
Hilda Mary Voss

Rita Mae Weaver
Yvonne Rita White
Eunice Rita Whittaker
Beverly Fleuriet Wilson

Masal Gladyse Wilson
Adele Wood
Elaine Woodcock
Amelie Jane Woolfolk

Memery Alyne Wyman
Mary Madison Ziegler
Doris Zilberman

SOPHIE WRIGHT HIGH SCHOOL-MID-TERM CLASS OF 1939

Mary Argote
Sylvia Berniker
Matile Sara Block
Hattie Wurtz Bowie
Florence Rita Cangelosi
Norma M. Cepraro
Gloria Joyce Dantin
Pearl Elizabeth Demarest
Hazel Florence Doell
Audrey Mary Eastin
Carmalite Louise Eble
Katherine Rebecca Franklin
Adrienne Louise Gaudin
Gladys Naomi Gould
Lucille Corinne Guidry
Davis Mae Hava
June Lois Hava

Grace Henrietta Houin
Florence Hudson
Marcelle Julian
Ethelyn Gloria Kane
Janie Kennedy
Dorothy Hazel Kern
Sarah Koretzky
Shirley Mary Lasseigne
Marcia Julia deLassus
Rosemary Marasen
Tracey E. McGuire
Theodosieus Montegudo
Grace Edith Moore
Mallie Louise Norris
Naomi Arthemise Oser
Doris E. Parmentel
Ethyl Marie Pennington

Stella Mae Rachal
Anita Radford
Doris Thea Rooker
Hildaruth Schroeder
Adelaide Shannon
Lillian Mae Smith
Alice Sarah Stuart
Adelel Kathryn Thon
Catherine Ford Tinnin
Ampara Margarita de la Vega
Hilda A. Watermeier
Charlotte Elizabeth Weaver
Dorothy Pearl Weisfeld
Audrey Cecilia Wiltbank
Melisa Stranton Wright
Jewel Marion Zibilich

SOHIE WRIGHT HIGH SCHOOL-JUNE CLASS OF 1939

Margaret Lois Ardoin
Mary Lucille Bankston
Margaret Mary Barry
Daiusy F. Bate
Elizabeth Lida Beard
Norma Elizabeth Behan

Rita Mae Bell
Nancy Parker Benhamn
Emma Isabel Bersault
Shirley Blanchard
Althea Boebinger
Jean LaRhiene Bonner

Dorothy Lucille Bonnett
Lillian Demarest Bott
Martha Ellen Boyd
Evelyn Margaret Breaux
Rosa Mary Brothers
Enid Anne Cain

Dorothy Aleene Carona
Elma Casey
Marion Clarice Chauvin
Metta Lelitia Coleman
Frances Bixland Connely
Teresita Marie Couturie
Vivian Cupero
Marie Louise Cuquet
Concetta Marie Danna
Lyndall Graham daFonte
Jimmy Franklin Dean
Marie Frances ld la Tour
Marie Louise Denny
Cynthia Graham Dodge
Martha Rose Doran
Cecille Francis Doran
Eva Carlla Douglns
Muriel Salome Draube
Anabelle Margaret Dunckley
Ethyl Mary Ecuyer
June Lucia Elliott
Martha Miller Emmett
Catherine Loyola Ernst
Lorraine Fassmann
Suzanne Faust
Alma Lee Ferchaud
Constance Elizabeth Findlay
Alyce Falby Fink
Rose Mary Edna Folse
Rita May Forbes
Thelma Marie Francioni
Helen Lydia Gaboesb
Ann Ganucheau
Albertin Elise Goeddertz
Gracr Rita Goodspeed
Marianne Ferguson Greene
Lucille Dorothy Griffin
Elmira Janin Hancock
Thelma Irma Haney
Gloria Hanley
Anna Belle Rebecca Hardy
Doris Rita Hardy
Frances Sharris
Catherine Emma Haslauer
Margaret Haywood
Claire Health
Geraldine Henderson
Alice Mae Henry

Adelaide Suzanne Hill
Rose Marye Hodge
Lydia Maxine Hoffman
Azalie Laura Holmes
Mary Hom Hilda Huber
Linda Annette Hudson
Marie Elma Hummell
Alice Eleanore Janet
Elizabeth Clements Jones
Marie Louise Jones
Lucille Marie Judge
Geldys Mary Karrigan
Gloria Lorraine Kaul
Anna Klare
June Elizabeth Krantz
Estelle Lacaze
Doreas Larroix
Marie Louise Lanaux
Alice Donalie Landry
Helen Claire Langolis
Eugene Louise Lassale
Arloe Lillian Lasseigne
Lydia LeBlanc
Janet Levy
Patricia Levy
Mary Walker Lewis
Dorothy Evans Lindsay
Hilda May Livesey
Evelyn Louise Luehrmann
Mary Katherine MacGlashan
Marie Mandella
Margaret Jennie Masson
Miriam McCrary
Margaret Angeline McHargue
Rita Jane McPherson
Margaret Louse McWhorter
Rose Mary Mertzweiller
Ethyl Samuelson Midlo
Dora Mary Mire
Donna Louise Mitben
Aphra Vairin Morris
Norma Dell Morris
Florence Mouring
Irene Louise Muller
Verlyn Rolfs Murphy
Elsie Myrtle Nielson
Doris Anita Olsen
Gertrude Mae Osstendorf

Mildred Josephine Padgett
Enid Catherine Paisiant
Lula Peliar
Barbara Jeanne Perkins
Dorothy Mary Porche
Elise Ann Puderer
Marion Eugenie Pujol
Elizabeth Geraldine Ragas
Celina Rita Gagusa
Margaret Rita Rebenack
Winnie Ann Rester
Virginia Ann Riley
Elaine Ripp
Mirian Roder
Jacqueline Rohrbrough
Alice Josephine Rosenberg
Muriel Elizabeth Roshko
Vera Mae Salomon
Lois Marie Sapp
Clara Julia Saunders
Merrie Gayle Schmidt
Adele Helen Schneidau
Elsa Maude Schroeder
Josephine Scorotta
Vennie Marie Selph
Ruth Shaw
Miriam Fieda Shocket
Earline Mary Simoneaux
Gladlys Camille Soilberger
Dorothy Ellen Sorenson
Esther Lou Soyster
Winnie Hampton Stewart
Mary Louise Stock
June Claire Story
Corrine Rose Strauss
Camille Rose Terranova
Jeanne Clare Thibodaux
Mathilde Baldwin Thomas
Marcella Tatman Thompson
Irene Marie Uzee
Marion Lorretta Ventura
Petrine Vittorino
Terry Douglas Walker
Myrtis Delorea Walters
Bernadette Margaret Weber
Regina Adele Weigand
Wennie O. West

Lucy White
Inez Ellen Withmeyer

Margaret Louise Wood
J. Coe Woodward

Mazie V. Yung

SOPHIE WRIGHT HIGH SCHOOL-MID-TERM CLASS OF 1940

Lillian Francis Andel
Helen Irene Anderson
Mildred Elizabeth Maradell
Edith Eve Bierhorst
Gloria Mae Brandenburg
Yvonne Mary Carriere
Marie Louise Clemmer
Mary Miles Coe
Claire Rusha Cook
Irene Marie Daigle
Elaine Rita Decker
Ruth Inez DeWailly
Evelyn Rosalle Domingo
Alma Claire Eble
Athea Mary Ernst
Anais Legendre Eshelman
Pauline Emma Ezell
Norma Ziona Finegold
Thelma May Froeba
Doris Marie Graver
Dorothy Bailey Green
Eulah Charlene Helm

Frieda Hebert
Olga Anna Hoehn
Isabelle Mary Hoffman
Marion Bertha Huber
Orris Catherine Huet
Rose Mary Iannazzo
Malvina Mary Jones
Florence Ann Kelly
Gloria Mary Ruth Koeneke
Gloria Athea Kreger
Carroll Marguerite Labit
Numge Cecilia LaGrange
Marilyn Fay Langston
Rita Mary LaPorte
Claire M. Laussade
Delores Ruth LeJeune
Nancy Elizabeth Littrell
France Carolyn Martin
Jane Shirley Martin
Charlotte Clara Maurin
Esther Helva Jean Mock
Beverly Claire Nogues

Emelie Olympe Ory
Gloria Grace Pattison
Francis Rita Pompeneila
Helen Cora Pool
Anita Carmen Pradillo
Cecile Jane Pumilia
Delores Pumilia
Mildred Adelaide Ranson
Carmen Marguerite Roberta
Annabelle Ethel Seither
Virginia Mae Smith
Helene Marguerite Starliper
Enid Stevens
Shirley Elizabeth Stiles
Elise Talmage
Maria Margaret Tamporello
Helen Edith Tardy
Beryl Theresa Tarrant
Gloria Van Der Haar
Muriel Clair Wedig
Dorothy Mae Weidert
Edith Mae Wetzel

SOPHIE WRIGHT HIGH SCHOOL-JUNE CLASS OF 1940

Ellen Adams
Eunice May Addison
Marcelle D. Aldrich
Charlotte Morse Ashley
Neil Gertrude Atchley
Hilda Aufdamorte
Virginia Ayers
Gwendolyn M. Bickham
Gertrude Lucy Biegelsack
Ruth Evans Biggers
Eelda Frances Bivona
Thelma Elizabeth Bordelon
Elise Catherine Boudreaux
Daisy Blanche Buoyson
Esther Lydia Bowman
Dorothy Louise Braud
Jimmy Maree Breckenridge
Elaine Claire Broker
Emay Hart Buchanan
Betty Florence Burns
Dorothy M. Butscher
Marie Yvonne Cantrelle
Claire Margaret Carden
Elizabeth Thyra Caserta
Mary Castrinos
Grace Henrietta Charbonnet
Fay Chase
Mary Lois Chester
Ida Launjune Chunt

Elaine Eulalie Clark
Margaret Isabelle Coffey
Jane Elizabeth Conery
Jean Shirley Corse
Catherine Virginia Corte
Melvia Coste
Iona Madelyn Dahlgren
Pearl M. Daigle
Allison Hilda Danneman
Audrey Marie Dansereau
Rita Theresa Davenhaver
Rita Frances Davis
Edwina Agnes Dickey
Murray Patricia Dillon
Barbara G. Dodd
Winnifred Dorothy Driscoll
Iris Mae Dubuc
Beverly May Ducote
Shirley Elizabeth Eagan
Lydia Eaves
Eleanor Edwards
Ercell Anita Elrod
Myrtle Margaret Fast
Shirley Mary Fast
Shirley Marion Fath
Lucille Faust
Maria Rita Favaloro
Lois Frances Feibleman
Esther Finegold

Rose Marie Fourton
Ruth M. Frederick
Ellen Lucille Fromherz
Madeline Irene Gabosh
Emilie Josephine Gaudet
Althea Clemence Gaudin
Elizabeth Geary
Ruth Esther Gottesman
Carolyn Graham
Margaret Mary Guidry
Edith May Hardy
Alda Louise Harris
Betty Burton Hartman
Jacqueline Adeline Harvey
Rose Marie Hebert
Olla May Helmke
Marjorie Juanita Henderson
Janice Cecile Hinricks
Manolita Dominga Hoz
Erna Elisie Huber
Margaret Ann Hutchison
Jennie Clare Iannazzo
Helen Johns
Martha Jane Johnson
Betty Mae Johnston
Lynnelle Jones
Patricia Elaine Kane
Edith Humphrey King
Sarah Elizabeth King

Bertha Irene Koch
Magdalena Gertrude Koenig
Adelaide Helen Kron
Warrens Elizabeth Kuntz
Gloria Elsie Labat
Marian Elizabeth LaGarde
Helen Chinn Lai
Norma Shirley Lala
Marilynn Lois Larson
marion Florence de la Tour
Charie Natalie Leadman
Shirley Marie LeBlanc
Shirley LeCorgne
Rita Mary Leitz
Julie Mary Lemman
Dorothy Levin
Florette C. Levy
Virginia Senter Littrell
Mary Catherine Loughlin
Wilma Marguerite Luria
Bernice Edna Macke
Lucile Mae Malarcher
Edna Mary Marie
Sarah Janice Mariette
Mary Erette Martin
Douglass Fain Matthews

Mary Esther McGlathery
Lorraine Marie McGuire
Doris Helen LcLeod
Barbara Legendre McMillan
Emilie Belk McNeely
Mary Francis McWhorter
Doris Lorene Meadows
Gertrude Mary Meighan
Georgia Idooma Miller
Marie Loretta Mitchell
Anne Thida Moore
Mary Helen Moore
Mary Frances Morgan
Katherine Munch
Dorothy Frances Nettles
Irma Mary Oser
Joyce Mary Parks
Norma Claire Patterson
Martha Emily Petty
Shirley Eileen Pic
Edith Marie Platt
Sybil Rosaline Prindle
Betty Ragio
Audrey Anna Leigh Ramond
Lena Claire Rando
Rosemary Reimmuth

Dorothy Reynaud
Lolita Robinson
Julie Anne Rodrigue
Ruth Natalie Rosen
Gloria Ann Salomon
Katherine Saunders
Shirley Mary Scanlon
Marian Adele Schmitz
Beverly G. Sherman
Jeanne Sarah Shields
Florine Silverman
Gloria Rose Simmons
Doris Helene Smith
Elsiemore Smith
Mary Ann Smith
Gloria Merle Spencer
Shirley Louise Stapp
Florence Lorraine Steele
Mildred Carmelite Teeters
Dorothy May Thorwegen
Gretchen Mary Trufant
Katherine Viola Verlander
Audrey Agnes Voelkel
Florence Eva Wright
Katie Lee Waggoner
Helen Anna M. Wagner

Rose Ellen Walsh
Anna May A. Wang
Alice Miriam Ward
Elizabeth Waters
Norma Rita Webre
Geraldine Mercedes Weil
Rita Mae Weitkam

Edna Rita Welch
Louise Bertha Welman
Glora Fredericker Western
Mary Louise Whitty
Anita Belle Wilkes
Harriet Williams
Kathleen J. Williams

Dorothy Helen Wiltz
Shirley M. Woolen
Rosalie Yankelowitz
Jewel Florence Yost
LaVerne Rita Young
Margie M. Yung
Valerie Elaine Zimmerman

SOPHIE WRIGHT HIGH SCHOOL-MID-TERM CLASS OF 1941

Katherine Mary Ahrens
Lucille Mara Allain
Carmen Leona Anderson
Doris Rita Barreca
Noel Berney Beeson
Ola Mae Bennett
June Margaret Blanchard
Miriam Gene Bosworth
June Jane Boyle
Loretta Grace Briant
Marion Claire Byrne
Nina Marie Alvarez Cabellera
Gloria Marie Carambat
M'Liss Rita Casey
Cola Lee Crawford
Ella May Day
Annette Mae Elson

Frances Mary Gallo
Gail France Gaudin
Monita Garson
Edith Belle Givan
Shirley Claire Grant
Helen Mary Guise
Elaine Audrey Hagelberger
Lilian Hammond
Fannie Mae Hart
Iris Pearl Herkender
Elizabeth L. Hallenberger
Gloria Mary Huttner
Norma Rosemary Janet
Elaine Mary Jones
Georgette Irma Joubert
Esther L. Keiffer
Audrey Marie Kirscher

Doris Yvonne Legendre
Athea Rita Livaudais
Muriel Ann Livesey
Zelma Rita Martin
Mary Elizabeth McKinney
Myrtel May Maegher
Katherine Mae Munch
Merl Marie Myrick
Anna Mae Nogues
Marion Louise Nuoclo
Laura Jane Pendergrast
Dorothy Yvette Pumphrey
Mary Rita Quinlan
Mathilda Aurora Ramon
Betty Gertrude Reuter
Louise Marion Robert
Geraldine Mary Rothe

Radel Helena Schwartz
Katie Nell Singuefield
Harma Alice Skinner

Ruth Elizabeth Summers
Gloria Rose Thomson
Charlotte Henrietta Wagner

Shirley Mae Whittaker
Anna May Wiley
Beverly E. Woodruff

SOPHIE WRIGHT HIGH SCHOOL-JUNE CLASS OF 1941

Patricia E. Ahrens
Marian F. Allen
Clair R. Anderson
Gloria R. Arbo
Alice E. Arnold
Anna C. Ashbey
Norma N. Atkins
Sybilla C. Auer
Althea F. Baehr
Peggie Elizabeth Baker
Lois K. Barry
Betty Ann Bartlett
Lillian L. Batet
Mary R. Bauer
Sadie R. Becknel
Delores E. Behan
Maude M. Bendahan
Dorothy A. Benjamin
Shirley C. Bergeron
Patricia M. Binnings
Jane Boswell
Dorothy M. Boudreaux
Shirley R. Boudreaux
Helen R. Bourgeois
Rosemary C. Boyle
Mary W. Brandon
Violet L. Bravo
Betty E. Breaux
Marjorie C. Breaux
Virginia B. Bres
Barbera Brown
Beryl J. Buisson
Edith R. Burg
Eunice F. Burke
Rita J. Burtchaell
Margaret M. Cali
Gloria M. Cantelli
RoseMary Ann Caparo
Frances H. Caraway
Marjorie O. Carter
Peggy M. Case
Patricia B. Castell
Pauline Castrinos
Shirley C. Cater
Rosalie A. Centanni
Gloria L. Charles
Ida A. Chopin
Dorothy Clemmer
June R. Conravey
Ruth C. Conravey

Delores J. Conzelmann
Virgina E. Cooper
Emma D. M. Couvillon
Bonnie C. Cranford
Josephine M. Cutrera
Gayle P. Dahmer
May L. Daigle
Myrle E. Danner
Yvonne M. Demarest
Ruby Demoulette
Theresa M. DiMarco
Joel L. Dreyfus
Pamela Ducote
Lilyon E. Elfenbaum
Jacklyn Estopinal
Sara Ella N. Eustis
Shirley M. Fazande
Ellen V. Fitzgibbon
Jean L. Flower
Marie E. Fortier
Hazel M. Fourreux
Dorothy J. Frederick
Maria L. Fulham
Rosalie M. Galliano
Catherine L. Golladoro
Rebecca N. Gilbert
Mae Alice Gillespie
Marie L. Goodspeed
Rai A. Goodspeed
Lillian Goodwin
Laura J. Gordon
Jane A. Gottschall
Miriam L. Gottsman
Barbara J. Gauner
Mary C. Grabner
Jacqueline M. Graves
Wilma M. Green
Pauline Greenspan
Audrey C. Hall
Bess H. Hall
June R. Hartway
Katherine M. Hawkins
Shirley Heiman
Maurinetta E. Heinsz
Marian H. Weidell
Magdaline Hickey
Stella M. Hill
Pearl G. Hoelzel
Marion S. Hofmann
Norma M. Homes

Rita Holtgreve
Helen Hom
Nancy M. Hudson
Merle Huezo
Betty M. Iley
Margaret Ingraham
Marie A. Ingraham
Martha Jackson
Katherine M. James
Emily S. Johnsen
Gertrude M. Justice
Ruth M. Junes
Lois R. Jurad
Yvonne M. Keefer
Shirley M. Kramer
Margaret M. Krause
Helen P. Kury
Leolen LaFleur
Doris C. Lai
Noelie R. Lambert
Virginia L. Langston
Blanche M. Larue
Marian A. Laussade
Laurel B. Lawson
Harriet A. Lichtenheld
June F. Lipscomb
Marie Marguerite Livaudais
Virginia M. Lorblich
Elizabeth A. Long
Rosemary C. Louque
Betty M. Lyle
Isabel Mann
Ebella A. Marab
Gloria M. McAuley
Mary E. McConnell
Irma M. McGladdery
Betty Pratt McLeod
Carmella M. Meyer
Dorothy P. Mitchell
Ida L. Mock
Antoinette R. Monjure
Selma R. Monroe
Gloria L. Morsner
Elizabeth Morphy
Mary L. Morris
Dorothy M. Munch
Rita M. Murphy
Sybil I. Newton
Betty R. Nichols
Anne M. Nold

Irene A. Owen
Buelah Poilet
Margaret Parker
Elizabeth M. Pattison

Mildred R. Pechon
Hester B. Pierce
Marie A. Peters
Theresa F. Pies

Josie N. Pillart
Josie L. Pizzolato
Jane A. Potts
Orenita P. Powers

Helen M. Pradillo
Miriam C. Pringle
Iris C. Ray
Audry R. Regula
Catherine Reynolds
Alma C. Risso
Doris B. Ripen
Nellie M. Rittineer
Gloria M. Robinson
Martha A. Rodgers
Althea R. Roberts
Ethyl Rose
Julanne Rose
Geraldine Russert
Vera I. Russell
Barbara N. Sanchez
Lois R. Saucier

Naomie S. Schaefer
Florence L. Scherer
Ethyl L. Schilnas
Elaine A. Schneider
Audrey M. Schwartzenburg
Dorothy Silverpass
Shirley R. Simpson
Marion D. Smith
Rosemary C. Springer
Mattie Sue St. Amant
Frances J. Stinson
Freida J. Stock
Louise A. Stocke
Edwidge M. Stockton
Magdelene V. Strumm
Sylvia M. Sugarman
Violet E. Swayne

Audrey M. Tanet
Dorothy M. Tatford
Gloria E. Thibodaux
Elvalee G. Troxclair
Maridel R. Ulm
Elizabeth J. Vallas
Lorrainne C. Venture
Irene A. Vogt
Marie Elizabeth Waggaman
Lella S. Waters
Janet C. Watson
Doris R. Webre
Thyra G. Wilde
Elise E. Wilkinson
Annabeth Wood
Yvonne Young

SOPHIE WRIGHT HIGH SCHOOL-MID-TERM CLASS OF 1942

Clayre Catherine Ahern
Doris Elain Allen
Lucille Doris Arceneaux
Delores Marie Baquie
Evelyn L. Bertrand
Rosemary Katherine Birthright
Evelyn Estelle Bollingham
Betty Beverly Breaux
Francis Lillian Brewer
Noel Marie Brou
Everita L. Chisholm
Florence Mary Clement
Gloria June Collins
Theresa Adelind Cullota
May Theresa Cumbus
Mary Theresa D'Angelo
Vera O. Driggers
Inez Glory Eastin
Rosemary A. Eble
Dorothy Catherine Elstrott
Florence Carlimitte Farrell
Gloria Mae Fleckinger
Jeanne Elise Gaudet
Mary Angelina Gonzalez

Ruth Ann Gorrondona
Lillie Mae Gourges
Winnie Mae Hansen
Mary Leslie Harlee
Antonio J. Hebert
Bertha Rita Hebert
Elsie May Heffron
Mary Elizabeth Himes
Frances M. Hutchison
Lorraine Theresa Inquierdo
Florence Hedwige Kaeker
Helen Mary Kerth
Louise LaFortune
Merrill Rita LeBlanc
Audrey May Legendre
Ellen A. Lennox
Ruby Mary Lightell
Norma Elizabeth Lucas
Ida M. Maloney
Johanna Frances Maloney
Gloria Marie Mayeux
Lucille Blanche McAuliffe
Marion Louise McCants
Coyle Redditt McChesney

Peggy McCutchin
Ethyl Lee McKinney
Miriam Malancon
Gloria Rita Meyer
Shirleymae Miller
Frances Gertrude Morris
Charlotte Namias
Winnifred L. Nelson
Catherine Parker
Lynne S. Phelps
Emelda Ponder
Myrea M. Railey
Lorraine Wanda Ray
Grace Rigg
Doris C. Rome
Mary A. Salvazzio
Cervilia M. Schulte
Rea D. Silverstein
Anna Audrey Sullivan
Letty B. Taylor
Mary Virginia Terry
Joyce B. Ulmer
Marion A. Whittaker
Marcella Jane Wiss

SOPHIE WRIGHT HIGH SCHOOL-JUNE CLASS OF 1942

Carol Helene Adiger
Veller Ann Amadee

Martha Ashley
Patricia A. Atchley

Katherine Caffery Baker
Marjorie Helen Baker

Normajean Ballinger
Dorothy Mae Barber
Audrey Yvonne Barry
Marion F. Batty
Josephinee Bechdolt
Christina M. Bendana
Lorraine L. Bentley
Lorraine Bernadas
Betty Ann Beveridge
Virgina F. Biggers
Rita Mae Bode
Betty Gloria Bolen
Marie Elise Bosworth
Audrey Mae Boudreaux
Mary Ann Bouvier
Doris Claire Bowman
Edith Louise Bowman
Goldie Faye Breen
Emma A. Brierre
Jacqueline A. Buras
Marie Frances Burke
Janet Maria Cain
Mary Louise T. Carlson
Violet May Castelin
Beryl H. Chasez
Corinne C. Chisolm
Doris May Clark
Janet B. Clemons
Evelyn Mary Code
Alsia Louise Corbera
Claire Cornman
Carolyn Crandall
Beryl M. Cuccia
Alma Lee Cyprus
Betty Blanche Dahlberg
Betty Lew Darling
Louise M. Davis
Mary E. Dempsey
Carol T. Douglas
Katherine Janvier Douglas
Jane E. Dragon
Carlyn A. Draube
Marion M. Duenas
Evelyn M. Duplantier
Ruth Mary Duracher
Joy Marie Edwards
Nancy Eustis
Stella M. Evans
Alice Ida Eyestone
Erma M. Farrell
Glorianna Fiegel
Earline M. Fontenelle
Yvonne M. Fremin

Margaret M. Gabosh
Connie M. T. Gallagher
Wilma E. Gassie
Ruth Marie Gelpi
Marion R. Gemelli
Elaine A. Giffroy
Anna Martha Gilbert
Alice Pickslay Glenny
Shirley C. Golay
Audrey Lee Gorman
Marie Louise Gossom
Ruth Iola Gould
Georgianna Gros
Leddie C. Guillory
Patricia Joy Gutierrez
Marilyn C. Haney
Edma Grace Harvey
Mildred Louise Heimel
Margaret Rose4 Helmke
Gloria E. Helwig
Valeita Hill
Lorraine M. Honore
Sara Ann Hunt
Agnes Iannazzo
Kate E. Johnson
Dorothy Katz
Dagmar Y. Kern
Seme Shirley Kleger
Marion Rose Klundt
Marcella V. Knight
Edna M. Koffskey
Kathryn Johanna Krieger
Anita Krilov
Melba Doris Kuhn
Dorothy Mae Laiche
Janet Landry
Marie L. Langlois
Stella A. LeBlanc
Dorothy Sue Legendre
Dorothy Lennox
Paula Rose Levy
Soline Mirian Levy
Gloria Mary Lirette
Frances J. Loughlin
Gertrude Lyles
Daisy Lee Mann
Audrey Ann Marrero
Dorothy Marshall
Letitia McGee
Catherine McWilliams
Henrietta Menzio
Mary Middleton
Dorothy Miremont

Rae Moss
Ann Mouledous
Edith Munch
Claire Myers
Charlotte Myrick
Vita Navarro
Mae Newman
Belle Newton
Frances Newton
Alaid O'Brien
Mae O'Neil
Verna Osolnach
Pearl Ottendorfer
Gibson Parlour
Marie Parr
Louise Patch
Louise Patterson
Marcelee Patrick
Marie Parino
Mae Petrossi
Marie Pinson
Marion Porter
Jane Priester
Marie Raymond
Clare Rebenack
Mildred Reed
Marguerite Rein
Marie Riehl
Floria Rihner
Louise Robinson
Eileen Roehl
Theresa Rome
Nora Rosche
Virginia Rosche
Joy Rosenberg
Lois Rosenberg
Ruth Rosenbohm
Reanos Sandlin
Sara Sazer
Magdalene Schmid
Augusta Schmidt
Maria Schwarz
Beverly Seely
Celina Seghers
Gloria Segreto
Joy Sehrt
Patricia Shields
Ray Shoerman
Virginia Sidney
Stella Skinner
May Smith
Ann Stark
Marguerite Steebar

Patricia Stevens
Mary Dailphia Stewart
June F. Stratakos
Gloria Iola Stroemer
Elaine Tanet
Shirley Tessier
Gloria Thalsheimer
Shirley Theriot
Ruth Tindell
France Toney
Dorothy Tortorich
Hilda Tracey

Mary Rose Trapagnier
Sarah Tucker
Helen Eileen Turner
Betty Velten
Carol Lillian Velten
Dorothy Verlander
Josephina Villalobos
Malba Villavicencio
Lois Vollenwelder
Yvonne Ward
Clare Ward
Joan Ware

Betty Watts
Carolyn Weill
Runa Wexberg
Virginia Aylmar White
Marjory Whitty
Betty Witcher
Alma Wood
Joyce Yonkelwitz
Rose Zinser